The Party
That Came Out of
the Cold War

The Party
That Came Out of
the Cold War

The Party of Democratic Socialism
in United Germany

Franz Oswald

PRAEGER

Westport, Connecticut
London

Library of Congress Cataloging-in-Publication Data

Oswald, Franz, 1947–
    The party that came out of the Cold War : the Party of Democratic Socialism in United
Germany / Franz Oswald.
      p. cm.
    Includes bibliographical references and index.
    ISBN 0–275–97731–5 (alk. paper)
    1. Partei des Demokratischen Sozialismus (Germany) 2. Political parties—Germany. I.
Title.
    JN3971.A98P3767   2002
    324.243'072—dc21   2002022432

British Library Cataloguing in Publication Data is available.

Library of Congress Catalog Card Number: 2002022432
ISBN: 0–275–97731–5

First published in 2002

Praeger Publishers, 88 Post Road West, Westport, CT 06881
An imprint of Greenwood Publishing Group, Inc.
www.praeger.com

Printed in the United States of America

The paper used in this book complies with the
Permanent Paper Standard issued by the National
Information Standards Organization (Z39.48–1984).

10 9 8 7 6 5 4 3 2 1

Contents

Preface

A decade after German unification, the role of the Party of Democratic Socialism (PDS) and the resulting change of the German party system can best be understood by tracing the trajectory traversed by the PDS. The collapse of the German Democratic Republic left the successor of East Germany's ruling party out in the cold burdened by a heritage its remaining members did not want to identify with. Since then the PDS has functioned as a vehicle of integration, providing many East Germans with a political milieu facilitating their arrival in the social reality of the united Federal Republic of Germany. Culturally and psychologically German unification is not yet complete. Nevertheless, the PDS has—de facto, if not always intentionally—made a significant contribution to the integration achieved so far.

Writing about controversial topics of German politics from the safe distance of Australia has, I found, made it easier to fulfill the duties of the historian and political analyst while avoiding the demands placed on the polemicist. Texts about the PDS are often affected by a very close connection between analysis and strategy. For example, the need to justify an exclusion strategy toward the postcommunist PDS often encouraged a portrayal of the party as "extremist," as a party of nostalgic traditionalists longing for a return of East German "real socialism." On the other hand, the argument for an integration strategy can be bolstered by a portrayal of the PDS as a normal participant in Germany's competitive party system.

A decade after unification, it should be possible to avoid such polemical commitments. Instead, with the advantage of hindsight, the assessments of the

PDS of the early 1990s can be corrected as we now know the outcomes of the late 1990s.

I have structured this book as a diachronic narrative analysis. This is not just an excuse for sequential storytelling; it is required by the central argument. At any given moment, a static portrayal could present the PDS as internally divided and immobilized by these divisions. However, over time the sequence of these internal disputes shows interesting shifts in party consensus. A static portrayal of the PDS could also, at any given moment, highlight the distance of the PDS from the center of the German party system, but such static pictures cannot identify the trend toward integration. A decade after unification, the successor of the former ruling party of East Germany has become an almost "normal" party.

The diachronic analysis of a learning process also requires rather precise descriptors capable of identifying incremental change. These small changes resulted in major change over a decade that cannot readily be recognized by observers with blunter instruments. The most problematic dichotomy regarding the PDS is the subdivision of left-wing parties into social democratic and communist parties. Political practitioners and analysts have argued that the PDS had only two impractical options: either to be a communist party, be marginalized, and fail or to be a social democratic party and be superfluous because there was already a big social democratic party in Germany. Yet for the analysis of the PDS this dichotomy is not an appropriate cognitive tool because it cannot recognize the political space the party has come to occupy: It is a left-socialist party, neither social democratic nor communist.

The diachronic approach and the effort to interpret smaller shifts in party consensus over a decade make it possible to locate the PDS more precisely in the German party system compared to earlier polemic texts by "extremism" experts inclined to deny smaller changes and reluctant to admit major change.

According to former German President Richard von Weizsäcker, the integration of postunification Germany requires a combination of truth and reconciliation. Understanding and accepting the PDS should be a part of it.

I am grateful to colleagues in the Australasian Association for European History and the Contemporary European Studies Association of Australia who commented on earlier versions of chapters; to Professors Reinhard Kühnl and Georg Fülberth (Marburg, Germany) for their insights into German party politics; and to numerous others in Berlin and across Germany who gave their time for interviews and discussion providing an oral "reality check" on the written sources.

A special word of thanks to my friend Henner Michels, without whom this project would never have started, and to my partner Hanifa Deen, without whose support this book would never have been completed.

Introduction

The development of the Party of Democratic Socialism (PDS) is part of the postcommunist system transformation of East Germany; at the same time, it is part of the unification of the two Germanies: The Federal Republic of Germany (FRG; West) absorbed the German Democratic Republic (GDR; East) into a larger united Federal Republic of Germany. This dual discontinuity is the major difference between the German case and other cases of postcommunist system transformation in central and Eastern Europe that occurred in the framework of a continuing nation–state.

The successor of the Socialist Unity Party (SED), East Germany's ruling party until 1989, had to adapt to this situation. In Poland or Hungary, for example, major factions of the former ruling communist parties transformed themselves into social democratic parties, presenting themselves as technocratic reformers capable of managing government, whereas smaller factions continued as communist parties. In Germany, however, the political space available to the PDS was much more circumscribed. There was already the Social Democratic Party of Germany (SPD), a party with broad appeal and years of experience in national and regional government of West Germany. Finding the social democratic political space occupied but not intending to form a communist party, the PDS was on the verge of irrelevance and disintegration but survived as it managed to combine a regionalist appeal to East Germans and an identity as a left-socialist party.

THE "PARTY WITHOUT FUTURE" SURVIVED

A decade after the unification of East and West Germany, the German party system included a viable left-socialist party, the PDS. Its electoral support almost equaled that of the Alliance 90/Greens party. It was represented in national parliament and entrenched in 6 of Germany's 16 regional parliaments and in hundreds of local councils in the East of Germany. It was the junior partner in one regional government and gave support to a minority government of Social Democrats in another state. The survival of the PDS looked like a most unlikely scenario to observers in 1989 and 1990 expecting rapid disintegration of this "party without future."[1] Its predecessor, the SED, was so discredited at the end of 1989 that most of the 16 million East Germans were hostile to the party, whereas 90 percent of its 2.3 million members deserted within a few months.

In late 1989, as a prelude to the demise of the Soviet Union in 1991, the SED lost control over events in the German Democratic Republic it had ruled for four decades. The historical experiment with "real socialism" was coming to an end. The demise of the "first workers' and farmers' state on German soil" was also the moment when the party lost its raison d'être. SED leaders and members had regarded themselves as "the party of the working class," destined to lead East Germany through the long historical period of transforming society via socialism and "developed socialism" to communism. There were four other parties in East Germany, but their role was that of handmaidens assisting the SED in its historical mission. In the "epoch of transition from capitalism to socialism,"[2] the SED saw itself implementing world history in Germany, completing the project that had started with the Russian Revolution of October 1917.

Doubts about this mission had grown during the 1980s, not only among the 16 million East Germans at large but also among the 2.3 million SED members. Many of them had hoped that Gorbachev's perestroika and glasnost would also stimulate reform and innovation in the GDR. However, when SED Secretary General Erich Honecker decided that GDR socialism did not need thorough reforms, hopes for improvement were virtually extinguished.

For a few weeks, after the demise of the Honecker leadership on 18 October 1989, and the fall of Honecker's successor Erich Krenz on 3 December, it seemed possible to replace bureaucratic-centralist socialism by a thoroughly democratized and reformed model of socialism. In December 1989, when an extraordinary party congress transformed the SED into the Party of Democratic Socialism, the remaining party members assumed that reforming socialism was possible, while the GDR continued to exist as the other German state, next to the Federal Republic in the West. "For a new GDR, for democratic socialism"— this slogan summarized the hopes of congress delegates.[3]

This vision was revealed to be illusionary within a few weeks. At the end of January 1990, the Democratic Socialists and the government led by Prime Minister Hans Modrow were once more overtaken by events. German unification was to be unstoppable; there would be neither place nor time to try out democratic socialism. In early November 1989, the SED had reacted much too late to a rapidly changing domestic and international context. Granting GDR citizens the right to travel abroad was a belated response when demand had become absolutely irresistible. It was hardly surprising that the reform intentions of the PDS were also outpaced by change that had become even more rapid. After the Volkskammer (Chamber of Deputies) elections of March 1990, the PDS found itself on the opposition benches, backed by only 16 percent of East German voters, facing isolation and hostility from other parties and among the wider population.

This party without a purpose, facing the prospect of becoming totally insignificant after unification with a much larger West Germany, came close to self-dissolution at the extraordinary party congress of December 1989. Its continuing isolation and loss of members made its demise appear predictable and inevitable. However, the PDS succeeded in surviving and transforming the remnants of the SED into a viable left-socialist party, leaving behind ideology and party structures modeled on the Soviet communist party. From 1990 to 1992 the survival of the Democratic Socialists was always in doubt. By 1994 it was still possible to describe the PDS as "party without future" (title of M. Gerner's book), although by the end of 1994 the party had survived a second national election.

By 1998, however, the PDS had consolidated its position in East Germany and had become somewhat less marginal in West Germany. It had, for the first time, gained 5 percent nationwide in the 1998 Bundestag elections. And it had broken through the isolation imposed on it by all other parties since 1990. For the first time, the PDS had been accepted as junior partner of the Social Democrats in a state government, in Mecklenburg–West Pommerania.

The survival of the PDS introduced a new element into the German party system: a left-socialist party, neither communist nor social democratic. According to PDS election campaign manager André Brie, "[T]he Socialist People's Party of Denmark and the Party of the Left of Sweden have demonstrated for several decades . . . that it is possible . . . to develop politically effective parties beyond the social democratic and the communist type of party."[4] The left-socialist PDS could function—in a way past communist parties (Communist Party of Germany [KPD], German Communist Party [DKP]) could not—as a "strategic reserve" of the Social Democrats.[5] Although the result of the 1998 elections gave Social Democrats and Greens a majority in the Bundestag without requiring the support of the PDS, the new constellation in the party system made future "Swedish majorities" possible in Germany, that is, minority governments of Social Democrats and Greens relying on parliamentary support by a left-socialist party.

THE CHANGING PLACE OF THE PDS IN THE PARTY SYSTEM

The place of the PDS in the German party system has changed significantly in the decade since its foundation in 1989. In a very short period in late 1989, the SED's role as the ruling party of the GDR ended. The SED had lost its constitutionally guaranteed "leading role" by decision of the Volkskammer (1 December 1989), although it still led government under Prime Minister Modrow. In January 1990, it became obvious that the Modrow government would only have the transitional task of winding down the GDR in preparation for unification with West Germany. After its defeat in the Volkskammer elections of March 1990, the PDS found itself on the opposition benches under new threats of survival. The Volkskammer majority appointed an "Independent Commission for the Investigation of the Property of Parties and Mass Organizations of the GDR" (31 May 1990) to investigate how much, or how little, of the SED's real estate and cash was to remain legitimate property of the PDS.[6] This Independent Commission threatened the financial viability of the PDS as organization.

At the same time as the former ruling party was becoming a marginalized opposition within East Germany, it also had to adjust to the unification of the two Germanies. In the months before unification was officially completed, West German parties were expanding east by absorbing existing minor East German parties or, in the case of the Social Democrats, by founding a new party organization. Only the PDS had its core strength in the East attempting to find an organizational base in the West.

In the early 1990s, the PDS survived in isolation by learning to identify with its role as opposition.[7] By 1994, the PDS had proven its capacity to survive and to transform itself. It also had reduced its isolation to some extent, when a minority government of SPD and Alliance 90/Greens accepted "toleration" by PDS parliamentarians in the Land parliament of Saxony-Anhalt. By 1998, the PDS had consolidated its electoral support and won 5 percent in nationwide elections. It had further reduced its isolation when it was, for the first time, accepted as junior partner in a state government coalition in Mecklenburg-Vorpommern. Within a decade, the PDS had become an almost normal party, a participant in a competitive party system in a parliamentary democracy, in stark contrast to its predecessor, the SED, exercising the "leading role" during four decades of "real socialism," and in a surprising recovery after half a decade of barely surviving as marginalized opposition.

NEW PARTY SYSTEM: REGIONALIZED PLURALISM AND TILT TO CENTER-LEFT

The survival of the PDS affected the party system in two ways. First, the existence of an additional party increased fragmentation. In West Germany, a three-party system consisting of the Christian Democratic Union/Christian Social Union (CDU/CSU), the SPD, and the Free Democratic Party (FDP) had prevailed since the 1950s, modified to a four-party system by the rise of the Greens in the 1980s. The post-1990 fragmentation did, however, not amount to "polarized pluralism" threatening democratic stability through the rise of left and right extremes. Instead, as argued convincingly by David Patton, the outcome was "regionalised pluralism,"[8] that is, a continuing four-party system in the West and a three-party system of CDU, SPD, and PDS in the East. Second, the entire party system shifted to the left through the inclusion of 16 million East Germans and the survival of the PDS. The delayed impact of unification had ended the center-right hegemony of the Christian Democrats, which had lasted from 1949 to 1998. Since 1998 a center-left government led by Social Democrats was as likely as a centre-right election victory.

Initially, it appeared that the impact of the PDS on the German party system would be temporary and minimal. Other parties aimed to marginalize and eliminate the party. For the Christian Democrats, it was an ideological enemy, representative of a socialist and communist tradition. The PDS had to be excluded from the consensus of democrats, possibly even banned as extremist and anti-constitutional. The only useful aspect of the PDS's existence was that it would split the electoral potential of the left, depriving the Social Democrats of part of the East German vote.

For Social Democrats, the PDS was the successor of a communist dictatorship that, in 1946, had destroyed the East German SPD when the Soviet Military Administration and the KPD forced the SPD to merge into the Socialist Unity Party of Germany (the SED). The PDS was also an awkward reminder of the embarrassing fact that many East German Social Democrats had, at least initially, welcomed this formation of a united party. Thus the SPD had to decide whether it would treat the entire PDS as a hostile successor of the communist tradition or accept parts of the PDS because they represented a social democratic potential finally returning to the SPD.[9] Initially Social Democrats adopted a strategy of marginalization and elimination, treating the PDS as hostile and excluding former SED members from joining the SPD. In an ironic twist, this very exclusion strategy may have forced many potential social democrats to find a political home in the PDS. Thus the Democratic Socialists retained many competent local councillors and administrators. This enabled the PDS to become entrenched in East German local government and to survive as a viable party.

Without the survival of the PDS, the party system of united Germany would have been an exact replica of the West German party system. Of the major West German parties, the Christian Democrats had expanded by absorbing the East German CDU as well as the Democratic Farmers Party (DBD), whereas the Social Democrats had supported the foundation of a new Social Democratic Party (SDP) in the East in late 1989 that later merged with the Western SPD. Of the relevant minor parties, the West German Free Democrats had merged with the East German Liberal Democratic Party of Germany (LDPD) and the National Democratic Party of Germany (NDPD), whereas the Greens had found a partner in Alliance 90, a collection of diverse East German dissident groups.[10] The likely outcome of this process was a party system with two major parties, CDU/CSU and SPD, as well as two minor parties, FDP and Greens, as in West Germany since the 1980s.

The survival of the PDS, however, created a different situation. In the five East German Länder and in Berlin, it regained, by 1994, 20 percent support to become the third largest party, after CDU and SPD. The Greens and the FDP, on the other hand, could not repeat the initial successes of 1990 and lost representation in all East German regional parliaments. In the East, the PDS was a major party accepted as normal by most voters. This quantitative fact had normative implications. By the late 1990s it had become impossible to treat the PDS as extremist outsider because this would have alienated too many East Germans, even those not voting for the PDS. Acceptance of the PDS in the East also affected its position in the West. If other parties had to cooperate with the PDS in the East, at the local or regional level, they could no longer portray the PDS as totalitarian. This eased the negative image of the PDS among West German voters.

The consolidation of the PDS in the East also changed the strategies of other parties toward the party, shifting from marginalization and elimination toward various forms of partial cooperation. This new situation also changed the political climate within the PDS. When other parties offered nothing but marginalization and pressure, the Democratic Socialists had no other choice but to identify with an opposition role. However, the transition of Social Democrats and Greens to a strategy of partial cooperation and integration also created new options for PDS politicians as the opportunity arose to modify the party's opposition role. Since 1994, the arguments for greater integration into the political system have gained strength within the PDS.

In the first half of the 1990s, the PDS had adopted a role as "societal opposition," using its parliamentary positions to campaign for East German grievances and for pacifist, ecological, feminist, and social justice themes. In the second half of the 1990s, the leaders of the PDS, "modern socialist" intellectuals, and pragmatists in local councils and Land parliaments were repositioning themselves: Their objective was no longer to criticize society from outside but to implement reform policies from within parliament, possibly from within government, in alliance with Social Democrats and Greens.

The survival of the PDS signaled that the absorption of East Germany by the larger West German Federal Republic had changed, to a noticeable extent, the party system of the united Federal Republic. The inclusion of 16 million East Germans initially favored the CDU/CSU when many East German voters supported Helmut Kohl, the "chancellor of unification," in the elections of 1990 and 1994. By 1994, however, the long-term impact of unification had become visible: Catholics no longer constituted almost half of the population, as was the case in West Germany. Christian Democrats were disadvantaged by the inclusion of the historically Protestant, now largely secularized East German electorate. Social Democrats had to share this secular, socialist potential with the PDS. Greens and Free Democrats could not stabilize their initial successes in the East and remained relevant only in the West, whereas the PDS remained largely confined to the East.

The 1998 elections brought, for the first time in the history of the Federal Republic, an arithmetic majority of the left (SPD, Greens, PDS). This raised the question whether this constituted "a structural realignment of the electorate which can be expected to establish the foundations of a red-green majority for the foreseeable future, or merely the situational response to circumstances uniquely favourable to the SPD and the Greens."[11] Padgett asserted that "the centre-left majority was situational in character" while acknowledging long-term change to the extent that the CDU/CSU had "lost the structural dominance which has exercised in the party system" as partisan attachments weakened in a more fluid electorate.[12] Padgett's assessment appears to underestimate the structural change resulting from unification. He himself mentions situational factors affecting the 1990 and 1994 elections when Kohl's coalition of CDU/CSU and FDP was "rescued from the full effects of its electoral decomposition by unification in 1990 and by economic upswing in 1994."[13] These unique situational effects of unification favoring the incumbent had subsided by 1998, and the long-term effects of including a secularized East German electorate appeared.

The structural dominance of the CDU/CSU in the electorate had ended largely because the share of Catholics in the electorate had declined from 42.9 percent in West Germany to 34.7 percent in united Germany because in East Germany Catholics were a minority of no more than 5.9 percent. While the share of Protestants had been affected only marginally (West, 38.1 percent; East, 27.0 percent; Germany, 35.7 percent), the share of no religion/other religions had increased from 19.0 percent in West Germany to 29.6 percent in united Germany because a majority of 67.0 percent of East Germans had no religious affiliation.[14] Thus the CDU/CSU now had to supplement its core support group of Catholic churchgoers to a much larger extent from among voters without any strong loyalties. The PDS, on the other hand, was drawing most of its support from irreligious East Germans.

The survival of the PDS had two effects: The party system in the five Eastern Länder and in the capital Berlin differed significantly from that in the 10 Western Länder. And the whole party system had, to some extent, shifted to the left. The CDU/CSU had lost its predominance, which had allowed it to lead governments for 28 out of 41 years before unification and for another 8 years after unification. By the late 1990s, a majority to the left of the CDU/CSU had become more likely. Center-left governments, led by Social Democrats, including the Greens, and supported by a left-socialist party, could become as frequent in Germany as they had been in Sweden for decades. The postunification electorate had made a majority of SPD, Greens, and PDS an arithmetic possibility in 1998. However, this was not yet a political possibility due to the remaining marginality of the PDS in the party system. In 1990, the PDS had been a total outsider. By 1998, the party had become acceptable enough to serve as junior coalition partner in the regional government of Mecklenburg-Vorpommern led by Social Democrats. Should the process of demarginalization continue at the same pace as in the 1990s, the inclusion of the PDS in a national government with SPD and Greens could be possible after the 2006 elections.

TRACING THE TRAJECTORY

The development of the PDS from extreme marginality in the early 1990s to acceptability as potential and actual partner in state-level government is presented in the next seven chapters. Chapters 1 and 2 discuss the development of the PDS during the last year of the GDR (1989–1990) when unification with West Germany was imminent but not yet completed. Chapter 1 analyzes the transformation of the PDS at and after its foundation congress of December 1989. Chapter 2 summarizes the role change of the PDS in the transitional East German party system, from governing party to marginal opposition, and its attempts to come to terms with imminent German unification.

Chapter 3 focuses on the decline of the PDS and its marginalization during 1991–1992, a time when portrayals of the party as extremist served to justify exclusion strategies promising to accelerate the demise of the PDS. Chapter 4 summarizes the consolidation period of 1993–1994 in which the PDS stabilized its support base in East German society and developed a programmatic identity and a critical semidistance to GDR history. The survival and stabilization of the PDS prompted analysts to suggest that an integration strategy could replace the marginalization of the PDS.

The analysis of the repositioning of the PDS during 1995–1997 in Chapter 5 is central to the argument. As the survival of the party appeared secure by late 1994, the debate about the future role of the party became relevant. The PDS redefined its opposition role. As SPD and Greens began to accept the PDS as an almost normal party, the PDS released itself from its earlier role as outsider opposition. The controversies of 1995–1997 shifted party consensus away from a role as critical outsider toward a less ambitious reform strategy. The party adopted a rather pragmatic strategic objective: to replace the neoliberal-conservative government of Chancellor Kohl by a center-left coalition of SPD and Greens, supported by the PDS.

Chapter 6 summarizes the practical consequences of the earlier consensus shift. By early 1997 the PDS was ready to join regional governments, and as it was one of three major parties in Germany's East, together with CDU and SPD, its inclusion in Land government coalition had become a viable option. Chapter 7 charaterizes the place of the PDS in the German party system a decade after unification, together with the change of the entire party system resulting from the inclusion of the East German electorate and the survival of the PDS. A brief chronology after Chapter 7 lists selected events illustrating developments from the foundation of the PDS to its entry in the Berlin state government in January 2002.

NOTES

1. Manfred Gerner, *Partei ohne Zukunft? Von der SED zur PDS* (Munich: Tilsner, 1994).

2. "Programm der Sozialistischen Einheitspartei Deutschlands," in *Dokumente zur Geschichte der SED. Volume 3 (1971–1986)* (Berlin: Dietz, 1986), p. 102.

3. PDS, *Materialien. Außerordentlicher Parteitag der SED-PDS, Berlin Dezember 1989* (Berlin: Dietz, 1990), p. 127.

4. André Brie, *Ich tauche nicht ab. Selbstzeugnisse und Reflexionen* (Berlin: Edition Ost, 1996), p. 258.

5. Alexander Gauland, "Konservativ sein heißt," *Blätter für deutsche und internationale Politik* 44, no. 1 (January 1999): 11.

6. Gregor Gysi, *Das war's. Noch lange nicht!* (Düsseldorf: Econ Verlag, 1997), p. 197; Helmut Zessin, Edwin Schwertner, and Frank Schumann, *Chronik der PDS: 1989 bis 1997* (Berlin: Dietz, 1998), p. 24.

7. Gysi, *Das war's*, pp. 156–157.

8. David Patton, "The Rise of Germany's Party of Democratic Socialism: 'Regionalised Pluralism' in the Federal Republic?" *West European Politics* 23, no. 1 (January 2000): 144–160.

9. Peter Glotz, "Wir Sozialdemokraten wären am liebsten die einzige linke Partei," in *Die PDS—Phönix oder Asche? Eine Partei auf dem Prüfstand*, ed. Heinz Beinert (Berlin: Aufbau-Verlag, 1995), p. 102.

10. Oskar Niedermayer, "Das intermediäre System." in *Politisches System. Berichte zum sozialen und politischen Wandel in Ostdeutschland*, ed. Max Kaase et al. (Opladen: Leske + Budrich, 1996), 3: 172–175.

11. Stephen Padgett, and Thomas Saalfeld, "Introduction." *German Politics*, Special Issue on *"Bundestagswahl '98: The End of an Era?"* 8, no. 2 (August 1999): 1–9; Stephen Padgett, "The Boundaries of Stability: The Party System before and after the 1998 *Bundestagswahl*," *German Politics* 8, no. 2 (August 1999): 88–107.

12. Padgett, "The Boundaries," p. 102.

13. Ibid.

14. Wolfgang G. Gibowski, "Election Trends in Germany: An Analysis of the Second General Election in Reunited Germany," *German Politics* 4, no. 2 (August 1995): 42.

Abbreviations

Alliance 90/Greens	Formed by merger of West German party "Die Grünen" and East German "Bündnis 90"
BHE	Bund der Heimatvertriebenen und Entrechteten (League of Expellees and Dispossessed)
CDU	Christlich Demokratische Union (Christian Democratic Union; major party in FRG; minor party in GDR)
CPSU	Communist Party of the Soviet Union
CSU	Christlich Soziale Union (Christian Social Union; sister party of CDU in Bavaria)
DBD	Demokratische Bauernpartei Deutschlands (Democratic Farmers Party of Germany; minor party in GDR)
DGB	Deutscher Gewerkschaftsbund (West German trade union federation)
DKP	Deutsche Kommunistische Partei ([West] German Communist Party, founded in 1968 by members of the banned KPD)
DVU	Deutsche Volksunion (German Peoples Union)
FAZ	*Frankfurter Allgemeine Zeitung*
FDP	Freie Demokratische Partei (Free Democratic Party; minor party in FRG)
FRG	Federal Republic of Germany (1949–1990, West Germany; since 1990, united Germany)

GBM	Gesellschaft zum Schutz von Bürgerrecht und Menschenwürde (Association for the protection of civic rights and human dignity)
GDR	German Democratic Republic (East Germany; 1949–1990)
HBV	Handel, Banken und Versicherungen (commerce, banks, and insurance employees's union)
IM	*informeller Mitarbeiter* (informal contributor)
ISOR	Initiativgemeinschaft zum Schutz der sozialen Rechte ehemaliger Angehöriger bewaffneter Organe und der Zollverwaltung der DDR
KB	Kommunistischer Bund (Communist League; founded by West German Maoist students)
KPD	Kommunistische Partei Deutschlands (Communist Party of Germany; merged 1946 in East Germany with SPD to form SED; banned 1956 in West Germany)
KPF	Communist Platform
LDPD	Liberal-Demokratische Partei Deutschlands (Liberal Democratic Party of Germany; minor party in GDR)
MdB	Mitglied des Bundestages (Member of Parliament)
MEP	Member of the European Parliament
MF	Marxist Forum
NATO	North Atlantic Treaty Organization
NDPD	National-Demokratische Partei Deutschlands (National Democratic Party of Germany; minor party in GDR)
NPD	Nationaldemokratische Partei Deutschlands (National Democratic Party of Germany; far right party in West Germany)
NSDAP	Nationalsozialistische Deutsche Arbeiterpartei (Nazi Party)
OWUS	Offener Wirtschaftsverband für kleine und mittelständische Unternehmen (Open business association for small and medium enterprises)
PCF	French Communist Party
PDS	Partei des Demokratischen Sozialismus (Party of Democratic Socialism)
SDP	Sozialdemokratische Partei (Social Democratic Party founded in East Germany in late 1989; merged with SPD in 1990)
SED	Sozialistische Einheitspartei Deutschlands (Socialist Unity Party resulting from merger of KPD and SPD in 1946; ruling party of GDR 1946–1989)
SPD	Sozialdemokratische Partei Deutschlands (Social Democratic Party of Germany)
SRP	Sozialistische Reichspartei (Socialist Reich Party)

PART ONE

DURING THE LAST YEAR OF THE GDR, 1989–1990

1

More Than a New Label: The Transition from SED to PDS, December 1989–March 1990

THE FOUNDATION CONGRESS: FROM SED TO PDS

The first congress of what was to be the PDS was, at the same time, the last congress of the SED. The extraordinary congress convened for 8–9 December 1989 had to negotiate a difficult path between continuity and discontinuity. The SED was collapsing and disintegrating. The morale of party members had been sapped for several years in the 1980s. While many SED members found some cause for optimism in Gorbachov's perestroika, they were at the same time disheartened by the refusal of the SED leadership under Secretary General Erich Honecker to acknowledge any need for change.[1]

Even a more innovative SED leadership would not have saved the GDR, as the preconditions of its survival disappeared. International factors such as the economic exhaustion of the Soviet Union, forcing it to relinquish control over Eastern and central Europe, as well as domestic factors such as the untenable economic situation of the GDR (external debts, trade deficit, underinvestment of the last 15 years) had made the existence of the second Germany precarious. This situation was exacerbated by the refusal of Honecker and Günter Mittag, the Politburo member responsible for the economy, to face realities and to act accordingly.

The replacement of Honecker as SED leader by Egon Krenz, on 18 October 1989, resulted in halfhearted, insufficient gestures. SED party members reacted in two ways. A wave of resignation swept party branches in all regions, while other members finally called for drastic changes. In the last months of 1989, the SED lost 900,000 of its 2.3 million members,[2] and these losses continued throughout 1990. At the same time, many critics of the leadership from the second and third ranks of the party organization as well as many rank-and-file members called for a complete overhaul and convened an extraordinary congress.

This congress began on 8–9 December and continued its unfinished business of 16–17 December. At that time, and even at the congress of 24–25 February 1990, delegates still assumed that socialism in the GDR could be reformed, democratized and modernized. However, by late February it had become obvious that unification with West Germany had become inevitable. Thus the GDR government under Hans Modrow could do no more than preside over the winding down of the East German socialist experiment.

The central question at the extraordinary congress was whether to dissolve the SED or to continue and reform the party. The groups favoring dissolution, most prominently the Platform Third Way (Plattform Dritter Weg), hoped that a clear break with the past would offer better conditions for a new left-socialist party, free from the structures and mentalities ingrained in the SED.[3] The eventual majority favoring continued existence of the SED had to map out a course of reform that would, over time, produce a credible new party. While delegates were considering these options, thousands of members were leaving the party. Hostility in the population against the SED was rising as every single member was held responsible for the deeds of the Honecker leadership and for the actions of the hated Stasi (State Security).

The extreme fragility of the party project was confirmed by renewed calls for dissolution in January 1990. These came from intellectuals who preferred a clean sweep, a new program, and a new structure. However, renewed calls for dissolution were rejected by the new party executive on 20 January. The demand for continuity was also based on the moral argument that it would be dishonest and incredible to shirk historical responsibility. Finally, there were very pragmatic reasons for organizational continuity. The SED was the owner of substantial assets (real estate, printing presses, vehicle fleets, etc.), and there were the personnel working in the party apparatus at the central, regional, and local levels. New party chairman Gregor Gysi[4] argued that one could not sack instantly 44,000 full-time party workers. Instead, the apparatus had to shed personnel in a more humane way. There was also the unspoken argument that the party would, of course, benefit from still holding the assets of the SED.

The complete exchange of leadership personnel was a strong indicator of discontinuity between SED and PDS. Before the party congress, an extraordinary meeting of the Central Committee (3 December) had excluded Erich Honecker and other members of the Politburo from SED membership. Then the Politburo and the Central Committee stepped down to be replaced by a working party preparing the extraordinary congress.

The new leaders elected at the first session of the congress (8–9 December) symbolized a break with the past. Party President Gregor Gysi, a lawyer who had defended dissidents in the 1980s, was a newcomer "not shaped by the party apparatus."[5] Deputy Chairman Hans Modrow, former regional SED secretary in Dresden, had been appointed prime minister of the GDR on 13 November. Unlike other SED leaders, Modrow was not suspected of abusing material privileges but had a reputation of honesty and modesty. The other deputy chairman was Wolfgang Berghofer, mayor of Dresden, enjoying a reputation as modern technocrat. It underlined the fragility of the party project that Berghofer left the PDS only a few weeks later, on 21 January, followed by another 39 prominent members of the Dresden SED, the mayor of the city of Magdeburg, and many other administrators.

The congress almost split over the question of the name of the party. In spite of the failures of four decades of GDR history, many members still identified with the name "Socialist Unity Party of Germany." For Hans Modrow, expressing the feelings of many older members, this name expressed ideals that could be salvaged in spite of the history associated with the GDR under Ulbricht and Honecker. Other delegates wanted to signal more discontinuity by adopting the name Party of Democratic Socialism. After long discussions, the congress decided to defer the decision and to adopt, for the time being, the name SED-PDS. A congress resolution tried to give meaning to the compromise over the name: "Those who today are still members of this party acknowledge its history and have no intention of eschewing responsibility. However, they profess that a break with Stalinism and a serious new beginning have been completed here. To do justice to both aspects, we have decided to carry temporarily a double name, i.e., to supplement our previous name."[6]

This decision was indicative of a pattern that was to be repeated in the next ten years of PDS history. Many changes introduced by Gregor Gysi, by his successor as party chairman Lothar Bisky, or by party strategist André Brie initially met with reluctance and resistance especially by older party members. These changes were then introduced gradually and with compromises. This careful timing of innovation allowed substantial change over several years without splitting the party. At the same time, it gave outside critics the opportunity to accuse the PDS of being nostalgic for a Stalinist past and not serious about reforms. This cautious method of guiding change was motivated by the need to hold the party together as a viable quantity. There was also the humane motive not to leave too many behind without a political home. Instead, older SED members could adjust to the new realities in a united, capitalist Germany at their own pace, in their familiar party subculture, while around them German unification was changing the social and economic environment for East Germans at an incredible pace.[7]

At the end of the extraordinary December congress, the party had a new name, new leaders, and a new party constitution. The SED-PDS was still leading the government of the GDR, although Prime Minister Modrow made it clear that he was governing at a distance from his own party, seeking consensus with all parties in the Volkskammer, and entering into dialogue, in a "round table" approach, with dissident groups formed in late 1989.

TOLERATING FACTIONAL DIVERSITY: "THIRD WAY" VERSUS "COMMUNIST PLATFORM"

The emergence of numerous "platforms" in December 1989 and January 1990 was symptomatic of this period of transition in which all critics of the Honecker Politburo were searching for new directions. These platforms were also indicative of the extent of change in the transition from SED to PDS. For seven decades, since 1920, when the Bolsheviks banned organized factions, the leaders of communist parties had insisted that the formation of factions was incompatible with the Leninist party of the "new type." The PDS broke with this tradition. Its new party constitution explicitly allowed platforms and associations, formed by members sharing a particular view, to organize across the branch structure of the party.[8] It even gave them official status by allowing them a quota of delegates to party congresses. This structural device guaranteed a voice at party congresses to minorities unable to find local or regional majorities for the election of delegates.

These platforms indicated the range of opinions in the PDS and shaped discussions. The most important ones were the "Platform Third Way" (Plattform Dritter Weg) and the "Communist Platform" (KPF). The Platform Third Way was initiated by the "modern socialists," a group of intellectuals who were to be most influential in the development of party programs and strategy. The Communist Platform, on the other hand, marked the left, traditionalist margin of the PDS.

The Platform Third Way advocated, in December 1989, the dissolution of the SED and a completely new beginning, thus maximizing the distance from old structures and old habits. This was the only occasion when the modern socialists clearly failed. In the following years several modern socialists exercised great influence on party programs and strategy. André Brie became PDS election campaign manager and party strategist; Dieter Klein, Michael Schumann, and Michael Brie influenced programmatic thinking.

The conceptual framework of modern socialism had been developed in the late 1980s by dissident SED intellectuals at Humboldt University in the "Project Group Modern Socialism," led by Michael Brie. They combined a "reception of Western theories of modernity" and a rather abstract, system theoretical approach arguing that modern societies had "the ability to a permanent development of societal structures . . . which . . . apparently is tied to the differentiation and autonomy of sectors of society into subsystems with relatively strong autonomous dynamics and only weak hetero-synchronisation." The main cause of stagnation in state-socialist society was identified in the subordination of subsytems to the whole of society and a subsequent loss of the ability of self-development.[9]

A short summary of the tenets of modern socialism could be found in the 1999 "Theses towards a Programmatic Debate," which also illustrated the continued hegemony of modern socialist ideas in the PDS. "Modernity," in this approach, was more than capitalism. "Modern bourgeois society" included achievements such as "pluralist democracy," the "market" as an "inexpendible decentral selection mechanism," and the "Rechtsstaat" (rule of law). These core institutions were supplemented by characteristics such as "the differentiation of society into efficient subsystems," "internationalisation of economy and society," and "individualisation."[10] These aspects of present society made it possible to pursue a reform strategy aiming to overcome the dominance of the profit motive.[11]

While modern socialists were to provide the analytical framework and mapped out PDS strategy, the KPF had very limited influence. It was successful on one occasion, when it joined others in opposing the dissolution of the SED at the December 1989 congress. Since then it was on the defensive, losing out on many strategic issues. The first of these numerous defeats occurred in mid- and late 1990 when the Communist Platform suggested that the natural ally for the PDS in West Germany was the German Communist Party (DKP). The PDS majority, however, kept its distance from the DKP and decided to build PDS party branches in the West. This decision made it clear that the Communist Platform was restricted to the role of a communist minority within a left-socialist, noncommunist party.

For a short time, there was a Social Democratic Platform offering a broad ideological orientation in competition with the Platform Third Way and the KPF. Founded in January 1990, it claimed to represent the social democratic tradition that had survived all repression since the 1946 merger of communists and social democrats. These social democrats within the PDS identified with the traditions of Karl Kautsky and Eduard Bernstein. The grouping did not last long,[12] disoriented as it was between attempts to find a place for social democrats in the PDS and the wish to leave the PDS for the SPD, which, however, did not allow former SED members to join.

PROGRAMMATIC BREAK WITH SED THINKING

Significant steps in a new programmatic direction were made at the foundation congress of the Party of Democratic Socialism. First, it distanced itself clearly from a failed model of socialism, from Stalinism, and from the structures and habits that shaped "real socialism" for decades even after Stalin's death. Second, it also distanced itself from an interpretation of the history of German working-class politics canonizing the tradition of the KPD and SED and, even within this tradition, canonizing only the "correct" line to the exclusion of critical voices and dissident minorities. Instead the PDS identified with a wider range of traditions, including social democratic ones. And third, the PDS distanced itself from the analysis of capitalism prevailing in the SED. Instead of describing capitalism as entirely negative, the Democratic Socialists acknowledged achievements of bourgeois society such as rule of law and parliamentary democracy that had made it superior to GDR socialism lacking modernity. These "civilizing achievements" made it possible to adopt a radical reform strategy within capitalism.

This break with SED thinking was underestimated or even denied by analysts focusing on continuity between SED and PDS. Patrick Moreau and Jürgen Lang claimed that the PDS was "an extremist and modernized communist party. . . . The camouflage is almost perfect" as the PDS presented a "seemingly moderate program."[13] Other experts acknowledged by 1994 that the PDS was dominated by a noncommunist, reform socialist leadership. To be more precise: The discontinuity between SED and PDS was significant and visible even as early as 1990.

The title of Michael Schumann's speech to the foundation congress signaled a clear intention: "We are breaking irrevocably with Stalinism as a system!" The main characteristics of this system included: concentration of power in one hand; administrative command over the entire economy; bureaucratic regulation of culture, science, and education; and a political culture of tutelage over all citizens.[14] In the mid-1990s the PDS was to debate whether this rejection of Stalinism as system referred only to the period of Stalin's rule until 1953 or whether "Stalinism" was meant to include the post-Stalin period as well. In spite of these differences, the anti-Stalinist consensus of the PDS was never seriously in doubt since neo-Stalinist positions were never shared by more than a few marginal individuals.

Dieter Klein's speech mapped out a "Third Way beyond administrative socialism and [a] profit dominated economy." Klein distanced the PDS from past strategies of communist parties expecting "an explosive revolution" leading from capitalism to socialism. Instead, he suggested a reform strategy aiming for a "turn away from the dominance of the profit motive in the regulation of societal and economic development."[15] These concepts increasingly dominated programmatic statements of the PDS, culminating in the draft for a new party program presented in April 2001.[16]

In the hectic atmosphere of the extraordinary congress, many motions were accepted by delegates more concerned with saving the party somehow than with details of the programmatic reorientation pronounced by Schumann and Klein. For many members it was impossible to realize what it meant to accept Kautsky and Bernstein as ideological forefathers whom they hardly knew except as renegades rejected by Lenin and the Communist Party for many decades. And it would take the whole party half a decade to explore the practical possibilities of radical reform politics as opposition party in a parliamentary democracy within a capitalist economic environment.

At its congress of February 1990, the PDS adopted not only a platform for the elections to the Volkskammer one month later but also a party program. Unlike the program adopted in 1993, this one was not the result of lengthy debates but was rather hastily stitched together. The 1990 program fulfilled two functions: It confirmed the break with past SED programs, and it was broad and imprecise enough to integrate a range of views.

The 1990 program distanced itself from the requirements in SED programs that party members adhere to a monolithic Marxist-Leninist worldview. Instead, it linked the PDS to a broad range of social democratic, socialist, and communist traditions. Including names such as Bernstein and Lenin certainly indicated diversity, although not necessarily consistency. Nevertheless, Manfred Gerner's conclusion that this indicated irreconcilable contradictions within the party[17] was not stringent. It was possible for a party closer to the ideas of Kautsky and Bernstein, such as the PDS, to tolerate a few non-Stalinist communists, provided they postponed their revolutionary expectations while assisting in more limited reform efforts. This was, indeed, the only realistic choice for the Communist Platform minority. For them, staying in the PDS remained more attractive, in spite of many defeats by the reform socialist majority, than a separate existence as a very small communist party.

Already in 1990, three important themes were visible that remained central to PDS programmatic thinking. First, there was ideological pluralism, the renunciation of any obligatory worldview, admitting instead a wide range of left approaches. This pluralism was not easily defined and required clarification, especially at the congress in January 1995, which confirmed the exclusion of Stalinist positions from PDS pluralism.

Second, there was the appreciation of the civilizing achievements of "modern capitalist society." This differed from earlier communist and socialist thinking that simply rejected capitalism and expected socialism to be better. The concept of "capitalist modernity" modified this assessment. It acknowledged that deficient forms of socialism could be inferior to some forms of capitalism. It pointed out that "real socialism" had failed because of its own shortcomings, especially because of the lack of "modernity," the absence of civilizing achievements that Western society had developed over several centuries. The "modernity" aspects of modern capitalist society were the starting point for the reform strategy proposed by the modern socialists in the PDS.[18] Modernity had achieved rule of law, individual human rights against the state, and formal democracy, and it had retained an evolutionary potential by allowing subsystems of society their relative autonomy, whereas the "monosubject" of real socialism, the all-commanding party state, had stifled the evolutionary potential of social subsystems.

The programmatic and strategic thinking of the PDS for the next ten years was influenced by this distinction. It was possible to criticize capitalism while at the same time acknowledging that democracy, rule of law, individual rights, and the relative autonomy of various social spheres from the state were achievements to be appreciated under capitalism and to be retained in any model of socialism. This distinction between "modernity" and "capitalism" as analytically separate aspects of bourgeois society was capable of guiding a critique of the deficits of failed "real socialism" as well as a reform strategy under capitalist conditions.

Third, there was the reformist strategy of transformation differing clearly from the Leninist model of revolution exemplified in the Russian Revolution of October 1917. This reform strategy was advocated in Dieter Klein's speech at the foundation congress in December 1989, and it was still relevant a decade later when PDS theorists suggested a "democratisation of democracy"[19] acknowledging the value of existing parliamentary democracy, which had to be retained and defended but also improved. Democratization was desirable on its own, but it could also be regarded as a step in a socialist transformative strategy.

The recognition of the evolutionary potential of modern capitalist society implying a reformist strategy was central to the thinking of the modern socialists dominating PDS debates. This approach was there in the speeches of Dieter Klein and Michael Schumann at the foundation congress in December 1989, in the program of February 1990, in the second program of 1993, in the *Kommentar* of early 1997, in the theses of the program commission majority of November 1999, and again in the draft for a new party program of April 2001. The "modern socialism" of Michael Brie was the theoretical guide for the reform socialists increasingly dominating the PDS executive as well as programmatic discourse.

STRUCTURAL BREAK WITH SED PAST: ELECTORAL PARTY WITHOUT WORKPLACE BRANCHES

The discontinuity between SED and PDS could be demonstrated most convincingly by the changes to the party constitution and its organizational structure. The Party of Democratic Socialism built a party structure more akin to social democratic parties equipped for election campaigns. Its predecessor, the SED, had the structure of governing communist parties aiming to retain control of the economic, administrative, and military branches of state power, whereas nongoverning communist parties such as the KPD had structures enabling them to intervene in economic class conflicts. The structural discontinuity between SED and PDS was perhaps the strongest argument against claims by Patrick Moreau and others that the PDS was merely the SED in "camouflage."[20]

The most important structural changes were the reduction of the full-time party apparatus and the shift from workplace branches to locality branches. The SED, like the Soviet Communist Party, had been dominated by the Politburo and a massive apparatus of full-time party officials, especially those working in the departments of the Central Committee. This Central Committee apparatus was replaced by several small commissions with minimal full-time staff working for the party executive. By mid May 1990, the number of full-time party staff had been reduced from 44,000 in late 1989 to circa 10,000.[21]

The shift from workplace to locality branches changed the nature of the party. The PDS had moved out of the arena of economic class conflict into the arena of electoral competition by basing the entire organization on locality branches. It was a distinctive characteristic of communist parties to give priority to workplace branches while relying on locality branches only if inevitable. Generally,

parties with workplace branches are geared toward working-class-focused economic and political class struggle. Locality branches, on the other hand, facilitate
activities such as election campaigning and highlight issues such as housing,
education, or public transport rather than industrial disputes between capital and
labor. For nongoverning communist parties, workplace branches were necessary
instruments of class struggle. For governing communist parties, workplace
branches in enterprises secured economic power, while party branches in state
institutions (administration, police, armed forces) safeguarded political power.
On the other hand, for the Party of Democratic Socialism, abolishing workplace
branches meant a structural break with past priorities. It also meant that it would
not exercise its future opposition role in the manner of past communist parties.

Internal pluralism within the party was secured not only by programmatic
guarantees but also by structural devices. Neither program nor party constitution
expected members to adhere to a particular worldview, whereas the SED had
required of its members allegiance to Marxism-Leninism. The PDS broke with
the monolithical ideological unity expected by past communist parties. These
had banned the formation of factions since 1920, whereas the PDS gave a recognized place in the party constitution to platforms and associations of members
sharing a particular view. In communist parties any factions across party
branches were banned. The PDS constitution, on the other hand, allowed such
groups, giving them the right to elect a number of delegates to party congresses.
These constitutional guarantees made possible the survival of the Communist
Platform as a minority within the left-socialist PDS. When the party leadership
attempted in January 1997 to remove or reduce this right of platforms, there
was enough support for this structural guarantee of internal pluralism,[22] even
among those PDS delegates not close to the Communist Platform, to defeat this
proposal.

In an attempt to emphasize continuity between the SED and PDS, conservative analyst Uwe Backes admitted some structural change but pointed to its
limitations: "On the one hand, past democratic centralism was broken up through
the admission of 'working parties' and 'platforms' with diverse ideological pro-
files; on the other, there emerged an almost all-powerful party presidium, and
the severely limited 'pluralism' included, right from the beginning, dyed-in-the-
wool communists."[23] Yet the existence of a powerful party executive did not
prove structural identity with the SED. A powerful executive also existed in the
Social Democratic Party of Germany (SPD) or in any other democratic mass
membership parties. In the PDS, the party executive was much weaker than it
had been in the SED because the full-time apparatus of the party was much
smaller. The balance of power had shifted, in the transition from SED to PDS,
in favor of elected bodies against the previously absolutely dominant apparatus.
This shift still left the executive in a strong position but not more so than in
other large parties.

The PDS strengthened elected party bodies such as the party congress compared to the party executive. For example, party chairman Gregor Gysi was

elected by the whole congress in December 1989, whereas previously in the SED the congress elected the Central Committee and left it to this smaller body to elect the general secretary and the Politburo. This procedure was still followed in December 1989 for the election of Gysi's deputies who were elected by the Parteivorstand (new name for the Central Committee). By January 1991, however, at the second party congress, the right to elect the deputy presidents had also shifted to the congress as a whole.[24] Thus the party executive was no longer as insulated from the will of the delegates as in the past. Later experience was to show that the executive still could dominate the wider elected bodies such as the Parteivorstand (wider executive) and the party congress. However, this was only the case to the extent almost inevitable in any party structures, for example, in social democratic and labor parties. There was no longer the absolute dominance of the Politburo over the Central Committee and party congress whereby the executive was capable of virtually naming the delegates to party congresses.

These structural changes constituted significant evidence of discontinuity between the SED and PDS. The PDS had become, in its organizational anatomy, a mass party based on membership in locality branches, not workplace branches. This structure redirected the party away from the conflicts of labor and capital experienced in the workplace toward the greater variety of issues experienced in localities. It also reshaped its capacity to act. Mass parties based on locality branches are geared for electoral campaigning, not toward influencing industrial conflicts.

NOTES

1. Documents illustrating tensions over the 1988 decision to ban distribution of Soviet publications are reprinted in Manfred Behrend and Helmut Meier, eds., *Der schwere Weg der Erneuerung. Von der SED zur PDS. Eine Dokumentation* (Berlin: Dietz, 1991), pp. 43–53.

2. Heinrich Bortfeldt, *Von der SED zur PDS: Wandlung zur Demokratie?* (Bonn: Bouvier, 1991), p. 155.

3. Gregor Gysi and Thomas Falkner, *Sturm aufs Große Haus: Der Untergang der SED* (Berlin: Edition Fischerinsel, 1990), p. 125.

4. Gregor Gysi, *Das war's noch lange nicht!* (Düsseldorf: Econ Verlag, 1997), p. 136.

5. Heinrich Bortfeldt, *Von der SED zur PDS—Aufbruch zu neuen Ufern? Sommer/ Herbst 1989–18 März 1990* (Berlin: Kommission Politische Bildung des Parteivorstandes der PDS, 1990), p. 24.

6. PDS, *Materialien: Außerordentlicher Parteitag der SED-PDS, Berlin, Dezember 1989* (Berlin: Dietz, 1990), p. 149.

7. By 1997, commentators were to acknowledge that the PDS had contributed to social integration at a time of rapid transformation. For example, see Sigrid Koch-Baumgarten, "Postkommunismus im Spagat. Zur Funktion der PDS im Parteiensystem," *Deutschland-Archiv* 30, no. 6 (1997): 864–878.

8. Section of the party constitution regarding "Zusammenschlüsse," in *Partei des Demokratischen Sozialismus: Programm und Statut* (Berlin: PDS, 1998), p. 34.

9. Rainer Land and Ralf Possekel, "PDS und moderner Sozialismus," in *Die PDS: Postkommunistische Kaderorganisation, ostdeutscher Traditionsverein oder linke Volkspartei? Empirische Befunde und kontroverse Analysen*, ed. Michael Brie, Martin Herzig, and Thomas Koch (Cologne: PapyRossa, 1995), pp. 115–116.

10. PDS Programmkommission, "Thesen zur programmatischen Debatte," *Pressedienst PDS*, no. 47 (26 November 1999): 4.

11. André Brie et al., eds., *Zur Programmatik der Partei des Demokratischen Sozialismus. Ein Kommentar* (Berlin: Dietz Verlag, 1997), p. 123.

12. Manfred Uschner, *Die roten Socken* (Berlin: Dietz Verlag, 1995), p. 19.

13. Patrick Moreau and Jürgen Peter Lang, *Linksextremismus: Eine unterschätzte Gefahr* (Bonn: Bouvier Verlag, 1996), p. 244.

14. Michael Schumann, "Wir brechen unwiderruflich mit dem Stalinismus als System!" in PDS, *Materialien*, pp. 41–56.

15. Dieter Klein, "Fertige Lösungen—das wäre wieder der Anfang von alten Strukturen," in PDS, *Materialien*, pp. 69, 67.

16. PDS, *Programm der Partei des Demokratischen Sozialismus. Entwurf* (Berlin: PDS, 27 April 2001).

17. Manfred Gerner, "Antagonismen der PDS. Zum Pluralismus der SED-Nachfolgepartei," *Deutschland-Archiv* 29, no. 2 (March–April 1996): 228.

18. Land and Possekel, "PDS und moderner Sozialismus," pp. 115–116. By 1997 this approach had become clearly dominant in PDS publications. For example, Michael Brie, "Die moderne kapitalistische Gesellschaft," in Brie et al., *Zur Programmatik der Partei des Demokratischen Sozialismus: Ein Kommentar*, pp. 25–42.

19. PDS Programmkommission, "Thesen zur programmatischen Debatte," pp. 21–22 (section on "Demokratisierung der Demokratie").

20. Patrick Moreau, "Das Wahljahr 1994 und die Strategie der PDS," *Aus Politik und Zeitgeschichte*, B1 (7 January 1994): 21.

21. Helmut Zessin, Edwin Schwertner, and Frank Schumann, *Chronik der PDS 1989 bis 1997* (Berlin: Dietz, 1998), p. 24.

22. Manfred Gerner, "Widerspruch und Stagnation in der PDS," *Zeitschrift für Politik* 45, no. 2 (1998): 166–167.

23. Uwe Backes, "Überblick: Linksextremistische Parteien in Deutschland: Sehnsucht nach 'Sinnstiftung,' " *Das Parlament* 44, no. 1 (15 April 1994): 2.

24. PDS, *Partei des Demokratischen Sozialismus: Programm und Statut* (Berlin: PDS, 1998), p. 37.

2

Coming to Terms with Opposition Role and German Unification, February–December 1990

At the extraordinary congress in December 1989, PDS delegates had still assumed that it was possible to modernize the socialist system of the GDR. The delegates still thought it likely that two German states would coexist in a confederation, perhaps preparing unification. The Democratic Socialists were still leading the government of the GDR, through Prime Minister Modrow. It appeared possible that a reformed PDS, with new leaders, new structures, and new ideas, could still play a significant role in the GDR. However, within a short time the political environment changed dramatically, in two respects. First, the party whose predecessor had governed the GDR for four decades was forced to learn all about an unaccustomed role as opposition after the Volkskammer elections of 18 March 1990. Second, the West German government was setting the pace for rapid unification, including currency union on 1 July, official constitutional union on 3 October, and the first election of a united parliament on 2 December 1990. Thus the PDS had to adjust to a role as marginalized opposition and to the absorption of a collapsing GDR by a much larger Federal Republic.

By late January it had become obvious that decisive internal and external prerequisites for the GDR's continued existence were no longer there. Internally, the overwhelming majority of GDR citizens wanted unification with West Germany; externally, the Soviet Union no longer had the will or the capacity to maintain the GDR, neither as junior partner in a socialist bloc nor as Western outpost in a strategic buffer zone serving Soviet security needs. Soviet leader Mikhail Gorbachev made this clear to Prime Minister Modrow in late January.

Modrow acknowledged the inevitable, on 1 February, in his declaration "Deutschland, einig Vaterland" (Germany, United Fatherland),[1] suggesting a confederation of the two Germanies as transition to unification. On the same day, the PDS abandoned its earlier policy of arguing for a continued existence of the GDR as part of a confederation. The party began to advocate a slower, negotiated process of unification without, however, being able to slow down the speed of the unification process, which effectively extended the economic, constitutional, and political structures of the Federal Republic to include East Germany.

The Party of Democratic Socialism had lost the initiative like its predecessor, the SED. After several years of inaction under Honecker, the SED had, in October and November 1989, begun to respond to change, albeit hesitantly and late. Similarly, the PDS was still merely reacting to changing international and domestic conditions in January 1990. Yet, unlike the SED under Honecker, the PDS at least realized it needed to adjust to a rapidly changing environment.

ELECTIONS MARCH 1990: GETTING USED TO THE OPPOSITION ROLE

In preparation for the elections to the Volkskammer on 18 March 1990, the Democratic Socialists held their election congress on 24–25 February. The last elections for the parliament of the GDR were also the first elections in which SED victory would not be guaranteed by a leading position on the unity tickets of all GDR parties. The PDS had to prepare itself for an opposition role. Electoral strategist André Brie pointed out that the party was not participating in the elections in order to win but to contribute to the development of a functioning democracy in the GDR.[2]

Opinion polls in January and February had identified the Social Democrats as the most popular party among East Germans, although their popularity declined when Chancellor Kohl gained a profile as the historical leader unifying Germany and bringing to East Germans the benefits of joining the Federal Republic. Eventually the Party of Democratic Socialism received a disappointing 16.4 percent of the vote on 18 March, while a majority supported Kohl's conservative Christian Democrats and their allies.

These elections were the end of the Modrow government and the beginning of an unaccustomed opposition role for the PDS. This included not only the usual frustrations that oppositions have to endure in parliamentary democracies. There was also the hostility of many East Germans and of the other parties toward the PDS. Its very survival was under threat, due to electoral unpopularity, loss of members, and active measures by government and parliamentary majority to weaken the party. The crucial instrument was to be the "Independent Commission for the Investigation of the Property of Parties and Mass Organizations of the GDR," which had to assess how much of the considerable assets of the SED were illegitimate and should be turned over to the state and how much could be retained by the PDS as successor of the SED.

For several years, the investigations by the Independent Commission together with well-timed demands by the tax office as well as internal financial scandals brought the PDS repeatedly to the brink of financial collapse. The question of the assets legitimately to be retained by the party out of the SED's massive property was to be settled not before July 1995.[3]

Electoral support for the Democratic Socialists declined further from the 16.4 percent achieved in March, down to 14.6 percent in local government elections on 6 May and further to 11.6 percent in elections for regional parliaments on 14 October. After four decades of a constitutionally entrenched government role for the SED, the PDS found itself on the opposition benches, marginalized by other parties, threatened in its financial survival by the Independent Commission, facing declining electoral support and membership numbers.

SEARCHING FOR A FOOTHOLD: NO ALLIANCE WITH WEST GERMAN COMMUNISTS

The decision by the PDS not to adopt the DKP as its West German ally and counterpart was of long-term significance for the place of the party in German politics, although it was barely noticed by observers at the time. In the long term, it allowed the PDS to overcome marginalization and to occupy a space in the party system as a left-socialist party capable of entering coalitions. In 1990, the PDS had to look for potential partners in West Germany as it became clear that unification of the two German states was proceding rapidly, with the currency union in mid-1990, the legal-constitutional unification in early October, and the first national elections on 2 December. For all other parties, the unification of the party systems consisted in a West German party expanding into East Germany or absorbing a preexisting East German sister party. Besides the ruling SED, there were four minor parties in East Germany. Their role was limited to the exercise of minor roles in the administration of the GDR without ever challenging the SED, yet each of the four had circa 100,000 members and an extensive branch structure. Although the leading personnel of these minor parties had participated in junior roles in the SED system, their branches and members were too valuable an asset for Western parties to treat them as enemies because of their past association with the SED.

The West German CDU absorbed the East German Christian Democrats as well as the Democratic Farmers Party of Germany (DBD). The Free Democrats absorbed the Liberal Democrats (LDPD) and National Democrats (NDPD). The West German Greens found partners in the Alliance 90 formed by some of the 1989 dissident groups. The Social Democrats were without an established East German partner because the East German SPD had ceased to exist in 1946 when it merged (or was forced to merge, depending on the interpretation of this controversial process) with the Communist Party to form the Socialist Unity Party of Germany. Thus the SPD depended on cooperating with the new Social Democratic Party founded in East Germany in the last weeks of 1989.

The Party of Democratic Socialism had three options regarding West Germany, none of which promised many short-term benefits. The PDS could either enter into an alliance with the (West) German Communist Party (DKP) or start its own PDS branches in the ten West German Länder (relying on West German left-wing splinter groups to provide personnel and structure). Initially, however, a third option was taken, and the Linke Liste (Left Ticket) was formed as an electoral alliance of individual West Germans.

The PDS benefited from a judgment of the Federal Constitutional Court (29 September) ruling that the 5 percent threshold for representation in parliament was to be applied for East and West Germany separately, not for the whole of Germany. This guaranteed parliamentary representation for the PDS, as it was certain to win more than 5 percent in the East, whereas its lack of support in West Germany made it very unlikely to win 5 percent for the whole of Germany. On the other hand, the PDS experienced a setback when electoral laws adopted by the Bundestag on 4 October disallowed electoral alliances between different parties in East and West ("Listenverbindungen"),[4] thus making it impossible for the PDS to combine its electoral efforts with an improvised West German Linke Liste. Instead, the party now had no choice but to set up its own party branches prematurely and hastily in West Germany.

The PDS leadership rejected cooperation with the DKP in order to keep other options open. The West German Communists had declined from their peak of circa 50,000 members in the 1970s and suffered from splits in the late 1980s, but they still could provide a branch network of almost 10,000 rather active members, certainly more effective than the hastily assembled 500 members of the Western branches of the PDS. Nevertheless, the PDS declined all offers by the DKP. Heinrich Bortfeldt pointed out that "cooperation with the . . . discredited . . . DKP would have immediately destroyed all other alliance options . . . on the left."[5]

The long-term significance of this decision was even greater. By rejecting the alliance with the DKP, the PDS majority kept open a future position as a left-socialist party for the whole of Germany. Within the PDS, only the minority Communist Platform demanded cooperation with the DKP, regarding it as an obvious West German partner. The leadership of the PDS, on the other hand, envisaged a different future for the party. The consequence of cooperation with the DKP would have been a permanent role as marginal opposition party, perhaps capable of mobilizing ten thousands of loyal activists but locked into a marginal electoral position below 1 percent, just like the DKP. A broader left-socialist party, on the other hand, would have the chance of attracting more electoral support and to be represented in parliaments and local councils. Rejecting the offers of the DKP meant that the PDS would adopt an identity as a left-socialist party, not as a communist party. It also meant prioritizing electoral success and parliamentary activity over the communist tradition of ideological, economic, and political class struggle. In the long run, this decision by the PDS was to facilitate future cooperation with Social Democrats and Greens eventuating several years later, beginning in 1994.

Many political analysts overestimated the continuity between the SED and PDS. Patrick Moreau, for example, asserted that the PDS was "dominated by continuity" and remained a thinly disguised communist party.[6] In the late 1990s, quite a few analysts had abandoned this aproach and defined the PDS more precisely as a left-socialist party. However, it was already possible to notice in 1990 that the PDS was very different from the SED. The strongest evidence for this discontinuity was the structural change of the party organization and the rejection of an alliance with the DKP.

HOW MUCH OF THE SED'S PROPERTY WAS LEGITIMATE PDS INHERITANCE?

The Socialist Unity Party had accumulated vast assets during four decades of governing the GDR. The Party of Democratic Socialism, as legal successor of the SED, was in possession of these assets, including real estate, printing works, a fleet of vehicles, holiday homes, and bank accounts. The question of which of these assets the PDS could legitimately claim as its own was raised, within the party and, more forcefully, from outside. As a new party, it could only distance itself from the past and gain credibility if it ceded most of this inheritance, retaining only a fraction of these assets necessary to allow the PDS to function. From here on the PDS embarked on temporary orderly administration of these assets, ceding most of them while struggling to defend its essential assets by political means and in the court system.

The party executive decided, on 13 January 1990, to cede SED property, including 11 of 16 newspaper publishing houses, 21 of 26 printing presses, and 22 of 37 guest houses. On 4 February, the executive resolved to give 3,041 million Mark (GDR), originating in the profits of SED enterprises, to the budget of the GDR government, in order to return illegitimate SED assets to the people of the GDR. If the PDS hoped to regain credibility among GDR citizens, this hope was not fulfilled. Quite to the contrary, this decision created mistrust, as people assumed that a party that "could cede so readily more than 3000 million Mark, was likely to have much more in reserve."[7]

After the Volkskammer elections of 18 March, the new parliamentary majority also raised the question of SED assets in the hands of the PDS. The Volkskammer appointed, on 31 May, the Independent Commission for the Investigation of the Property of Parties and Mass Organizations of the GDR. In spite of the broader brief indicated by its title, the commission was to focus on the assets of the SED now held by the PDS. The motives for the establishment of the Independent Commission were mixed. On the one hand, there was the interest in returning the illegitimate assets of the SED to the people of the GDR, through the state budget or by allocating them to local government. On the other, there was also the motive to make life difficult for the PDS, perhaps to destroy the party financially.

The other institution involved in decisions over former SED assets, besides the Independent Commission, was the Treuhandanstalt. This body was founded by the Modrow (PDS) government, on 1 March 1990, in order to administer nationalized property but also to transform some of it into private enterprises. Later, the Treuhand was given the task of privatizing the entire East German economy. Besides this main task, the Treuhand also administered the former assets of the SED.

On several occasions the actions of the Independent Commission, the Treuhand, and the Tax Office came close to eliminating the Party of Democratic Socialism by simply destroying its economic viability as an organization.

The PDS sought to retain as much property as could be considered its legitimate inheritance, including assets owned by the Communist Party before 1933 when it was banned by the Hitler regime. The PDS also had claims to sufficient assets to enable it to continue the legitimate work of a political party. At the same time, one can assume there was also the motive just to retain as much as possible of the SED assets. To demonstrate goodwill, party treasurer Wolfgang Pohl informed the press about PDS assets, and on 20 July a statement about these assets was handed to the Independent Commission.[8] This started very lengthy proceedings that only ended in July 1995, five years later.

In late 1990, illegal financial transactions by party officials triggered a financial scandal that damaged the credibility of the PDS. It also revealed some of the fears and misperceptions about West Germany that some of the older generation of party leaders had inherited from past historical experience. Wolfgang Pohl, party treasurer and one of the three deputy chairmen, had transferred the massive amount of DM107 million to an account in Moscow. The police searched PDS headquarters in the Karl-Liebknecht-House in Berlin, on 18 and 26 October, for evidence. Pohl admitted the transaction and was arrested on 26 October.[9]

Pohl stated that he and other party officials feared that the party would be driven into illegality,[10] like the SPD under Bismarck from 1878 to 1990, or the KPD for shorter periods during the Weimar Republic, for the entire 12 years of the Nazi dictatorship and, again, from 1956 to 1968 in West Germany. In order to guarantee the survival of the party in illegality, Pohl had attempted to secure assets. This financial scandal triggered further losses of party members. It also damaged the image of the PDS just before the Bundestag elections of 2 December.

Pohl's assumptions about the situation of a socialist party in bourgeois democracy were based on historical experience. In the communist tradition, bourgeois democracy was always considered an insecure place for a working-class party that could never securely enjoy democratic rights. Behind bourgeois democracy there was always the dictatorship of capital that could quite easily take on less democratic forms, forcing a working-class party underground. In order to be prepared for this, a party would have to take precautions as soon as threats to its survival began to appear.

On the other hand, there was the social democratic tradition of committing the SPD to a reform strategy under the conditions of bourgeois democracy. It had not enabled the Social Democrats to withstand the onslaught of Nazism in 1933, but it had allowed the SPD to grow in strength in postwar West Germany and to lead government from 1969 to 1982.

Many members of the Party of Democratic Socialism did not know what to expect in late 1990. A decade later it was clear that bourgeois democracy in West Germany could accommodate a left-socialist party. The PDS had experienced attacks by the media and suffered other disadvantages, but it enjoyed the benefits of legality and was represented in local, regional, and national parliaments throughout the 1990s. In the first weeks after unification, however, after 3 October, the historically engrained reflex of preparing for illegality was triggered in PDS treasurer Pohl, at a time when the GDR had ceased to exist, popular hostility toward the PDS intensified, and threats of unemployment affected former GDR officials.

This financial scandal contributed to a clarification of political thinking in the PDS. The theoretical issue of the reliability of bourgeois democracy took on practical relevance. If "capitalist modernity" meant more than just capitalist exploitation, if it also meant "civilizing achievements" such as rule of law, formal democracy, and individual human rights, then a left-socialist party such as the PDS could find a place in the political system and embark on a radical reform strategy without abandoning its identity and without having to fear illegality.

The financial scandal around the illegal transfer of funds threw light on the practical relevance of subsequent theoretical discussions. The PDS understood itself as "societal opposition," but it had to find out what the political options for such "societal opposition" were. The party also had to become familiar with the new political environment; it had to "arrive in the Federal Republic," as party strategist André Brie was to formulate later.

Pohl's historically grounded fears made it impossible for him to perceive "bourgeois democracy" as anything else but the thinly disguised "dictatorship of capital." On the other hand, the experience of the PDS in the following decade, and the accompanying theoretical debates, showed that bourgeois democracy was a significant civilizing achievement of capitalist modernity, there to be enjoyed even by a "societal opposition" such as the PDS.

The PDS officials involved in illegal financial transaction were sentenced, on 20 March 1992, by the Landgericht Berlin to suspended prison terms, two years for Pohl and 21 months each for Wolfgang Langnitschke and Karl-Heinz Kaufmann. These sentences were squashed by a federal court on 21 October 1993, and finally on 20 June 1995, the three were found innocent of the original charge of acting against the interests of their employer, the PDS.[11]

FIRST ALL-GERMAN ELECTIONS OF 2 DECEMBER 1990

The first elections in united Germany on 2 December 1990 resulted in a majority for the governing coalition of Christian Democrats and Free Democrats.

The voters, especially in East Germany, expressed their confidence in Chancellor Kohl, who had brought them rapid unification. The warnings of Social Democratic leader Oskar Lafontaine highlighting the costs of rapid unification were rejected by the electorate. For the Party of Democratic Socialism the elections signaled continuing decline. Compared to the Volkskammer elections of March 1990, PDS support in East Germany had gone down from 16.4 percent to 11.1 percent, and in West Germany, the PDS/Linke Liste had achieved no more than 0.3 percent, for a national total of 2.4 percent. Only the separate application of the 5 percent clause to East Germany allowed the PDS to cross the representation threshold and to win 17 seats in the Bundestag, out of a total of 662.

This result, together with the continued rapid decline of PDS membership, seemed to indicate that the party was heading for certain extinction. Political analysts confidently predicted that it would not be represented in the Bundestag after the next election in 1994, when the 5 percent clause would be applied to Germany as a whole.[12] One year later, in October 1991, opinion polls predicted even lower results for the PDS, as low as 6.5 percent in the East and 1 percent for the whole of Germany. Patrick Moreau predicted "a certain 'out' at the next Bundestag elections,"[13] even expecting the knockout perhaps earlier in the East German local government elections of 1992.

For the time being, however, the PDS was represented in the Bundestag. It had one direct mandate, in the East Berlin electorate of Berlin-Hellersdorf/Marzahn where chairman Gregor Gysi attracted a relative majority of 31.8 percent. The other 16 seats were the result of proportional distribution according to the votes supporting the PDS tickets. Much of its electoral support came from white-collar workers and the intelligentsia, whereas few blue-collar voters had supported the PDS. While its predecessor SED had claimed to be the party of the working class, the PDS had become a party of the socialist intelligentsia; its electoral strongholds were the suburbs of East Berlin housing the "service class" of the GDR. This weakness of the PDS encouraged other parties to adopt a strategy of marginalization hoping to accelerate the imminent demise of the PDS. The 17 PDS parliamentarians were an isolated minority experiencing hostility in all facets of life in parliament.

In December 1990, the PDS had been saved by a quirk of the electoral system: the application of the 5 percent representation threshold separately to East and West Germany, a once off rule for the first election immediately after unification. The end of the PDS appeared imminent, most likely at the 1994 Bundestag elections when the 5 percent threshold would be applied for the whole of the German electorate.

NOTES

    1. Hans Modrow, *Aufbruch und Ende* (Hamburg: Konkret Literatur Verlag, 1991), appendices 5 and 6, pp. 184–188.

2. Heinrich Bortfeldt, *Von der SED zur PDS: Wandlung zur Demokratie?* (Bonn: Bouvier, 1991), p. 153.

3. Helmut Zessin, Edwin Schwertner, and Frank Schumann, *Chronik der PDS 1989 bis 1997* (Berlin: Dietz, 1998), p. 273.

4. Bortfeldt, *Von der SED zur PDS: Wandlung*, p. 224.

5. Ibid., p. 216.

6. Patrick Moreau, *PDS—Anatomie einer postkommunistischen Partei* (Bonn and Berlin: Bouvier, 1992), p. 454; Patrick Moreau and Jürgen Peter Lang, *Linksextremismus: Eine unterschätzte Gefahr* (Bonn: Bouvier Verlag, 1996), p. 244: "The camouflage is almost perfect."

7. Bortfeldt, *Von der SED zur PDS: Wandlung*, p. 174.

8. Zessin, Schwertner, and Schumann, *Chronik*, p. 29.

9. Bortfeldt, *Von der SED zur PDS: Wandlung*, p. 233; Zessin, Schwertner, and Schumann, *Chronik*, pp. 34–5.

10. Bortfeldt, *Von der SED zur PDS: Wandlung*, p. 234.

11. Zessin, Schwertner, and Schumann, *Chronik*, p. 86, 144, 267.

12. Thomas Ammer, "Die Parteien in der DDR und in den neuen Bundesländern," in *Parteien in der Bundesrepublik Deutschland*, ed. Alf Mintzel and Heinrich Oberreuter, 2nd ed. (Bonn: Bundeszentrale für politische Bildung, 1992), p. 458.

13. Moreau, *PDS—Anatomie*, p. 458.

PART TWO

SLOWING DOWN THE DECLINE, SURVIVING ON THE MARGINS, 1990–1994

3

Decline of PDS Encourages Exclusion Strategy, 1991–1992

THE WEAKNESSES OF THE PDS IN 1991–1992

In the first two years after unification the Party of Democratic Socialism experienced a prolonged period of weakness during which its end as an organization and as an electoral party seemed imminent. Most serious was the continued dramatic decline of its membership. In 1989 the SED had 2.3 million members, that is, about 1 in 5 adult GDR citizens. By February 1990, the PDS had only 650,000 to 700,000 members. Half of these had deserted by early June 1990 when the party counted 350,941 members. One year later, in June 1991, membership stood at 242,000. At the end of 1991, only 172,579 remained. The age structure of party membership added to this picture of imminent collapse. In 1994, two-thirds of all members were older than 55 years.[1] The membership of the PDS was either defecting or dying out.

Administrative and financial measures threatened the financial survival of the PDS even after it had weathered the scandal of November 1990 over the illegal transfer of DM107 million to Moscow. The Treuhand took control of all real estate owned by the party in Brandenburg (June 1991) and in Berlin, including party headquarters in the Karl-Liebknecht-House, on 12 July. Legal proceedings over this matter continued for a year until the Berlin Administrative Court decided on 24 August 1992 that the Treuhand had to return the Karl-Liebknecht-House to the PDS without any restrictions. On 27 June 1991, the Treuhand took control of all accounts of all PDS executives on all levels. Even payments of less than DM10,000 were subject to approval by the Treuhand. This financial control was intensified on 1 September when the Treuhand informed the PDS that all monies had been withdrawn from all accounts of the PDS. For the time being, the Treuhand had granted a loan of DM5.5 million, which the PDS had to pay back by the end of 1991.

The Independent Commission for the Investigation of the Property of Parties and Mass Organizations of the GDR decided in November 1990 that even the membership fees collected by the SED had been illegitimate. This decision implied that the PDS was not entitled to any part of the property inherited from the SED. To prevent the elimination of the party by administrative means, the executive appealed to members and supporters (23 November) to help the party to survive.[2]

Although the PDS contributed to a clarification of the financial situation by renouncing any claims to SED property outside Germany in favor of the Treuhand, the disputes with the Treuhand, the Independent Commission, and the Tax Office over the former property of the SED were to continue until mid-1995. The financial survival of the party was threatened repeatedly by rather arbitrary measures of the authorities. However, at the same time the PDS reaped the benefits of the Rechtsstaat (rule of law), as it could use the system of administrative courts to appeal successfully against these administrative decisions.

The foundation of the Committees for Justice in mid-1992 was an attempt by the Democratic Socialists to break out of their isolation by initiating a social movement with an appeal broader than the party itself. These committees were meant to be the core groups of a wider movement for social justice, for the redress of injustices and deficits of the unification process. This purpose was not achieved, nor did the committees become the core of a broader political party. They succeeded, however, in consolidating the connections between the PDS and its clientele organized in groups defending specific East German interests. These links were further consolidated with the foundation of the Ostdeutsches Kuratorium der Verbände (East German Coordination of Associations), launched on 2 October 1993 in East Berlin.[3]

In this period of membership decline, financial pressures, and marginalization, the PDS also saw its electoral appeal decline further, beyond the losses it had suffered between the election results of March 1990 (16.4 percent in the East) and December 1990 (East, 11.1 percent; West, 0.3 percent; nationwide, 2.4 percent). Opinion polls on 9 June 1991 indicated support for the party was as low as 6.5 percent in the East and 0.5 percent in the West. When an opinion poll in late 1991 gave the Democratic Socialists no more than 1 percent nationwide, Patrick Moreau predicted the end of the party not later than at the 1994 Bundestag elections but probably even earlier, during the local government elections in East Germany in 1992.[4]

Yet these local government elections became the first indicator that the party could survive, although everything else was pointing to a rapid demise. In the Eastern districts of Berlin, the PDS achieved 29.7 percent of the vote (24 May 1992), showing that it had consolidated support in its stronghold areas. Although the party as a whole was still unpopular, its candidates were accepted by many East Berliners as competent local government administrators.

Late 1991 and early 1992 was to be the period of lowest electoral support for the PDS. Signs of recovery were not recognizable at the time. It seemed that the PDS was losing voters and members in an unstoppable process, although it demonstrated some resilience in a subculture concentrated in several districts of East Berlin. It appeared likely that the PDS would soon be no more than a "milieu party" representing a small subculture of former GDR public servants and party officials, localized in East Berlin.

By late 1993, however, this period of lowest electoral support had been over-come. An opinion poll by the Allensbach Institute in late December showed 5.3 percent support for the PDS for Bundestag elections,[5] indicating that the party had a remote chance to overcome the 5 percent threshold to qualify for representation in the Bundestag after the 1994 elections.

MARGINALIZED BY OTHER PARTIES: ELIMINATION STRATEGY

The objective to marginalize and eliminate the Party of Democratic Socialism was shared, in the early 1990s, by all other parties represented in national and regional parliaments. It was somewhat ironical that the PDS had become the target for all negative feelings about the GDR and the Stasi, after these no longer existed. The SED, on the other hand, while it was still governing the GDR, had been a sought-after dialogue partner, in government-to-government relations with the CDU/CSU and in party-to-party relations with the SPD during the 1980s. After the collapse of the GDR, the bitterness about the SED, the Stasi, and Honecker had to find an outlet. There was only the PDS as target for deep-seated emotions, which made it difficult to acknowledge that the party was very different from its predecessor, the SED.

For the conservative Christian Democrats and the neoliberal Free Democrats, a negative portrayal of the PDS continued the anticommunism of the Cold War period. Anticommunism was one of the themes holding together the Catholic, liberal, and national-conservative currents united in the CDU/CSU since the late 1940s; it served to delegitimize not only the West German communists but anything loosely connected with "socialism," including the Social Democrats. After German unification and the disintegration of the Soviet Union in 1991, the anticommunist theme lost some of its power. Nevertheless, it was still useful for the CDU/CSU to use memories of communist rule in East Germany and the Soviet Union as long as possible to create a negative image for the democratic socialists in the PDS, which might also damage the social democratic SPD.

The Social Democrats had somewhat different motives for marginalizing the PDS. First, like the Christian Democrats, the SPD had a tradition of anticom-munism readily applied to the PDS as well. Second, the SPD harbored painful memories of 1946, when Communists and Social Democrats in the Soviet Occupied Zone merged to form the Socialist Unity Party of Germany (SED). For most West German Social Democrats and for those East German Social Democrats who opposed this merger and fled to the West, the Socialist Unity Party meant the destruction of the Eastern branches of the SPD forced to submit to a *Zwangsvereinigung* (coercive merger) by the Soviet Occupation Administration and the KPD. And third, the PDS was a competitor in the electoral arena competing for voters on the left margin of the SPD and of the Greens.

The merger of KPD and SPD in 1946 had initially been welcomed by many Social Democrats in the East, because it promised to end the division in the German working-class movement that had occurred after World War I and was regarded by many as an important cause for Hitler's victory over the left in 1933. However, even many of those who initially wanted the merger were disappointed by 1949 when the SED had been transformed from the expected broad left-socialist mass party into a highly centralized, ideologically narrow Marxist-Leninist party following the model of the Stalinist Communist Party of the Soviet Union (CPSU). Memories of this merger were kept alive in the West German SPD by a cohesive group of former Eastern Social Democrats who could not forget or forgive the elimination of Social Democracy as an organization for over four decades. The anniversary of this merger in 1996 was to provoke another heated debate about the relations between SPD and PDS.

However, unlike the Christian Democrats, the center-left SPD could not have the same uncomplicated relation to the PDS. For the Christian Democrats, the PDS would always be a distant, far left opponent. For the SPD, the PDS was the successor of an enemy that had destroyed the Eastern SPD in the 1940s, and it was a competitor for similar sections of the electorate. Yet the PDS was also a potential source of members for the SPD. Finally, the PDS was even a potential ally of the SPD. If the PDS was to develop into a possible junior partner of the SPD, just like the formerly marginalized Greens had done, the combined potential of the German left could outnumber the electoral support of the CDU/CSU and FDP.

In 1990, the SPD had the option to reclaim social democratic potential in East Germany by inviting former members of the SED to join the SPD, especially those organized in the "Social Democratic Platform" of the PDS. For several reasons the SPD decided against this option and preferred to support the newly founded "SDP" (Social Democratic Party),[6] although this meant to restrict itself to a very narrow membership base in the East. To invite former SED members to join the SPD would have been an admission that the SED had included a social democratic component since 1946 that survived as a continuing undercurrent in the SED for four decades.

The SPD was attractive to former SED and PDS members, such as Wolfgang Berghofer, mayor of Dresden and one of the deputy chairmen of the SED-PDS, elected at the extraordinary congress of December 1989. When Berghofer left the PDS in January 1990, dozens of competent administrators left with him.

However, the SPD maintained the taboo against SED personnel—a decision that was to make life difficult later in the 1990s.[7]

The taboo against former SED personnel was more costly for the SPD than for the CDU/CSU. The Christian Democrats readily absorbed the Eastern CDU, including all personnel that had served in the GDR as mayors and administrators. The SPD, on the other hand, had to rely on the rather inexperienced personnel of the newly founded Social Democratic Party in the East.

A strategy of marginalizing and eliminating the PDS made sense for the center-right CDU/CSU, and the center-left Social Democrats had even more reasons for this strategy in the early 1990s. If there were any Social Democrats speculating whether the PDS could, one day, function as junior partner of social democrats, just like in Sweden or France, they certainly did not discuss this option openly in the early 1990s.

There were also very pragmatic reasons for a strategy of exclusion and elimination. Any cooperation with the PDS in the early 1990s would have alienated most East German and virtually all West German voters. And because the PDS was on the verge of extinction, a strategy of marginalization seemed rewarding. At that stage, a portrayal of the PDS as a merely superficially reformed Stalinist party was compatible with the preferred strategy of the day. Yet as soon as the PDS showed that it could survive and retain regional relevance in the East, perhaps even gain some national relevance, the portrayals of the party by political analysts changed toward a justification of partial cooperation. This made it very difficult to assess the extent of change within the PDS. All assessments of the PDS as a whole and all comments about its wings and platforms were affected by the strategic preferences and partisan sympathies of the commentators.

PORTRAYALS OF PDS COLORED BY STRATEGY TOWARD PDS

The portrayal of the PDS by political analysts was clearly associated with the strategies recommended by these experts. In the early 1990s, the "totalitarianism" concept served to justify the marginalization of the PDS, suggesting that the democratic parties of center-right and center-left had to keep a distance from all extremist parties, both left and right. On the other hand, by 1996–1997 a "modernization theoretical" approach appeared that ascribed to the PDS a useful function "for the political regulation of the transformation process"[8] of East Germany. As the established Western parties could not achieve social and political integration of all East Germans during this difficult period of transformation, partial cooperation with the PDS could be justified as the party offered a "necessary and useful, nevertheless . . . in the long run superfluous" supplementary function during a transition period.[9] Instead of characterizing the PDS as extremist and dysfunctional, these modernization theorists argued that the party system was stabilized as the PDS contributed to its representativity and integrative capacity. These two major conceptions appeared in several variations of exclusion and integration strategies, each supported by a corresponding portrayal of the PDS.

Four more specific approaches combining a portrayal of and a strategy toward the PDS can be distinguished. First, a strategy of marginalizing the entire PDS could be justified by a portrayal of the whole party as extremist or, at least, as tainted by its extremist components. This approach led analysts such as Patrick Moreau, Eckhard Jesse, or Jürgen Lang to exaggerate the continuity between SED and PDS. In several books by Moreau, for example, the PDS as a whole was portrayed as a thinly disguised, superficially and cleverly reformed communist party that still had revolutionary and violent intentions but was capable of deceiving an unsuspecting electorate.[10] This portrayal suggested that the PDS should perhaps be banned as anticonstitutional or at least be observed by state authorities. Other parties should continue to exclude the PDS from cooperation as "German democracy should renew its antitotalitarian consensus and take notice of the danger from the extreme left, not only from the extreme right."[11]

Second, a strategy of marginalizing and splitting the PDS was predicated on an analysis of the PDS as deeply divided internally between reform socialists and traditionalist communists. Here the PDS was to be kept isolated and quarantined until it had shed its left wing. According to Manfred Gerner, only the KPF and other minorities within the PDS were extremist, whereas the extremist character of the whole PDS was deducted from the fact that it included the KPF as well as a silent majority of older members full of nostalgia for the GDR and quietly supporting the KPF against PDS reformers. Although reformers occupied all leading positions in the PDS, Gerner argued that they could not really reform the PDS because of the mentality of the nostalgic silent majority and because of the impact of the KPF.[12] Gerner emphasized the diversity within the PDS, pointing to serious differences between leading reform socialists, Communist Platform, older members, and more pragmatic local councillors. This analysis suggested a strategy of placing the PDS in quarantine until its internal differences had been sorted out. Once the communist wing was split off and isolated, the reform socialist wing could be absorbed into the electoral support base of the SPD.

Third, a strategy of partial integration of the PDS was also based on portraying the party as internally divided. However, here the split was to be accelerated by partial cooperation with the party. Thus the PDS could be induced to shed its unacceptable radicals, after which the acceptable components could be integrated. Jürgen Raschke was an early advocate of elimination by integration. He pointed to the French precedent where the Socialist Party had included the French Communists into a government coalition depriving them of their role as vocal opposition. In this approach, the PDS was described as paralyzed by divisions, with a detachable left wing. The dominant reform socialists were portrayed as rather similar to Greens and Social Democrats in many respects,[13] implying they could be made superfluous.

A fourth approach appeared only slowly and hesitantly: It positively emphasized the overlap between PDS programs and ideas of left Social Democrats and Greens. The greater these similarities, the more the Democratic Socialists could be portrayed as harmless and nonthreatening. If this analysis were right, the PDS was perhaps superfluous as just another version of left social democracy and environmentalism but not dangerous.[14] However, this more accepting portrayal of the PDS remained a small minority position for several years. This approach could justify cooperation with a PDS interpreted as a harmless regional variant of SPD and Greens. And should the PDS survive, its proximity to Green and left social democratic ideas could justify the inclusion of the party as junior partner in broad left alliances.

Many analyses of the PDS were shaped by a conceptual dichotomy subdividing the left into social democrats versus communists. This classification was certainly valid between 1917 and 1991, when European working-class parties could be readily classified into social democrats and communists, into Second International and Third International, although this had always neglected smaller currents. However, this dichotomy gradually lost its validity with the development of Eurocommunism, and in the 1990s, it became misleading. The development of the PDS into a left-socialist party was difficult to notice for observers guided by the dichotomous distinction between "communists" and "social democrats."

Statements by leading Social Democrats Oskar Lafontaine and Erhard Eppler illustrated this misconception. PDS Chairman Gysi reported suggestions by Erhard Eppler in 1991 "either to pursue traditional communist politics or, in case of a social democratic direction, to dissolve the PDS as superfluous." Oskar Lafontaine made similar suggestions to Gysi: "After all, I pointed out, we already had social democratic policies in place, and he had declared that he no longer subscribed to communist principles."[15] This logic could also be applied to components of the PDS, labeling them either social democratic or communist. This dichotomous approach obscured changes within the PDS and made it difficult to understand the PDS as a whole. The existence of left-socialist parties such as the Socialist People's Party of Denmark or the Party of the Left of Sweden had demonstrated for several decades that a left-socialist party, neither communist nor social democratic, could be a viable political project.

As the PDS changed internally and regained strength after a period of extreme weakness, the electorate grew less hostile to the PDS, especially in East Germany. While other political parties realized the failure of their strategy of marginalization and elimination, political analysts also modified their portrayal of the PDS as moribund and extremist. In the late 1990s, analysts began to ascribe to the PDS positive functions: They acknowledged that the party had provided many East Germans with "a 'political home' in a counterculture milieu"[16] during a transformation phase, helping them to get used to a new society and a new political system.

SHOULD THE AUTHORITIES BAN THE PDS AS "EXTREMIST"?

The Party of Democratic Socialism was regarded as an extremist party by the Federal Authority for the Protection of the Constitution and by its Land-level counterparts, dangerous enough to warrant observation, by overt and covert means. Every year, the PDS was included in official reports on the state of "extremism," on parties of the far right and far left. Such observations could provide the material for a ban of a party as anticonstitutional. The classification of a party as extremist by the authorities affected not only its legal standing but also its political standing insofar as other political parties were expected to shun any cooperation with such extremists.

Initially the authorities of every Land observed the PDS. After several years, the practices began to differ between the Länder. The party governing the most conservative Land, the CSU in Bavaria, repeatedly called for a ban of the PDS and for continued close observation. On the other hand, the head of the Authority for the Protection of the Constitution of Brandenburg (governed by Social Democrats) asserted (28 July 1995) that the PDS was a democratic party that did not warrant any observation.[17] By 1995, the treatment of the PDS by Social Democratic regional governments had begun to depart from the earlier marginalization strategy. Even Christian Democrats, especially in the Eastern branches, began to doubt the wisdom of calling for a ban of a party that was accepted by most Eastern voters as very normal.

Declaring a party illegal was made difficult by the German constitution of 1949 explicitly protecting the existence of political parties as parts of a functioning democracy. In the 1920s, the Weimar Constitution had treated parties like any other club or association: They could be banned by government decisions or by lower courts. From 1933 to 1945, under Hitler's Third Reich, all parties except the Nazi Party (NSDAP) were banned. In response to this experience, the Basic Law of 1949 prescribed that only the Constitutional Court (Verfassungsgericht) had the competence to declare a party illegal. In the Cold War climate of the 1950s, the Communist Party of Germany (KPD) was banned in 1956. This judgment was still in force decades later and made the existence of the German Communist Party (DKP) rather precarious when it was founded in 1968. The Constitutional Court could have easily found that the DKP was implicitly illegal as an obvious successor to the banned KPD. However, it was politically inopportune, in an international climate of detente, to bring the matter before the court. On the far right, the neo-Nazi Socialist Reich Party (SRP) had been banned in 1952, although this did not stop the foundation of other far right parties such as the NPD.

In this context, the analyses of the PDS by academic experts were not just exercises in political science. Any portrayal of the PDS by Moreau, Jesse, Lang, or Neu as an extremist party continuing the dictatorial traditions of the SED also justified continued observation and possibly a ban of the party. These authors published, for example, the *Jahrbuch Extremismus und Demokratie* (Yearbook on Extremism and Democracy),[18] an annual volume about political organizations they regarded as extremist. These materials supported the practice of some Land governments to observe the whole PDS or parts of it, especially the youth wing or the Communist Platform.

The more a party could be portrayed as extremist, the less legitimate it was for other parties to form coalitions with such extremists. Not only potential voters or members were warned off. More important, other parties were reminded that such extremists had to be excluded from the "antitotalitarian consensus" of German democracy.[19]

When the Bavarian minister Günther Beckstein (CSU)[20] stated in April 1995 that the PDS was just as extremist as the "Republikaner" party, he signaled to Social Democrats that they were to abstain from cooperation with the PDS, just as the center-right CDU/CSU was abstaining from any cooperation with the national-populist Republikaner. Several far-right parties (NPD, DVU [German Peoples Union], Republikaner) had managed to win seats in Land parliaments, usually taking electoral support away from the CDU/CSU. It was impossible, however, to form right-wing coalitions between the Christian Democrats and these parties, for two reasons. First, although the national-conservative wing of the CDU/CSU might have wanted an alliance with the right, the Catholic and liberal wings always resisted such calculations. Second, there was a broad consensus that the major parties were never to form alliances with extremist parties. In an apparent symmetry of left and right, the CDU/CSU had to keep NPD, DVU, and Republikaner isolated, and the SPD had to keep the DKP isolated. By classifying a party as extremist, it was no longer available as ally for its more centrist neighbors.

The governments of Bavaria and Berlin were most consistent in advocating observation of the PDS by overt and covert means. As the PDS was tiny in Bavaria, the warnings by the Bavarian CSU government were intended to keep the PDS on the margins nationwide, not just in Bavaria. On the other hand, the government of Brandenburg was the first to cease observation of the PDS. There were several reasons for this decision. First, the government of Premier Manfred Stolpe (SPD) had a more realistic assessment of the PDS as a legitimate left-socialist party than other Land (state within the German federal structure) governments. Second, the PDS was supported by circa 20 percent of the electorate and was accepted by a majority of voters as a legitimate party. Third, Stolpe owed the PDS some gratitude for saving his career when he had been accused of past cooperation with the Stasi secret police in the GDR. A parliamentary investigative committee, constituted on 27 February 1992 and chaired by Lothar Bisky (PDS), had found Stolpe innocent.[21] In this situation Stolpe had to reciprocate to some extent. Individual PDS members still had their real or alleged Stasi connection discussed publicly, but the PDS as a whole was no longer observed by the Brandenburg authorities as an extremist party.

The demarginalization of the PDS over the next few years was also accompanied by a reduction of observation by the central and regional Authorities for the Protection of the Constitution, at least officially. It remained, however, a useful tactic to remind the public at the right time of the allegedly extremist character of the PDS, for example, in late 1996 and early 1997, when Social Democrats and Greens were reassessing their relations to the PDS. At that time, several East German SPD leaders had expressed the view that partial cooperation with the PDS had become inevitable, at least in the East,[22] and similar views were voiced among the Greens. The Erfurt Declaration by prominent intellectuals and union leaders was to go further (9 January 1997), suggesting that SPD and Greens include the PDS in an "alliance for social democracy."[23] These debates were preparing the ground for decisions to be made about coalition options for elections due in 1998. The crucial question was: In case the CDU/CSU government lost its majority, should the SPD enter a "grand coalition" with the CDU, or should the SPD risk a coalition with the smaller Green party, possibly requiring the support of PDS parliamentarians?

Precisely in this situation the CDU, as senior partner in the Berlin Land government, pointed out that the observation of the PDS as extremist party might have to be stepped up. So far the Berlin authorities were observing several components of the PDS, including the Communist Platform and the youth wing of the party. Now the authorities were assessing whether the entire PDS had to be observed by covert means, including the use of informers. The reason given for the observation of groupings within the PDS was that some had contacts with the militant "Autonomen" youth subculture, whereas others had links to organizations of the Kurdish minority among immigrants from Turkey.

Support for this announcement by the Berlin CDU came from Germany's leading conservative daily, the *Frankfurter Allgemeine Zeitung (FAZ)*. Editorial comment in the *FAZ* warned against being guided by "political opportunity" in their assessment of the PDS. The latter had a harmless "Eastern face—as pedestrian regionalist party," whereas Social Democrats tended to forget the other face of the PDS as a "gathering point of left radicalism with connections to the terrorist milieu."[24]

Irrespective of the real activities and intentions of the PDS, the public image of the PDS had become a crucial component of German politics as soon as a majority to the left of the CDU was conceivable, formed by SPD and Greens, possibly requiring PDS support. Without a gradual gain of legitimacy by the PDS during the mid-1990s, it would have been impossible to form a coalition of SPD and PDS governing Mecklenburg–West Pommerania in 1998. If the PDS was really the left extremist counterpart to right extremist parties such as NPD, DVU, or Republikaner, a coalition of SPD and PDS was a breach of a taboo as repugnant as a coalition of CDU/CSU with the Republikaner. If, on the other hand, the PDS was a legitimate left-socialist party, the SPD could work with the PDS, whereas the CDU/CSU still could not form alliances with the far right.

HOW IMPORTANT WAS THE COMMUNIST PLATFORM (KPF)?

The Communist Platform attracted media attention far beyond its actual significance as a small minority within the PDS. Even more disproportionate was the media attention given, for several years, to the neo-Stalinist positions presented by Sahra Wagenknecht, a philosophy student in her twenties who was among the most quoted, most photographed, and most commented upon PDS members. The statements and writings of Wagenknecht were evidence for the media that the PDS included a silent majority of unreformed neo-Stalinists. It will be argued here that the neo-Stalinist positions of Wagenknecht were unrepresentative of the PDS. They were not even representative of the entire Communist Platform of which she remained a prominent member even after her demise from the wider party executive (Parteivorstand) of the PDS in January 1995.

To exaggerate the influence of the Communist Platform was a popular practice among journalists. This was still the case in 1998 when its influence had declined further than ever before. Author Christian von Ditfurth described the KPF as insignificant, as a group of merely 500 older members, according to his own research, although others gave estimates of 2,500 or 5,000. Whichever figure one accepted, "the KPF would be an insignificant sect in a party of 100,000 members." Nevertheless, von Ditfurth claimed that there were two factors giving the KPF significance. "On the one hand, it reflects in its theses what majorities in the party believe; . . . But just as important as this partial congruence between party majorities and KPF is, on the other hand, the spectacle which . . . media staged around Sahra Wagenknecht."[25] Ironically, von Ditfurth himself contributed to this spectacle of highlighting the tiny KPF and the neo-Stalinist individual Wagenknecht by dedicating the entire first chapter of his book to them.

The claim that the KPF minority represented the views of a silent majority of party members was made not only by journalistic authors such as von Ditfurth but also by more scholarly analysts such as Manfred Gerner.[26] However, it was a misleading assumption that all criticism of reform socialist leaders Gysi, Bisky, and Brie indicated KPF influence. The fact remained that most changes suggested by these leaders were usually accepted by the party, albeit after protracted debates.

Exaggerated claims regarding its influence were made by the Communist Platform itself. The KPF claimed that it spoke for the majority of PDS members resisting leaders intent on social-democratizing the party. The mirror image of these claims was presented by analysts arguing that the PDS could not be social-democratized by its leaders because a silent majority together with the KPF defended the crypto-communist character of the PDS. Both claims were evidently wrong. They ignored the variety of views in the PDS not reducible to a dichotomy of social democratic versus communist.

For a short time, during the foundation period in late 1989 and early 1990, the KPF had been an important component of the majority that opposed self-dissolution of the SED. After it had helped to preserve organizational continuity in the transition from SED to PDS, the Communist Platform found itself regularly in a minority on all strategic issues for the next decade, resisting in vain what it considered to be the gradual and consistent social-democratization of the PDS.

In 1990, the Communist Platform failed in its attempt to move the PDS into an alliance with the (West) German Communist Party (DKP), when the PDS was searching for partners in unifying Germany. Instead, the PDS majority kept the DKP at a distance and opted for the laborious formation of PDS branches in the West, thus keeping open the option of future alliances with SPD and Greens. In 1992–1993, the Communist Platform failed when it presented a draft for the party program, an alternative to the draft presented by the program commission of the party. The 1993 program, which the KPF criticized at the time, was later to become its defensive position when it tried to resist further change in the late 1990s. The pluralism enshrined in the PDS constitution and confirmed by the 1993 program was to become the Communist Platform's guarantee of survival.

That KPF influence continued to decline was shown at the party congress in January 1995 when Sahra Wagenknecht was not reelected to the wider executive. The fact that she received the support of about a third of the delegates[27] did not measure KPF influence. It rather indicated disagreement with the methods used by party leaders to prevent a reelection of Wagenknecht.

In mid-1995, the Communist Platform was replaced as the most relevant critic of the reform socialist leadership by the Marxist Forum (MF). [28] Unlike the KPF, the MF did not just appeal to a narrow spectrum identifying with the label "communist" but to a broader range of Marxist positions. The existence of the Marxist Forum marginalized the KPF further, as it could no longer claim to be the voice of all party members opposed to the Gysi-Bisky-Brie leadership.

The variety of views within the KPF can be illustrated by a comparison between Michael Benjamin and Sahra Wagenknecht. Benjamin rejected Stalinism as repressive, as undemocratic, and as a failed economic model. He attempted to find acceptable communist positions in a Leninism separated from Stalinist distortions inflicted after Lenin's death and advocated an evaluation of alternative communist traditions eliminated by Stalinism.[29]

Wagenknecht, on the other hand, defended the Stalin period of Soviet history.[30] While the anti-Stalinist communist Benjamin pointed to defects of "real socialism" as the main causes of its defeat, Wagenknecht emphasized two different factors. First, there were the antisocialist strategies of imperialism, beginning with outright pressure in the early phases of the Cold War, then shifting to the more indirect strategies of softening up the socialist world. Second, it was not Stalinism that had failed domestically. To the contrary, the decline of "real socialism" in the Soviet Union and Eastern Europe started with the revisionism of Nikita Khrushchev criticizing Stalin in 1956. Subsequently the domestic development of the Soviet Union deviated from the course toward communism, and in international relations the Soviet Union neglected the vigilance against the machinations of imperialism. This naïveté of "peaceful coexistence," which began with Khrushchev, was brought to completion by Gorbachev, who finally sold out to imperialism. In Wagenknecht's analysis, the failure of Soviet socialism was caused by external factors and by revisionist, opportunist aberrations from the precedents set by Stalin.

Wagenknecht's position ignored the inherent flaws of the Stalinist and post-Stalinist model of socialism. All other currents in the PDS criticized Stalinism—some more consistently than others—and shared the anti-Stalinist consensus developed in the PDS since its foundation. Wagenknecht, on the other hand, together with parts of the KPF, argued that loyalty to Stalin's approaches would have given socialism and communism a better chance of success.

Altogether, the difficult act of defining and maintaining a communist identity, which was credibly distant from the history of Stalinism, attracted only limited support in the PDS. The KPF was tolerated because a majority of the party regarded a democratic communist position as conceivable. On the other hand, neo-Stalinist or antidemocratic communist positions were clearly declared incompatible with PDS membership at the 1995 congress. The left-socialist PDS did not leave out in the wilderness this minority that insisted on calling itself communist, as long as it shared the anti-Stalinist consensus of the PDS.

THE STASI PROBLEMATIC: ALLEGED AND REAL PAST ENTANGLEMENTS OF PDS MEMBERS

The most hated institution of the East German regime was the State Security Service, abbreviated "Stasi" in German. Long after the end of the GDR, the Stasi problematic affected the public image of the PDS. The credibility of the party suffered by revelations that a number of PDS politicians had, before 1990, served the Stasi as part-time informers. In other cases, the damaging allegations were unfounded or could never be proven. Another aspect of the Stasi problematic was the close connection between the PDS and ISOR, a group representing the interests of former Stasi employees in conflicts over their pension entitlements and in legal proceedings. The collection of Stasi files administered by the Commissioner for the Records of the State Security posed a severe threat to the credibility of individual politicians and to the party as a whole. This will be illustrated briefly in reference to PDS politicians Wolfram Adolphi, André Brie, and Gregor Gysi and to the social democratic leader of the Brandenburg government, Manfred Stolpe.

Former Stasi officials found themselves completely marginalized in the last months of the GDR in 1990 and even more so after unification. Besides these full-time officials, the Stasi had made use of thousands of part-time spies, known under the abbreviation "IM" (*informeller Mitarbeiter* = informal contributor). In united Germany, any revelations about a past as IM could be a mortal blow to any political career. This affected not only former SED members now in the PDS but also former members of the East German CDU or LDPD joining the West German Christian Democrats or Free Democrats. There were also East German artists who had spied on dissident fellow-artists, or church officials who had reported on religious circles.

Information gained from the files of the Stasi was used to prosecute former GDR officials after German unification. These files were administered by the Commissioner for the Records of the State Security. A staff of 3,000 was employed to evaluate a massive collection of files that became the main source of accusations regarding past associations with the Stasi.

The credibility given to notes in Stasi files without requiring further evidence led to the ironic claim that the Stasi exerted some of its greatest impact after its dissolution. This was the view of eminent writer Günter Grass[31] who deplored that Stasi files were treated as if the notes were without any errors. The destruction of many Stasi files soon after November 1989 should be taken into account, as missing files could lead to different interpretations of existing files. And many notes reflected the need of Stasi officials to exaggerate their success in attracting part-time informers. Yet the files were often treated as irrefutable evidence rather than as indicative sources.

The case of Wolfram Adolphi, the chairman of the Berlin organization of the PDS, was of relevance for the whole party because the Berlin branch included more former GDR officials than any other branch. On 22 May 1991, Adolphi revealed that he had worked as IM for the Stasi producing analyses about the situation in East Asia while working there as a journalist. The subsequent congress of the Berlin PDS (8–9 June 1991) expressed its confidence in Adolphi; however, a debate continued over whether or not he should resign. The congress also adopted a resolution requesting party officials to be open about their pasts, including possible Stasi connections. In the end this case was solved by Adolphi stepping down as chairman of the Berlin PDS and as a member of the Berlin parliament.[32]

The national party congress of the PDS (21–23 June) responded to this situation by adopting a similar resolution demanding that all bearers of party offices and all candidates for public office should come clean about Stasi associations beforehand. This would not automatically exclude them from nomination but would, of course, be a severe handicap. A later party congress (29–31 January 1993) confirmed the "Stasi resolution."

The implementation of these decisions was very inconsistent. The most embarrassing case was that of André Brie, deputy chairman of the PDS and chairman of the Berlin organization. He had to admit that he had violated the congress resolution of June 1991 by not revealing his past activities as a Stasi IM. In December 1969, a young André Brie had volunteered to work as an IM. His activities as IM had been rather harmless, not causing harm to the human rights of any individual. However, he had not revealed his IM activity, contrary to the congress resolution of June 1991. Thus he had to step down as chairman of the

Berlin PDS (25 October 1992) and as deputy chairman of the entire PDS (26 October 1992).[33]

Yet the revelations affected Brie's career only to a limited extent. He could no longer act as the public face of the party as deputy chairman, possibly a future chairman. Nevertheless, he retained enormous influence in his new positions as election campaign manager and as chair of the committee in charge of developing party programs. Brie survived his IM scandal without having to face the end of his political career.

The social democratic leader of the Land government of Brandenburg, Manfred Stolpe, also came under attack for alleged Stasi connections in his past work as church official for the Brandenburg Protestant church. These allegations were investigated by a parliamentary committee, constituted on 27 February 1992, chaired by Lothar Bisky, a member of the Brandenburg Landtag and chairman of the PDS parliamentary group. The outcome of the committee's investigations was that Stolpe had never been an IM, that any contacts with Stasi officials had been inevitable in his work as church official and had not involved any illegitimate reporting.

SPD leader Stolpe was cleared and continued political life as premier of Brandenburg. Assuming that the committee's 1994 report was right in clearing him, it would still have been possible for the committee to treat the allegations in a more protracted and more damaging way, destroying even an innocent. In this respect, Stolpe had to be grateful to PDS leader Bisky who chaired the committee in a way that minimized damage to Stolpe—for example, by not presenting the report before local elections in Brandenburg in late 1993.[34]

The most tenacious pursuit of IM allegations was directed against Gregor Gysi, by far the most popular of all PDS politicians. First allegations against Gysi, then party president, emerged in January 1992. In mid-1995, by then parliamentary leader of the PDS, Gysi came under renewed attack and, once more, in 1997–1998, before the 1998 elections. Allegedly Gysi had served the Stasi as IM under the code name "Notar."

These allegations, if proven, could have inflicted massive damage on the PDS. Gysi was virtually the only PDS politician with any popularity among West German voters; election campaigns relied heavily on his witty and entertaining media performances. Gysi was also a symbol of a new beginning in the PDS, elected as party president in December 1989 because he was not a product of the old SED party apparatus.

Gysi's democratic credentials were based on his role as defense attorney acting for a number of dissidents in the last years of the GDR. It was precisely this reputation as courageous lawyer taking on East German authorities that came under attack. Allegedly Gysi had used his role as defense attorney to inform the Stasi about the intentions of the dissidents he was supposed to defend.[35] The accusations failed to take into account that the small number of defense attorneys in the GDR had to operate in the gray area between the GDR justice system and the Stasi, especially if they defended political dissidents.

The allegations reappeared again in 1997 and 1998. The parliamentary committee of the Bundestag investigating the allegations sidestepped the legal requirements of the court system by producing a report in May 1998 that portrayed Gysi as guilty. The report arrived at the conclusion that Gysi had worked as an IM for the Stasi from 1975 to 1986. In an attempt to clear his name, Gysi indicted himself under a procedure allowing lawyers to request an examination of alleged derelictions of duty. This self-indictment was, however, not admitted because Berlin justice authorities had already decided in July 1998 that Gysi had not breached his duties as defense attorney.[36] Thus Gysi was caught between legal authorities not allowing him to clear his name because he was not guilty of the charges and a parliamentary committee majority finding him guilty, conveniently during an election campaign.

A different aspect of the connections between Stasi history and the present PDS is shown by the interest groups representing former party and state officials of the GDR, including those employed by the Ministry for State Security. One of these groups was ISOR, the "Initiative for the Protection of Social Rights of former members of armed organs and of the customs administration of the GDR." About 100,000 of these officials had their postunification pension entitlements reduced by 30 percent by a government decision. Resistance to this "pension penal code" was the main motivation for ISOR. On 1 January 1997, the pension penalty was lifted for most former GDR officials but was retained for former Stasi officials, irrespective of their past function, whether they had operated as secret police proper or whether they had served as cooks or drivers.

ISOR had 25,000 members in the late 1990s and was part of a network of East German interest groups coordinated by the Ostdeutsches Kuratorium der Verbände.[37] The PDS regarded these groups as legitimate defenders of East Germans disadvantaged by the unification process. PDS politicians and lawyers provided the former Stasi officials in ISOR with political and legal support in their disputes with the social security administration. Therefore, these former GDR officials were among the most loyal supporters of the PDS.

Disputes about GDR history were more than just academic assessments of the shortcomings of "real socialism." For these former GDR officials, it concerned their own biographies. If the GDR was nothing but an *Unrechtsstaat* (state of injustice), then their lives had been wasted serving a criminal government. If, on the other hand, the GDR had been, at least in its beginnings and in its intentions, a legitimate response to German history, then former GDR officials could retain their self-respect. There was a biographic, personal dimension to debates in the PDS whether the term "Stalinism" should be applied to the GDR history after Stalin's death in 1953. The members of ISOR regarded themselves not as criminals but as defenders of an attempt to build a Germany free from Nazism.

Thus the PDS had to live with the "Stasi problematic." It was a new party led by critics of the GDR system. Yet some of these leaders had a past as IMs of the Stasi, while thousands of members and supporters had been deeply involved with the Stasi or other parts of the state apparatus. Many of these defended their biographies by defending GDR history. While the PDS carried the burden of real and alleged links with a problematic past, it provided an environment in which many East Germans could integrate into the society of united Germany, even those not at all welcomed by the new Germany.

MARGINALIZATION BY SPD IRONICALLY HELPED TO CONSOLIDATE PDS

The Party of Democratic Socialism survived its period of weakness in 1990–1992 because marginalization strategies against the party backfired and contributed to its stabilization as an organization instead of leading to its elimination. The electoral support base of the PDS was also consolidated by the punitive approach taken by the new government against many employees of the East German public service or the SED party apparatus. As these lost employment, careers, and much of their pension entitlements, they were forced into a defensive subculture, into a network of interest groups attached to the PDS as the only political force supporting these unification losers.

To welcome former SED members into the Social Democratic Party was a course of action SPD leaders could, hypothetically, have taken in 1990. Manfred Uschner[38] argued that such former SED members could have made a significant contribution to the SPD, which, unfortunately, rejected them. He pointed out that in 1946, at the time of the merger of KPD and SPD to form the SED, the 700,000 social democrats formed a majority among SED members. In spite of the SED's domination by communist personnel and ideas, the social democratic tradition survived in many families. Even in the early 1980s, when Margot Honecker wanted to change the name of the SED to "Communist Party of the GDR," this was not implemented because the SED still had some characteristics of a unity party.

A further reason for the existence of social democratic potential within the SED, according to Uschner, was the attractiveness of the West German SPD in the 1970s during Willy Brandt's Ostpolitik and in the 1980s during the interparty dialogue between SPD and SED.[39] Uschner, a former party official assisting SED leaders in conducting the dialogue with the SPD, was influenced himself. He was surprised, in 1990, by the turnabout in SPD practice, rejecting SED members who had previously been wooed as dialogue partners when they still were part of the governing SED.

It is plausible to assume that an invitation by the SPD to former SED members or current PDS members identifying with social democracy would have attracted thousands. This would have provided the SPD with competent personnel for local and regional politics and administration. It would also have given to the SPD an East German identity. If the defection of Wolfgang Berghofer and dozens of expert administrators in January 1990 had been followed by an exodus of thousands of PDS pragmatists to the SPD, the PDS would not have been able to gain strength in local government as early as 1991–1992. The Berghofer group even had negotiations with SPD representatives in Hamburg about an eventual transition, but these negotiations were aborted.[40]

The SPD had decided in December 1989 to select as East German ally a new party that had been founded in October under the name SDP (Social Democratic Party). This group included so many theologians that Uschner called it a "young pastors' movement."[41] Once this choice was made, it was next to impossible to allow an influx of former SED members into this new and small party, led by politically inexperienced pastors, without overwhelming this party completely.

A second reason for keeping former SED members out of the SPD, besides possible tensions between the new SDP and recruits coming in from the SED, was the historical animosity, since 1946, between the SED and the West German SPD. Welcoming former SED members into the SPD and accepting them as part of a surviving social democratic tradition in East Germany would also have amounted to a belated acknowledgment that in 1946 social democrats had joined the SED voluntarily in their hundred thousands. This would have destroyed the argument that the SPD in the East had been the victim of a *Zwangsvereinigung*, an entirely coercive merger.

A further unspoken reason for excluding former SED members was the difference between the West German SPD after the conversion to the Godesberg Program of 1959 and the older social democratic tradition suddenly reappearing among former SED members. The SPD had distanced itself from its Marxist socialist past and from its roots in class politics, becoming instead a center-left people's party. The social democratic potential among SED members, to which Uschner referred, was influenced by an older tradition. In January 1990, the new social democratic platform related to the tradition of Kautsky and Bernstein. Compared to the Communist Platform's reference to a non-Stalinist version of Leninism, the tradition of Kautsky and Bernstein was certainly social democratic. However, compared to the West German SPD after 1959 the East German social democratic potential was well to the left. The post-Godesberg SPD could not be thrilled by an influx of old-fashioned social democrats identifying with Kautsky, Bernstein, and Bebel, as well as Marx and Engels.

Thus the SPD found its Eastern partner in the "young pastors' movement" called the SDP, soon to be transformed into East German branches of the SPD. Later this decision was called a "historical mistake" by former SPD leader Willy Brandt.[42] In the climate of 1990, however, it would have required great courage and great foresight to risk the ire of the center-right parties if the SPD had decided to invite those SED members identifying with social democratic traditions to join.

With hindsight, an absorption of the pragmatic local councillors' component of the PDS by the SPD in 1990–1991 would have decisively weakened the PDS, depriving it of competent personnel that allowed the PDS in 1992 to regain the confidence of a part of the East German electorate. A PDS deprived of a large number of its local councillors and mayors would have been smaller, as an organization and electorally. It would have been located further to the left and in greater danger of political isolation. By excluding all former SED members, the SPD left these individuals with no other choice but the PDS. This left the PDS large and competent enough to rebuild itself from a strong base in local government.

Another effect of the exclusion of former SED members was that the SPD itself remained weak as an organization in East Germany. The SPD's electoral appeal in East Germany recovered from the defeat of 1990 as the CDU lost support in 1994 and 1998. However, this success was not stabilized by a corresponding development of the SPD organization in the East. By 1995, out of about 800,000 SPD members, only 28,000 lived in the East.[43] Thus the SPD's Eastern branches had only about a quarter of the membership of the PDS, which was more firmly rooted in East German society.

The exclusion of former SED members was supplemented by the marginalization of the service class of the GDR. The pattern of elite renewal after unification, which had sidelined and penalized the political, administrative, and scientific personnel of the GDR, had provided the PDS with a stable core of support from a subculture of unification losers. Although later, in the elections of 1994 and 1998, many PDS voters had above-average income and worked in white-collar occupations, there was still a widespread feeling of relative deprivation triggered by the influx of West German careerists taking over well-paid positions in the early 1990s.

Overall, the marginalization strategy against the PDS and the service class of the former GDR excluded a segment of East German society large enough to support a viable opposition party, eventually attracting about 20 percent support among East German voters. Furthermore, the widespread feeling among East Germans that their regions would remain disadvantaged for the foreseeable future contributed to a broader acceptance of the PDS from 1993 onward. A more selective strategy of marginalization together with an early strategy of integration could have reduced the PDS to insignificance. However, this strategy was not really available in 1990 or 1991. Nor was it apparently necessary as the blunt strategy of marginalization seemed to be successful without requiring more refinement. It was only after the consolidation of the PDS was becoming more obvious, by 1993, that a strategy of partial cooperation was suggested, still hoping for the eventual elimination of the PDS but accepting the fact of its medium-term survival.

NOTES

1. Patrick Moreau and Jürgen Peter Lang, *Was will die PDS?* (Berlin: Ullstein, 1994), p. 15; Dietmar Wittich, "Mitglieder und Wähler der PDS," in *Die PDS: Empirische Befunde & kontroverse Analysen*, ed. Michael Brie, Martin Herzig, and Thomas Koch (Cologne: PapyRossa, 1995), p. 67.

2. Helmut Zessin, Edwin Schwertner, and Frank Schumann, *Chronik der PDS 1989 bis 1997* (Berlin: Dietz, 1998), pp. 59–60, 64, 73.

3. Ostdeutsches Kuratorium der Verbände, *Mitteilungen Nr. 1* (Berlin: GBM, 1993); Ostdeutsches Kuratorium der Verbände, *Mitteilungen Nr. 2* (Berlin: GBM, 1994).

4. Patrick Moreau, *PDS—Anatomie einer postkommunistischen Partei* (Bonn and Berlin: Bouvier, 1992), p. 458.

5. Zessin, Schwertner, and Schumann, *Chronik*, p. 156.

6. Manfred Uschner, *Die roten Socken* (Berlin: Dietz Verlag, 1995), pp. 18, 180.

7. Ibid., pp. 180–189.

8. Sigrid Koch-Baumgarten, "Postkommunismus im Spagat. Zur Funktion der PDS im Parteiensystem," *Deutschland-Archiv* 30, no. 6 (1997): 865.

9. Gero Neugebauer and Richard Stöss, *Die PDS. Geschichte. Organisation. Wähler. Konkurrenten* (Opladen: Leske + Budrich, 1996), p. 299.

10. Patrick Moreau and Jürgen Peter Lang, *Linksextremismus: Eine unterschätzte Gefahr* (Bonn: Bouvier Verlag, 1996), p. 244: "The PDS is an extremist and modernised communist party. . . . The camouflage is almost perfect: With a pop image and a seemingly moderate program the PDS attempts to disguise its true intentions from the eyes of the public."

11. Moreau and Lang, *Was will die PDS?* p. 171.

12. Manfred Gerner, "Widerspruch und Stagnation in der PDS," *Zeitschrift für Politik* 45, no. 2 (1998): 179.

13. Jürgen Raschke, "SPD und PDS: Selbstblockade oder Opposition?" *Blätter für deutsche und internationale Politik* 39, no. 12 (December 1994): 1453–1464.

14. Hans-Georg Betz and Helga A. Welsh, "The PDS in the New German Party System," *German Politics* 4, no. 3 (December 1995): 103: "By 1994 the PDS had a strong resemblance to the West German Greens of the 1980s."

15. Gregor Gysi, *Das war's. Noch lange nicht!* (Düsseldorf: Econ Verlag, 1997), p. 250; Oskar Lafontaine, *The Heart Beats on the Left*, trans. Ronald Taylor (Cambridge: Polity Press, 2000), pp. 45–46.

16. Koch-Baumgarten, "Postkommunismus im Spagat," p. 876.

17. Zessin, Schwertner, and Schumann, *Chronik*, p. 276.

18. For example, Uwe Backes and Eckhard Jesse, eds., *Jahrbuch Extremismus und Demokratie*, vol. 9 (Baden-Baden: Nomos, 1997).

19. Moreau and Lang, *Was will die PDS?* p. 171.

20. Zessin, Schwertner, and Schumann, *Chronik*, p. 243.

21. Manfred Wilke, "Die Diktaturkader André Brie, Gregor Gysi, Lothar Bisky und das MfS," *Politische Studien* 49, no. 360 (July-August 1998): 50–55.

22. Wolfgang Thierse, "Strategiepapier 'Gesichtspunkte für eine Verständigung der ostdeutschen Sozialdemokraten zum Thema Umgang mit der PDS," *Frankfurter Rundschau* (19 December 1996).

23. "Erfurter Erklärung," reprinted in *Blätter für deutsche und internationale Politik* 42, no. 2 (February 1997); pp. 251–254.

24. *Frankfurter Allgemeine Zeitung*, 6 January 1997, p. 8.

25. Christian von Ditfurth, *Ostalgie oder linke Alternative: Meine Reise durch die PDS* (Cologne: Kiepenheuer & Witsch, 1998), p. 3.

26. Gerner, "Widerspruch und Stagnation in der PDS," p. 179.

27. Manfred Gerner, "Antagonismen der PDS: Zum Pluralismus der SED-Nachfolgepartei," *Deutschland-Archiv* 29, no. 2 (March–April 1996): 228.

28. Moreau and Lang, *Linksextremismus*, p. 124.

29. Michael Benjamin, "Über Kommunismus und 'Antistalinismus'—Antwort an Kurt

Gossweiler," *Kommunisten in der PDS. Sonderheft der Mitteilungen der Kommunistischen Plattform der PDS* (June 1995): 10–12.

30. Sahra Wagenknecht, *Antisozialistische Strategien im Zeitalter der Systemauseinandersetzung. Zwei Taktiken im Kampf gegen die sozialistische Welt* (Bonn: Pahl-Rugenstein Nachfolger, 1995).

31. Gisela Karau, *Die Affäre Heinrich Fink* (Berlin: Spotless, 1992), p. 96.

32. Gysi, *Das war's*, pp. 208–211.

33. Ibid., pp. 207–211; André Brie, *Ich tauche nicht ab. Selbstzeugnisse und Reflexionen* (Berlin: Edition Ost, 1996), pp. 72–85.

34. Manfred Wilke, "Die Diktaturkader André Brie, Gregor Gysi, Lothar Bisky und das MfS," *Politische Studien* 49, no. 360 (July–August 1998): 51–54; Zessin, Schwertner, and Schumann, *Chronik*, p. 143.

35. "Pakt mit dem Teufel," *Der Spiegel*, no. 24 (1995): pp. 40–44.

36. Sigrid Averesch, "Gysi beantragt Verfahren gegen sich selbst," *Berliner Zeitung*, 18 August 1998, p. 6.

37. Moreau and Lang, *Linksextremismus*, pp. 143–144; Ostdeutsches Kuratorium der Verbände, *Mitteilungen Nr. 1*, pp. 14–15.

38. Uschner, *Die roten Socken*, p. 95, 13.

39. Ibid., p. 15.

40. Ibid., p. 180.

41. Ibid., p. 180.

42. Ibid.

43. Ibid., p. 16.

4

Toward the 1994 Elections: Survival and First Steps out of Isolation, 1993–1994

REPRESENTING ALL EAST GERMANS, NOT ONLY UNIFICATION LOSERS

The consolidation and recovery of the Party of Democratic Socialism in 1993 and 1994 was possible because it was anchored in East German society: in local government, in broadly based welfare organizations, and in a network of interest groups responding to East German grievances. The party gained acceptance as "indicator and expression of East German identities." The PDS was the only relevant institution in the East that was not the result of a transfer of West German institutions but the outcome of "endogenous transformation."[1] The post-communist transformation of East Germany differed from that in other central and East European countries in that the end of "real socialism" was also the end of the GDR as a sovereign state. In the German case transformation involved not only system change but also unification of two countries. This made the transformation of the political and economic systems simpler in one respect: West German institutions were ready to be expanded into the East. The GDR was transformed by a "transfer of external institutions," a process characterized by "the dominance of 'ready made actors.'"[2] At the institutional level, German unification was a largely successful and smooth operation. The impact of trans-formation and unification on political culture and everyday life, on the other hand, was more contradictory. There was no "coincidence of systemic and bi-ographic transformation." Instead, Rudolf Woderich argues that "the radical sys-temic discontinuity of transformation effected a continuization of individual biographic patterns."[3] As the certainties of daily life were problematized by system change, East German identities based on everyday experience became more important for individuals.

This reassertion of East German identities became visible by 1992. Initially in 1990, almost all East Germans simply wanted to be Germans and supported rapid unification. Their new German identity amounted to an identification with all things West German, so strong that in 1990–1991 West German consumer goods were preferred to anything produced in the East. However, when East Germans began to feel that their luckier Western cousins looked down on them as somewhat unsophisticated and not used to the wheeling and dealing of a free-enterprise economy, only then did most "Ossis" realize that four decades of shared experience had created a common Eastern identity. When West German companies took over East German media, the incoming journalists from the West were not familiar with their audience's identities as Mecklenburgers, Brandenburgers, or Thuringians, let alone with their feelings as East Germans being taken over by West Germany. At this stage, an "Ossi" identity was reasserted. This was visible not only in opinion polls but also in everyday life, for example, in a rediscovery of East German consumer goods. In politics, the PDS was the main beneficiary of this reassertion of East German identity because it was the only party "at home" in the East. Other parties were perceived as Western, although the Christian Democrats managed to benefit from an assertion of regional identities in Saxony and Thuringia.

By 1993, the PDS could draw support from three social categories. First, it was anchored in a secular, socialist, urban subculture in East Berlin and other cities in the East. Second, it had a core of stable support from interest groups of unification losers from the former state and party apparatus who had lost employment, career prospects, and status during postunification elite replacement while also attracting support from qualified white-collar employees with above-average income. Third, it could gain popularity as the only party expressing East German interests, whereas all other parties were dominated by their Western branches.

The PDS survived its weakness of 1990–1992 not because there was an obvious need for a nationwide left-socialist party but because it became a credible representative of regional East German interests. This clashed in two ways with its proclaimed role as nationwide left-socialist party. In the West, it had limited appeal because it was perceived as East German. And in the East, many PDS members were tempted to abandon the effort to build a party in the West in favor of concentrating on the more rewarding role as a regionalist East German party.[4] At the same time, its regional strength made it possible for the PDS to claim some national relevance and to sustain the long effort of building the party in the West.

The credibility of the PDS as champion of East German interests resulted from the work of PDS members in local and regional parliaments. On 6 May 1990, in the last local government elections before unification, the PDS had achieved 14.6 percent of the vote and gained 9,300 seats in local representations.

Of these it had lost 500 by August 1991, and of 305 PDS mayors elected in May 1990, only 180 were still members of the PDS.[5] Nevertheless, the PDS had a base in local government. This was supplemented by local party branches setting up citizens' advice bureaus staffed by older PDS members with time on their hands due to early, involuntary retirement. There PDS members assisted East Germans not familiar with the workings of the new system, in their dealings with the bureaucracy of social security and local government. One of the most successful examples was Christine Ostrowski who began as campaigner for tenants' and residents' rights in the city of Dresden and later became an expert on housing issues and PDS member of national parliament. These grassroots activities translated into electoral success, noticeable for the first time on 24 May 1992, in the Berlin local government elections when the PDS gained 29.7 percent of the vote in Berlin's Eastern districts.

Older PDS members were also active in the Volkssolidarität (People's Solidarity), a welfare organization with hundreds of thousands of volunteer members, similar to the social democratic Arbeiterwohlfahrt (Workers' Welfare) in West Germany. In this prepolitical field of voluntary social work, the influence of the Volkssolidarität was due to be gradually reduced by competition from the Arbeiterwohlfahrt, the Catholic "Caritas," or Protestant welfare organizations. However, for a good number of years it provided PDS activists with local networks among East Germans.

The PDS also gave support to and received support from a number of interest groups expressing the interests of East Germans negatively affected by unification. These groups represented former state and party employees, Stasi and police officials, teachers, and academics sent into early retirement on low pensions. For example, it was estimated that 20 to 25 percent of those employed in the education system of the GDR were affected by mass dismissals.[6] Within the first two years after unification, until 3 October 1992, the unification treaty allowed for dismissals because of reasons such as "personal lack of suitability," "lack of qualification in the discipline," and "surplus to requirements." After this date, the official criteria for dismissal were narrower: Only violation of human rights or work for the Stasi were still reasons for immediate dismissal.[7] Yet in administrative practice the so-called individual case test still focused on questions about positions held in the GDR state or party organization, the holders of which were automatically disqualified as public servants.[8]

Although the foundation of the Committees for Justice, initiated by the PDS in July 1992, failed to develop a broad social movement against negative effects of unification and neoliberal attacks on the welfare state, these committees nevertheless served to consolidate existing interest groups. Another form of coordinating this multitude of interest groups was developed with the Ostdeutsches Kuratorium der Verbände which held its first congress in Berlin on 2 October 1993.[9] Besides these generalist organizations with a coordinating function, there were single-purpose groups with more specific themes. On 19 May 1993, the "Gesellschaft zur rechtlichen und humanitären Unterstützung" (Association for

Legal and Humanitarian Support) was founded.[10] This organization provided legal representation for former employees of government administration, the armed forces, and the justice system of the GDR confronted by the new legal system. The former GDR officials regarded this as *Siegerjustiz* (victor's justice), judging them under the laws of the FRG, which did not apply to them because they worked in another country, the GDR.

Other organizations represented citizens not involved with government or party under the GDR but nevertheless disadvantaged by the changes of property structures after unification. For example, many long-terms tenants of flats and users of land for gardening or recreational purposes were affected by the government decision to return real estate nationalized in the 1950s to former owners instead of compensating them financially while continuing existing tenancies and usage.[11]

The consolidation of its support base among East German interest groups and its appeal to an emerging East German identity allowed the PDS to survive in the early 1990s and to begin its recovery in 1993 and 1994.

PROGRAM OF 1993: "SOCIETAL OPPOSITION" AGAINST "PREDOMINANCE OF CAPITALIST PROPERTY"

A new party program was adopted by the third party congress of the PDS (29–31 January 1993) replacing the program hastily put together in January 1990. In long discussions throughout 1991 and 1992, three draft programs had been evaluated, one developed by the program commission of the party executive, a second draft put forward by the Communist Platform, a third draft developed by commission member Klaus Höpcke. The program debate had been a part of the long period of weakness of the PDS, during 1991, whereas the adoption of the program signaled a turn toward consolidation, beginning with the relative success in the Berlin local government elections of 24 May 1992.

Only the revised draft of the program commission was presented to the party on 19–20 December 1992, as the Communist Platform withdrew its text. While the debate before the congress had been controversial, an overwhelming majority of 96.3 percent of congress delegates voted in favor of the proposed text.[12] This left the Communist Platform and other opponents of the program isolated. In an ironic turn of events, the Communist Platform was to argue four years later that the reform socialist majority intended to undermine the consensus reached in 1993. By that time, the once unacceptable 1993 program had become a desirable defensive position for the KPF, attempting to ward off further change.

In the 1993 program, the PDS defined itself as "a socialist party in Germany." The indefinite article "a" signaled a break with past claims of KPD and SED that they were "the" party of the working class. The PDS also wanted to develop "the ability, to take up the ideas and experiences of other emancipatory movements," a wording that rejected claims to exclusive ownership of historical truth implied in "Marxist-Leninist" programs. The internal pluralism of the PDS was confirmed in its self-description as a "coalition of different left forces" including those "who want to offer resistance to capitalist society and reject the given conditions fundamentally, as well as those who connected their resistance with [efforts] to change the given conditions positively and to overcome them step by step."[13]

In an attempt to define the relative importance of parliamentary politics and extraparliamentary struggles, the program regarded "extraparliamentary struggle for social change as decisive."[14] This was interpreted by Manfred Gerner as a serious contradiction to the PDS's stated commitment to pluralist democracy, rule of law, and division of powers.[15] Here Gerner's critique failed to distinguish this emphasis on extraparliamentary activity from an attitude completely reject-ing "bourgeois parliamentarism." The 1993 PDS program acknowledged the relevance of parliamentary efforts: "The PDS strives for parliamentary strength and performs work in parliaments and in local government which is oriented towards the immediate problems of citizens." And even in this program empha-sizing extraparliamentary activity, the PDS signaled its willingness "to take on political responsibility for radical societal and ecological changes." This pro-grammatic guideline left open future participation of the PDS in government coalitions if tangible benefits for citizens and noticeable social or ecological change could be achieved. Priority, though, was given to a role of the PDS "as an oppositional force."[16] Later, after 1994, the emphasis clearly shifted. By 1997 the PDS was willing to join government coalitions.

The 1993 program never spelled out which economic order the PDS wanted. Gerner queried that it was "not transparent" whether the PDS "preferred a re-formed market economy or wanted some kind of planned economy."[17] Yet, while not excluding a future socialist economy the program could be regarded as guide for pragmatic reforms of the given economic system. The program favored a "plurality of property forms" and opposed the "predominance of pri-vate capitalist property." These apparently indecisive formulations left it open for traditional socialists to imagine a future society with a significant state and cooperative sector together with a substantial private sector. At the same time, this pluralism of property forms meant, for the foreseeable future, no more than a social market economy in which the PDS could assist Social Democrats in resisting the neoliberal drive toward privatization, in order to defend a public sector of limited size.

The "statism" of the PDS program was criticized by Gerner as it reminded him of SED programs.[18] It would have been more precise, however, to distin-guish between the SED's statism in a bureaucratic centralist model of socialism and a much more modest social democratic statism demanding state responsi-bility for welfare provision and regulatory intervention in the economy. The limited statism of the PDS program was much closer to social democratic in-terventionism than to the SED's centralist nationalized economy.

The program indicated, according to Gerner, deep splits between "two dia-metrically opposed currents" whom he identified as "social reformers" versus "orthodox Marxists."[19] The actual voting behavior of delegates at the 1993 congress did not support Gerner's claim. On the contrary, there was broad support for the program by 96.3 percent of the delegates. Contradicting his own claim of a deep split, Gerner admitted that there was a clear reform socialist majority among leaders and delegates. He suggested, however, that the "anti-reform minority" among leaders and delegates had the support of "a broad basis in the party" rejecting "social democratism" and concluded that "this asymmetric constellation–pro-reform majority in leadership and tradition-bound majority among the party rank-and-file–had a paralyzing effect on the party and had prevented radical innovation from the beginning."[20]

Here Gerner misunderstood the pattern of conflicts within the PDS. The Communist Platform was not the voice of a silent majority of members, although this was claimed by the KPF itself and by outside observers intent on overestimating the communist component of the PDS. The voting pattern at all congresses from 1993 on showed clearly that the KPF was a small and declining minority.

The bulk of the resistance against the reform socialist course of Gysi, Bisky, and Brie did not come from KPF positions, neither from the Leninist-Bukharinist position of Benjamin nor from the even more marginal neo-Stalinist position of Wagenknecht. The opposition came from an adherence to more centrist Marxist traditions, perhaps identifiable with the names of Bebel and Kautsky. A substantial part of the membership sympathized with positions expressed by intellectuals later organized in the Marxist Forum. They wanted to retain a more traditional Marxist approach emphasizing class issues, the property question, and a socialist perspective. This, they felt, was being abandoned by the "modern socialists" criticizing the "predominance of the profit motive" rather than capitalist property as such.

The 1993 program of the PDS struck an ill-defined compromise between these approaches. Like the modern socialists, it criticized "the dominance of the profit principle";[21] however, continuing the Marxist habit of focusing on property issues, it also recommended "that the dominance of private capitalist property had to be overcome." These arguments justified a strategy aiming to modify the dominance of the profit motive by political means and by introducing "a plurality of property forms."[22]

Compared to its predecessor of January 1990, the 1993 program was less decisive in its rejection of "real socialism" in the GDR and the USSR, although there was still a clear distance. In the mid- and late 1990s, minorities such as the Communist Platform and the Marxist Forum became defenders of the 1993 program against attempts by the modern socialists to shift party consensus further to the right by reducing the socialist elements in the program even more.

EVALUATING GDR HISTORY: WAS IT ALL WRONG?

The very existence and survival of the Party of Democratic Socialism was from the beginning dependent on finding an appropriate response to the history of East Germany under the SED. Was the history of the SED since 1946 so negative that a dissolution of the party was the only justifiable response? This was suggested by the Platform Third Way and supported by a large minority. Or was it possible to find positive aspects in the failed socialist project and in the traditions contributing to SED history? In the end, the foundation congress opted for organizational continuity and programmatic change. The justification was that organizational continuity was an act of honesty by not obfuscating responsibility for a negative past. The party tried a new beginning based on an open appraisal of a very problematic history.

Many critics of the PDS insisted that the party had never come to terms with GDR and SED history. In this view, the public statements distancing the party from Stalinism were less important than the defense of the past expressing the nostalgic mentality of many PDS members. Yet it will be argued here that all currents within the PDS, not only the reform socialist leadership, engaged extensively and critically with GDR history. The critical distance from the past varied, but it was noticeable in all cases, with few exceptions. Measured by the expectations of PDS critics, this distance from the past was not sufficient. To claim, however, that it was nonexistent or negligible would ignore all evidence.

The German term *Geschichtspolitik* refers to the politics of writing history or, more precisely, to conflicts over the interpretation of the past in order to legitimize present and future actions. After 1945, the German left had endeavored to widen the delegitimizing effects of Nazism's collapse by implicating not only the Nazi party but also conservative elites who had helped Hitler into power and benefited from armament, conquests, and "Arianization" of Jewish property. The right, on the other hand, focused blame exclusively on Nazi leaders while taking pro-Nazi elites out of the political firing line.

After 1990, *Geschichtspolitik* was again taking place on a massive scale. On the one hand, there was the effort to portray the GDR as "the second German dictatorship" besides the Third Reich, as *Unrechtsstaat* (a state characterized by injustice). This dominant interpretation was institutionalized in the Gauck authority administering the Stasi files and in the Enquete Commissions established by German parliament, in 1992 and again in 1995. The expected political effect of this version of *Geschichtspolitik* was twofold. First, it was meant to shape German political culture for the foreseeable future, delegitimizing not only Stalinist and administrative-centralist versions of socialism but all versions of socalist thinking. Second, it also served to justify the elite exchange undertaken in the East. If the GDR was "the second German dictatorship," more or less on a par with Nazi Germany, then it was justified to replace not only those who had committed human rights violations or other crimes but also most schoolteachers, university professors, and local government administrators who had not been part of the power elite of the GDR.

On the other hand, there was the effort of the PDS to combine a thorough critique of a failed, undemocratic, and inefficient model of socialism with a cautious defense of socialist ideals and of the individuals who had served these. This qualified critique of GDR history was intended to delegitimize Stalinist positions while opening up political space for left-socialist positions. The PDS had to undertake a careful sifting of historical traditions in its search for sources of legitimacy. This search for acceptable traditions was bound up with the psychological need to defend one's own biography.

Only a very small minority attempted an unqualified defense of the GDR together with a positive evaluation of Stalin's rule until 1953 and the subsequent period of centralist-administrative socialism, still shaped by the Stalinist past. This minority found itself on the margins outside the PDS, in small communist groups continuing a life of veneration for past leaders such as Ernst Thälmann. And there were individuals within the PDS, especially within the Communist Platform, who took this approach. The media paid attention to these marginal individuals, far beyond their objective relevance, because a quote from Sahra Wagenknecht made interesting news. Yet the defense of Stalinism by Wagenknecht, Hanns Heinz Holz, or Kurt Gossweiler was not representative for the evaluation of the past undertaken by PDS leaders, by "modern socialists," by the Marxist Forum, or by non-Stalinist communists in the Communist Platform.

Few agreed with Wagenknecht's claims that East European socialism had failed because of the betrayal by revisionists ranging from Khrushchev to Gorbachev. For all other currents in the PDS, the GDR had failed because of inherent systemic flaws. The Historic Commission of the PDS warned in a statement of 1993 against a selective, embellishing approach to GDR history overemphasizing periods of attempted reforms of the GDR system: "Attention is directed to the 'special German way' of the immediate post-war years, to the 'New Course' of 1953, the 'New Economic Policy' of 1963 as if in these conceptions alone there was sufficient evidence for the willingness of the SED to learn and for the reformability of GDR socialism."[23]

The dominant interpretation of East German history treated the GDR as the "SED dictatorship," the second German dictatorship besides the Third Reich.[24] This approach had massive institutional support in the Gauck authority and in the parliamentary Enquete Commissions of 1992 and 1995 but also among the West German historians taking over positions in East German universities in the early 1990s. On the other hand, PDS historiography had a weak institutional basis as historians close to the PDS were often in involuntary early retirement. Until 1991 to 1992, many East German historians had still held academic positions but had since then been *abgewickelt* (literally "wound down," i.e., dismissed during the transformation of the East German education system). The "PDS offered a protective roof to a number of social scientists dismissed after the collapse of SED rule which sheltered . . . an entire network of foundations, educational associations, research institutes and regular sessions of colloquia, quite apart from the Historical Commission with the Party Executive of the PDS."[25]

The claim that the PDS had not engaged in a critical analysis of East German history was made by many critics, for example, in an overstated and simplistic manner by Patrick Moreau: "In only six booklets . . . has the party tried to come to terms with its own history."[26] This quantitative claim can be refuted by the sheer number of conferences held and books published illustrating that the PDS made a significant effort to come to terms with history. In November 1990 a conference was held on "Stalinism in KPD and SED," followed by conferences on the Stasi and security policies of the GDR in October 1991, on the legal system of the GDR in October 1992, and on the use of political trials in united Germany in relation to the GDR past in November 1993.[27] From 1993 to 1998, the PDS published 11 volumes of *Ansichten zur Geschichte der DDR* (Views about the History of the GDR), which brought together the materials written by experts in support of the PDS minority in the Enquete Commission of the Bundestag.[28]

It was a different issue whether the quantity of PDS publications about GDR history also reflected a corresponding quality of critical analysis. Among party members there was a tendency toward a less-than-critical defense of the past. The Historical Commission of the PDS warned against this temptation to respond to "the wholesale condemnation of the GDR prevailing in the media" by "returning to old positions and shifting to an all-round defence of the GDR."[29]

Altogether, the PDS engaged with GDR and SED history quite extensively. In programmatic texts and historical publications the PDS developed a thorough critique and qualified defense of the past. If party members had a less precise response to the past, if the psychological need to defend their biography led to a more unqualified defense of GDR history, this should be noted but ought not be taken as evidence for an absence of historical critique.

A defense of the antifascist and socialist intentions of hundreds of thousands of East German social democrats and communists who joined the SED in 1946 was not an apology for the Stalinism in the Soviet Union until 1953 or the subsequent centralist-administrative socialism still shaped by Stalinism. For example, the publications of Uwe-Jens Heuer, a prominent member of the Marxist Forum, included a thorough critique of the lack of democracy in "real socialism," together with a critique of past socialist theorizing that expected all answers from changing economic power and class structure without exploring the need to democratize the political system.[30] Nevertheless, Heuer insisted on the distinction between "Stalinism" proper ending in 1953 with Stalin's death and the end of mass terror, and the subsequent period of "centralist-administrative socialism," deserving a lesser degree of critique.[31]

The greatest distance from the past can be found in the publications of modern socialists. Michael Schumann even distanced himself from those communists defeated and eliminated by Stalin because they still thought and worked within a communist framework.[32] Here the condemnation of the past was characterized by a broader notion of "Stalinism" including not only the period of Stalin's rule but "real socialism" after 1953 as well. André Brie acknowledged that the period after 1953 did not see the mass terror prevalent under Stalin, but structural continuities still justified extending the label "Stalinism" beyond 1953.[33]

Altogether, the PDS had come to terms with history to a relevant extent. This critical engagement with history linked the party with a variety of socialist, communist, pacifist, and radical-democratic traditions of German history. It attempted to salvage socialist ideals from a critically evaluated past. The critique of the past in PDS history debates was, however, less severe than in the dominant interpretation of GDR history as "the second German dictatorship" on a par with Hitler's Third Reich. In this respect, PDS history debates could not satisfy the critics of the party.

EVALUATING GDR BIOGRAPHIES: DISTANCE OR NOSTALGIA? PUNISHMENT OR RECONCILIATION?

Individuals responded to systemic discontinuity with an emphasis on biographic continuity. The transformation of East Germany had involved a change of the economic and political system as well as the end of a sovereign state. Thus systemic discontinuity was deeper, for example, than in postcommunist Poland, which continued as a sovereign nation. An additional psychological reason for East Germans to feel defensive about their biographies was the rediscovery of the continuing differences between East and West Germans. Within a short time after German unification, East Germans grew less enthusiastic about the slogan "We are one people." Unification remained welcome for an overwhelming majority; it became a settled habit much faster than division had. However, very soon many East Germans felt they were second-class Germans. The East would not catch up with the richer West soon but was to remain the poorer part of Germany for decades to come. The "Ossis" felt they were treated as slow-witted cousins who could not keep up with dynamic and streetsmart "Wessis," often behaving as "Besser-Wessis"—as Westerners who knew everything better.

This challenge to the individual self-respect of East Germans extended to their past. In the perception of many West Germans, East Germans had lived through four decades of a dictatorship as quiet accomplices, their biographies tainted by the very fact that they had lived so long under Ulbricht and Honecker. Thus the evaluation of GDR history was closely related to an evaluation of individual biographies. Had their lives been worthwhile living? This question affected those who had just lived their private lives in the niches of GDR society as well as those who had identified with the socialist project, either with its rather imperfect realization or with some imagined better version. For the officials of the East German state and of the former ruling party these questions were even more urgent as their careers had ended in early retirement with reduced pension entitlements. In many cases former members of police, military, and secret service also had to face the criminal courts of united Germany, accused of human rights violations.

The responses by two presidents of the Federal Republic illustrate the range of options for the treatment of former GDR officials. Both presidents, Roman Herzog and Richard von Weizsäcker, were members of the Christian Democrats.

Nevertheless, von Weizsäcker's emphasis on reconciliation differed clearly from the more punitive approach advocated by Herzog.

If the GDR had been a dictatorship on a par with Hitler's Third Reich, then the officials of party, state, police, and armed forces were to be punished like leading Nazis after 1945. If, however, the GDR had been, at least initially, a legitimate response to the German experience of Wilhelmine Empire, Weimar Republic, and Third Reich, then the punishment of GDR elites had to be much more selective. If the GDR project had some initial legitimacy, then only the perpetrators of human rights violations should face the courts. Other officials, who had only administered GDR laws without committing any particular human rights violations, should not be punished or sent into early retirement with reduced pensions. Even those who had been responsible for the construction of the border fortifications in August 1961 and for the guarding of this border until 1989 should not be treated as violators of human rights but be excused, as they had acted legally in an international context determined by Soviet interests in the East-West confrontation of the Cold War, far beyond the control of East German leaders, let alone individual border guards.

Rejecting calls for an emphasis on reconciliation and integration, German President Roman Herzog, a conservative Christian Democrat, still argued in 1998 for a punitive approach to officials of the former East Germany. Once before "those responsible for a dictatorial past" had benefited from a tendency to forget and to move on.[34] This misplaced leniency by the German justice system toward former Nazis in the 1950s should not be repeated with the personnel of the other German dictatorship. This argument by President Herzog distorted the basic legal principle that punishment should correspond to the seriousness of the crimes perpetrated. Whatever the "second German dictatorship" had committed, it was certainly not on the same order of magnitude as the Third Reich's extermination of millions of Jews and others on racist grounds, or the war of aggression it started in 1939.

In contrast to President Herzog's punitive approach, former President Richard von Weizsäcker recommended an emphasis on integration and reconciliation. Comparing the crimes committed by Hitler's Third Reich and by the GDR governed by the SED, he offered a realistic assessment of the proportions: "The SED state did not bear responsibility for a war of aggression or for a Holocaust."[35] Therefore, the necessary amount of punishment had to be much smaller in proportion. Comparing the GDR with South Africa, he argued: If Archbishop Tutu could emphasize reconciliation rather than punishment in his response to the Apartheid regime, then Germans could do the same much more easily, taking into account that the crimes against humanity committed by the Apartheid regime had been so much worse than anything that happened in East Germany.

Following the example of Archbishop Tutu, von Weizsäcker pleaded: "Reconciliation cannot succeed without truth. Truth without reconciliation, however, is inhumane."[36] In practice, the punitive approach advocated by Herzog prevailed for several years. Nevertheless, the liberal-conservative position of von Weizsäcker also achieved some influence.

Von Weizsäcker also argued that any accused should normally be tried by measuring his actions against the laws valid in his country at that time, not by retrospectively applying the laws of another country. Thus GDR officials should not be judged by West German law. The only exception to the rule "nulla poene sine lege" (no punishment without law) should be made in the case of extremely grave violations; for example, in the Nuremberg trials leading Nazi war criminals were judged by the standards of international law, not by the laws of Nazi Germany, which they had obeyed.[37]

East Germans who had served in the education system, in the health services, or in local administration all resented that their lives were devalued. They were denied recognition of their qualifications and services. If they still had jobs, they found themselves demoted; if they were in early retirement, their pensions were reduced. Finally, there were millions who had done their work and who had brought up their families. Were their lives worth less than those of West Germans who had done exactly the same except in far more comfortable circumstances?

Whether these arguments defending the value of East German biographies were fully justified can analytically be kept separate from the fact that there was a reassertion of East German identity driven by the individual need for self-respect. The economic beneficiaries of this assertion were the producers of East German consumer goods that regained popularity after an earlier period in which only West German goods were desired by East German consumers. And the political beneficiary was the PDS presenting itself as the only party defending East German interests and offering an environment in which East Germans could look back at their lives with some self-respect.

THE DIFFICULTIES OF BUILDING THE PDS IN THE WEST

In the hectic months of German unification in 1990, the PDS had gained a foothold in West Germany, in a mixture of improvised responses and strategic decisions. The PDS rejected an alliance with the (West) German Communist Party, although this alliance had been recommended by the Communist Platform within the PDS. Instead, an electoral alliance was attempted between the PDS and an improvised West German collection of individuals under the name "Linke Liste." This arrangement was, however, made impossible by rulings of the Constitutional Court against such electoral alliances between East and West German groupings. Thus the PDS improvised a third option. The groups around the Linke Liste turned themselves into Western branches of the PDS. By December 1990, this approach resulted in 0.3 percent or 100,000 votes in the first postunification elections. Party membership remained at an extremely low level in West Germany, with circa 600 members in September 1990, about 250 in early 1992, and over 1,000 in March 1993.[38]

From 1990 to 1994, the progress made by the PDS in West Germany was extremely slow. During 1991 and 1992, setbacks canceled out any achievements. Only during 1993 and 1994, when the party consolidated its position in East Germany, did it also experience a modicum of success in West Germany.

The decision of 1990 to start the PDS in the West, instead of continuing the search for an alliance between the Eastern PDS and a collection of Western Leftists, created lasting difficulties, according to Gero Neugebauer.[39] The Western Left remained skeptical about any PDS intentions to enter alliances without leadership claims; the PDS, on the other hand, had ongoing doubts about the ability of the left in the West.

The cultural gap between East German PDS members and West German leftists (to the left of the SPD) can be illustrated by the experiences of Christine Ostrowski, leader of the Dresden city organization of the PDS:

At the beginning of my closer contacts, about spring 1990, I was full of respect. . . . I imagined some immensely experienced "battle hardened revolutionaries," former 68ers. . . . Over time I realized then that my exalted ideas were misplaced. I encountered the Western Left as smaller groups of people—i.e. some invitations . . . created the impression of immense masses of people, when umpteen organizations had signed the paper, and when I got there, a mere handful of people sat there and each represented one of the organizations with only a few members each. . . . We have the responsibility that the GDR broke down. They, I think, have to consider why they have reached so little societal relevance.[40]

Ostrowski could also have considered whether the weakness of left socialists and communists in West Germany had less to do with their individual shortcomings than with the rather unattractive East German model of socialism and the successes of West German capitalism tempered by an energetic welfare state.

The cultural distance worked both ways. The exercise of power had been a distant historical project for Western Leftists, a hypothetical possibility. For many Eastern PDS members, on the other hand, the exercise of power and the occupation of influential position had been reality not a long time ago. Many PDS politicians had been local and regional administrators, university professors, or officials of a ruling party. The individuals joining the Western branches of the PDS could not understand that it was more important to get into local councils, Land parliaments, or Land governments than to criticize capitalism from a principled position. The different experiences of political socialization in the 1970s and 1980s resulted in different approaches to politics.

For the West German leftists, as for the Communist Platform and the youth wing of the party, radical politics was about mobilizing social movements and building a critical oppositional culture. On the other hand, for East German PDS politicians with experience in the state or party apparatus, politics was about exercising power—previously in the second or third rank of the GDR elites and now in local and Land government of united Germany, albeit in a totally different framework.

Surprisingly the PDS absorbed more individual members from small former Maoist, Trotskyite, or Green-Alternative organizations[41] than from the milieu of the German Communist Party, which had identified with East Germany before unification. The closest West German equivalent of the positions held by the "modern socialists" and by the Gysi-Bisky leadership was to be found as a left-socialist minority within the SPD. The radical reformism of Gysi and Bisky resembled the notions of "system-transcending reforms" or "structural reforms" advocated by the Young Socialists (the youth wing of the Social Democrats) in the late 1960s and early 1970s.[42] Yet these left-socialist SPD members had no reason to join the PDS.

Another close West German equivalent of PDS radical reformism would have been the "innovators" wing of the German Communist Party. However, these Gorbachovites had left the DKP in the late 1980s, only to disperse in disappointment and exhaustion. From this source the PDS could only attract a small number of individuals such as Wolfgang Gehrcke, former leader of the DKP "innovators,"[43] without recruiting much of the potential of circa 10,000 Gehrcke supporters who had left the DKP with him. The traditionalists in the remaining DKP organization were the preferred Western allies for the Communist Platform in the PDS. Yet PDS leaders consistently rejected any party-to-party alliance with the DKP, not only in 1990 but ever after.

In this situation, when several more natural counterparts to the PDS were not really available, the Western branches of the PDS recruited members from a surprising range of organizations. Groups that had criticized Soviet and GDR socialism from Maoist and Trotskyite positions had changed since their foundation in the 1970s by leftist students. These groups had deradicalized themselves sufficiently to make the PDS an acceptable option for joining either individually or en bloc. Some groups retained their organizational cohesion even after joining the PDS. Thus the party was used as a forum by much smaller groups, or it became a career path for those tired of far left fringe politics. For example, two activists of the previously Maoist KB (Communist League), Ulla Jelpke and Andrea Lederer, became members of the federal parliament for the PDS.[44]

Altogether, the PDS recruited a small but colorful spectrum of members in West Germany, forming party branches completely different from those in East Germany. The 100,000 East German PDS members and their leaders often had, to say the least, mixed feelings about the 1,000 or 2,000 West Germans in their party.

The difficulties of finding any members and voters in the West were compounded by the difficulties experienced with the party members the PDS did attract. For example, the Hamburg branch of the PDS decided twice to stand for Land parliament elections, in September 1993 and again in September 1997, both times against the advice of the central PDS executive. In both cases electoral support for the PDS was very low (0.5 percent in 1993 and 0.7 percent in 1997), considerably lower than the votes achieved by the PDS in Hamburg in the national elections of 1994 (2.2 percent).[45] Repeatedly the executive tried to mobilize those Western members willing to work more closely with the leadership in order to impose some discipline on other members using the PDS as a vehicle for the political practices of their groups of origin.

The construction of the West German PDS progressed exceedingly slowly and haltingly during 1991 and 1992. In June 1991, executive member Wolfgang Gehrcke[46] had to admit failure in his task of forming a pluralist alliance of West German groups ("Sammlungsbewegung") to be allied to the PDS. This might have served as a bridge to those West Germans left of the SPD but unwilling to be submerged in a much larger PDS. After the failure of this concept, expanding the PDS westward remained the only option, especially when the foundation of the Committees for Justice in 1992 failed to attract more than the narrow clientele of the PDS.

In spite of these experiences, the third Session of the second Party congress confirmed the intention that the PDS wanted to become a nationwide party (14–15 December 1991). This ambition experienced a setback when the PDS suffered a financial crisis in 1992 and 1993, resulting in a retrenching of full-time organizers in the West. However, since spring 1993 a reactivation of the Western Länder branches could be observed.[47] The number of West German members of the PDS rose from 1,180 members (1993) to 2,048 members (1994). By 31 December 1995, membership in the West had risen to 2,388.[48]

When the party congress of January 1995 confirmed the commitment of the PDS to attempt an expansion into West Germany, the worst was over. In the 1994 elections support for the PDS had tripled, from a very low 0.3 percent in December 1990 to a not-so-low 1.0 percent in 1994. Encouraged by this result, PDS leaders announced that the PDS definitely did not want to remain an Eastern regional party but would continue its expansion to the West.

A NEW IMAGE: CLOSER TO F.D. ROOSEVELT THAN TO MARX

The "Ingolstadt Manifesto" was launched by PDS chairman Gregor Gysi on 16 February 1994. With this document, Gysi made an effort to project an image of the PDS as a party for all Germans, not just a representative of East German interests. The text addressed "all people living in Germany," and this appeal was reinforced by the choice of the Bavarian city of Ingolstadt as the place of launching the text and as part of the title. Even most West Germans outside Bavaria would have to think twice before they could locate Ingolstadt, about 60 kilometers (40 miles) north of Munich on the Danube river. The act of launching this document in Ingolstadt said as much about the PDS as the content of the document. It illustrated the need for the party to get noticed in West Germany where its organization was still very weak, especially in Bavaria. For attention and publicity the party was dependent on the popular and entertaining Gysi. During election campaigns, the witty and talkative lawyer was the party's face in the media, the only PDS politician known by West Germans.

Although the title "Manifesto" alluded to the Communist Manifesto of 1848, the text used the language of nonsocialist political thinking. The demand for a "New Deal" literally alluded to U.S. President F.D. Roosevelt's attempt to rein in the unbridled capitalist market. Unlike the 1848 manifesto, Gysi's text did not express any intention of abolishing capitalism. His arguments "against the socially irresponsible state, against the absolute power of capital" differed from traditional Marxist demands to break the power of capital. Rejecting Thatcherite freemarket radicalism, he demanded a return to the social regulation of capitalism that had emerged in Western Europe and North America in response to the Great Depression and World War II. Reminiscent of J.J. Rousseau rather than Karl Marx, Gysi asked for a "New Social Contract,"[49] for a new agreement on an ethical-political framework to guide the market economy.

Within the PDS, Gysi's Ingolstadt Manifesto was soon attacked as a relapse into presocialist thinking, back to the liberal and democratic framework of Rousseau. The text had to be disappointing for Marxists expecting statements about the need to replace capitalism by socialism. Instead, the Manifesto addressed issues familiar to SPD and Greens. The text was not a summary of principles but a collection of urgent issues, many of which could also have appeared in social democratic or Green statements.

Parliamentary democracy was to be subject to reforms intended to deepen the democratic process. This approach differed from the traditional communist critique of bourgeois democracy demanding a change of the economic system while neglecting the issue of democratizing the political system. The traditional assumption was that breaking the economic power of capital would put an end to class society and thereby bring about real democracy and the withering away of the state. In Gysi's approach, on the other hand, democratizing the political system was identified as desirable in itself. It is also implicitly assumed that the end of capitalism was not a prerequisite for democratization.

A scenario of threats to peace, to ecological survival, and to social security was presented. At the same time, Gysi emphasized optimism if opportunities were grasped. "The great chances of the end of the Cold War were missed because the West did not want to change" (p. 3). He reminded the reader of the experience that "the welfare state, the reining in of the capitalist market by society, and the New Deal once successfully stood up against the socially irresponsible state, against the absolute power of capital in the labour market, and the ideology claiming that the market was ungovernable" (p. 4).

The manifesto also recommended new channels for the expression of the will of the people. Decision making by referendum, as in Switzerland, could introduce an element of direct democracy. The introduction of a second chamber representing nongovernment organizations elected by all voters, besides the elections to federal parliament, could give a voice to neglected interests. For this purpose, the electorate should not only vote for parties to be represented in the Bundestag. They could also allocate a second vote to nongovernment organizations competing for seats in a "second chamber" (p. 8) to represent interests neglected by parties and politicians.

Proposals regarding the future of work combined the traditional socialist priority of full employment with the ecological motive of sustainability.

For fifty years the industrial societies in West and East were driven by the demand for more consumer goods and more armament. This has to be a thing of the past. More life chances through less consumption and without armament are necessary for survival. . . . An ecological revolution of the way of production and the way of life is required. . . . Housing, public transport, education and culture, a total renewal of the entire infrastructure and communication, the creation of a society friendly to children and adequate for old people require our work. . . . There is almost too much work [to be done]. All these new social, ecological and cultural necessities have be turned into effective demand urgently. (p. 10)

The solution is another "New Deal, a new social contract" (p. 10). This economic and ecological New Deal is to be accompanied by pacifist policies: "Regional and transregional systems of collective security are the most important guarantees of a peaceful world. The ability of states to conduct war is to be abolished by demilitarisation" (p. 13).

The Ingolstadt Manifesto included the optimistic claim that "by 1994 the PDS had long time ago arrived in the Federal Republic." Here the party anticipated a desired outcome: that the regional East German PDS would succeed to arrive in the whole of Germany, including the West. The manifesto certainly expressed this intention. In reality, this intention was far from being achieved. The PDS was still trying to compensate for the weakness of its organization in the West by the skillful use of Gregor Gysi as a one-man show. Nevertheless, the outcome of the 1994 election proved that the party had moved another small step closer to its arrival in the West of the Federal Republic.

POSITIONING THE PDS FOR THE "SUPER ELECTION YEAR" 1994

The year 1994 was a "super election year" (*Superwahljahr*), as Germans had to vote in about a dozen elections for the European Parliament, the German Bundestag, several Land parliaments, as well as local government in several Länder. A PDS congress (Berlin, 11–13 March) adopted platforms for the European elections (12 June) and the Bundestag elections (16 October), confirming the image projected by the launching of the Ingolstadt Manifesto in February. The PDS tried to appeal to a West German audience and to a broader spectrum of voters beyond a traditional socialist left.

The election program included a variety of green, pacifist, and feminist themes besides traditional socialist concerns such as measures against unemployment and specific East German demands such as the raising of wages to West German levels. The treatment of women's issues indicated the direction of change. Besides the traditional socialist claims to equal wage for equal and equivalent work and to the right of legal abortion, there were also newer feminist themes such as the demand for subsidies for women's refuges.

The PDS also adopted ecological themes unfamiliar to the SED tradition, criticizing "expansionist economic concepts, destroying nature and culture."[50] While conservative political analyst Patrick Moreau dismissed these ecological concerns as disguised communist objectives posing as a "crusade for the salvation of the human race from global dangers," Hans-Georg Betz and Helga Welsh discovered similarities between the PDS and a more radically pacifist and environmentalist Green party of a decade earlier, while Manfred Gerner even accused the PDS of plagiarizing from SPD and Greens.[51]

Socialist traditionalists in the PDS rejected the party's draft election program as "merely radical-democratic." Instead, the KPF suggested greater emphasis on a socialist objective "because capitalism cannot solve the problems of humankind." The KPF proposed an alternative election platform with a more explicitly socialist preamble and stronger demands for social rights and taxation of higher incomes.[52]

The tensions between reform socialists and KPF emerged again during the selection of candidates. PDS leaders attempted to include a wide range of left-independent and radical-democratic individuals on the open tickets of the "PDS–Linke Liste." The KPF, on the other hand, wanted to include members of the German Communist Party (DKP) on the open ticket of the PDS. However, the PDS majority rejected, as in 1990, a party-to-party alliance with the DKP but conceded that its members could be included on the PDS ticket as individuals rather than as party representatives.

One example of the intended broad left candidate selection was the writer Stefan Heym, a dissident and long-standing critic of the GDR. Another was the Count von Einsiedel, a great-grandson of Prussia's "iron chancellor" Otto von Bismarck whose candidature was vocally opposed by party members with a traditional socialist mentality. Many found it disturbing that von Einsiedel had left the GDR in December 1948 and had criticized it vehemently. Von Einsiedel was perceived as antisocialist or as a nationalist because he had welcomed German unification as a positive step, not only as an inevitable necessity.

Letters to the daily paper *Neues Deutschland* questioned whether the PDS should use the "candidature of the 'Comrade Count' " to demonstrate a positive attitude toward German identity. Should not "class" be emphasized by socialists "to the exclusion of nation"? The "Comrade Count" had to establish his socialist credentials. During World War II, as a prisoner in the Soviet Union, he had joined the antifascist National Committee Free Germany of anti-Hitler officers and become a socialist. It was his firsthand knowledge of Stalinism that made him critical of the Soviet system several decades before most PDS members had turned anti-Stalinist.[53]

To judge from the Einsiedel debate, the PDS leadership found attitudes acquired in years of SED party life the hardest obstacle to the development of a broader left-socialist party. Nevertheless, the party entered the election year with programs and candidates confirming its broad left positions and its combination of traditional social justice issues with feminist, environmentalist, and pacifist themes.

RELATIVE SUCCESS IN THE FEDERAL ELECTION OF 1994

The results of several elections in 1994 confirmed that the PDS had become a viable party. It had achieved a stable role as a relevant minor party in national parliament and as a major regional party in Eastern Germany. After its precarious existence and decline during 1990–1992, the consolidation and growth of 1993–1994 had reached a level that appeared to guarantee its survival in the medium term. This consolidation forced other parties to rethink their strategy toward the PDS. The strategy of elimination through marginalization had not achieved the desired results, and new strategies would have to take into account the medium-term existence of the PDS. The elimination strategy was, nevertheless, tried once more at the end of 1994 when administrative measures of the Berlin taxation authorities took the PDS to the brink of financial destruction one last time.

In the elections to the European Parliament (12 June 1994), the PDS achieved a relative success with 4.7 percent of the national vote but stayed below the representation threshold of 5 percent, thus failing to get any seats. The result of 1,669,384 votes, or 4.7 percent, was significantly higher than the 2.4 percent achieved in the national elections of December 1990. This gave the PDS some hope for the Bundestag elections later in the year, although failure was still quite likely. Since participation rates of voters were always higher in Bundestag elections than in European elections, the PDS would need more voters just to achieve the same percentage again, let alone raise it to the required 5 percent. Local government elections in three Länder in the East were held on the same day as the European elections. The PDS improved its representation in local councils and increased its electoral support to 24.3 percent in Mecklenburg–West Pommerania, 16.3 percent in Saxony, and 15.7 percent in Thuringia.[54]

In the Bundestag elections of 16 October, the most important elections of 1994, the PDS achieved 4.4 percent (December 1990: 2.4 percent). This was not enough to overcome the 5 percent representation threshold. In the East, the result was 19.8 percent, compared to 11.1 percent in December 1990. In the West, the PDS had tripled its vote compared to the 1990 elections, albeit from a very low base. With 1.0 percent support, the PDS was still a very small party in West Germany.[55]

Although the PDS failed to reach 5 percent, the party nevertheless qualified for representation in the Bundestag by winning a sufficient number of direct mandates. Electoral law requires either 5 percent of the national vote or a minimum of three local seats won directly in order to qualify for the proportional distribution of seats. The PDS achieved this with victories in four East Berlin strongholds and reentered the Bundestag with 30 MdBs (MdB = Mitglied des Bundestages [Member of Parliament]). The writer Stefan Heym, who had won the seat of Berlin-Mitte/Prenzlauer Berg, was the oldest member of parliament. This made him the *Alterspräsident* ("father of the house"), entitling him to open the first session and to give the first speech.

The PDS was represented in parliament, but once more it had not achieved the status of *Fraktion*, that is, a full parliamentary party qualified by at least 5 percent of the vote. As it fell a few members short of *Fraktion* status, it had to be content with the lesser status of a *Gruppe* (parliamentary group), entitled to less speaking time, office space, and funding. The PDS also missed out on another advantage enjoyed by established parties. They received state finance for foundations pursuing political education and research (CDU: Konrad Adenauer Foundation; CSU: Hanns Seidel Foundation; SPD: Friedrich Ebert Foundation; FDP: Friedrich Naumann Foundation). Initially the Greens were also excluded from this form of party finance, but after several years of continued representation in parliament, their Heinrich Böll Foundation also received funding. The PDS contested their status as *Gruppe*, demanding the entitlements of a *Fraktion*, but the Constitutional Court rejected the case, recommending only a few minor improvements of the rights of a *Gruppe* in parliament.[56]

HUNGER STRIKE AVERTS TAX OFFICE THREAT TO FINANCIAL SURVIVAL OF PDS

The very existence of the PDS was threatened once more in late 1994, after two years of consolidation as organization during 1993–1994 and relative successes in several elections in 1994. The strategy of elimination was attempted a last time in late 1994 by the Berlin Tax Office and by the "Independent Commission" at a time when parts of the SPD and of the Greens were considering a shift to a strategy of integration by partial cooperation. It was the financial survival of the organization that was once more threatened, not through a scandal created by illegal transfers of funds, as in late 1990, but through demands from the Berlin taxation authorities.

This financial crisis illustrated the ambivalent attitude of Social Democrats and Greens to the PDS. Only a short time after the Magdeburg model of late June 1994, when the SPD and Alliance 90/Greens had formed a minority government in Saxony-Anhalt depending on support by PDS parliamentarians, the same parties started a media campaign against the PDS. While the relevance of the PDS had to be acknowledged in Eastern Land parliaments, it was still an object of outright attacks during national elections. CDU leader Chancellor Kohl labeled the PDS "red-lacquered fascists,"[57] while national SPD and Greens leaders still hoped to eliminate the PDS in the medium term by reducing it to regional East German relevance and by keeping it out of national parliament.

The climate was set in a media campaign launched by SPD and Greens in August 1994 suggesting that the PDS was financed from illegal sources. In this situation, the Independent Commission reneged on possible compromises with the PDS about former SED assets. When the PDS asked banks for credit to finance election campaigns, it was refused, as the banks were not sure whether the PDS would be able to repay after the elections, in case the election compensation monies were to be confiscated by the taxation office. The PDS had to ask members and supporters for personal credits to be repaid when election campaign compensation monies came in after the election.

The controversy over outstanding taxation went back to October 1992 when the Berlin Tax Office had asked the PDS to pay DM3.2 million taxes arising from the profits of former SED enterprises in 1990. Then the PDS had gone to court, arguing that the Treuhand was the proper addressee of the tax bill because this institution had been administering former SED property relinquished by the PDS in 1990. The Berlin fiscal court agreed with the PDS. The federal fiscal court, on the other hand, decided that the PDS was the right addressee of the tax bill but left open the question whether the PDS or the Treuhand would finally have to pay the bill.[58]

Two weeks after the national elections of 1994, the Berlin taxation office demanded, on 3 November, not only the DM3.2 million of October 1992 but a much bigger amount of DM67.4 million of tax for business activities during the first half of the year 1990. This demand came at the worst possible time for the PDS when it was financially exhausted by the election campaigns of 1994 and when it had not yet received the election campaign finance due to all parties.

The Treuhand expressed its willingness to be liable for all tax payments relating to former SED property that it administered since 1990. The Independent Commission, however, rejected this offer of the Treuhand and pointed to the PDS as the legal successor of the SED. The Berlin Tax Office then insisted that the bill be paid from the property that the PDS had retained out of former SED assets. "The ... Berlin fiscal court decided ... on the one hand, to defer the execution of the tax bill to the time of the effective decision about our appeal against the tax bill, but, on the other, connected this to the condition that the PDS would have to cede its incoming election campaign compensation as security to the tax office."[59] Chairman Gysi suspected that this action had been timed for maximum effect. At that time the PDS only had DM200,000 in hand, owed DM3.8 million to supporters in election loans, and had outstanding bills of about DM2 million for campaign costs. These loans and bills were to be paid from the election campaign compensation due on 1 December, which was, however, now threatened by the immediate demands of the Tax Office.

PDS leaders went public, on 30 November, against the demands of the Berlin Tax Office and of the Independent Commission for DM67.4 million to be paid from remaining PDS property instead of taking it from the much larger former

SED property now administered by the Treuhand. PDS leaders occupied premises of the Independent Commission and of the Treuhand, but police removed
them over night. Then PDS leaders continued their hunger strike in the premises
of the Berlin regional parliament, again, only to be removed by police. Finally
the hunger strike continued in the Berliner Volksbühne theater.

At the same time, the party appealed to the Berlin Administrative Court,
which decided, on 7 December, in favor of the PDS. Any outstanding tax payments were to be paid by the Treuhand as administrator of former SED assets,
whereas the confiscated election campaign compensation monies had to be
handed to the PDS. After this decision, the hunger strike of PDS leaders was
stopped.[60]

This episode was of political relevance beyond its financial and legal aspects.
Within the PDS, once more voices arose questioning the credibility of the "rule
of law" when the bourgeois state was using and abusing administrative and legal
processes to strangle a left-socialist party. For several years the reform socialist
wing of the PDS had argued that capitalist modernity had more to offer than
just the negative aspects of capitalism. Modernity in bourgeois society also included achievements such as formal democracy, individual human rights, and
the rule of law. This was significantly different from views held by German
socialists and communists in the past emphasizing that the promises of liberal
rule of law and bourgeois democracy were hollow. In this situation, the actions
of PDS leader Gysi tried to ensure that PDS members retained their newly found
appreciation of the rule of law (Rechtsstaat). The Berlin Tax Office made this
rather difficult; however, the decision by the Berlin Administrative Court must
have restored some faith in the rule of law among PDS members.

These events were also indicative of the conflicting strategies toward the PDS.
Any strategy of eliminating the PDS at all costs would have alienated a considerable minority of East Germans from the united Germany they had lived in
since 1990. A moderate conservative such as former Federal President Richard
von Weizsäcker pointed to the need for integration and reconciliation.[61] He was
aware of the political costs resulting from an excessively punitive approach to
the former GDR elites and state officials and from a marginalization strategy
toward the PDS. Once more, German socialists would have been pushed into a
role as outsider opposition. From a liberal-conservative point of view, it was
preferable to have the PDS and its clientele integrated into the political process
as a left-socialist party, compared to an administrative destruction of the PDS
that would leave a quarter of all East Germans with the experience that bourgeois democracy was a very thin cover for capitalist class rule.

German democracy was learning to live with its left-socialist minority, while
PDS members and supporters were learning the role of a party competing with
others in a parliamentary democracy. The Berlin Tax Office and the Independent
Commission came close to destroying this learning process.

The dispute over former SED assets ended finally when an agreement between
the Independent Commission and the PDS of 16 June was confirmed by the

Higher Administrative Court of Berlin on 18 July 1995.[62] Five years after the PDS had ceded most of the SED's vast assets to the GDR government, and after the last parliament of the GDR established the Independent Commission of the Property of Parties and Mass Organizations of the GDR, the controversy over the SED's illegitimate assets was settled. The PDS had secure possession of a small part of former SED property. The party was the legal and political successor of the SED but was no longer responsible for its predecessor's vast assets administered by the Treuhand since 1990.

NOTES

1. Rudolf Woderich, "Ost-Identität—Residuum der Vereinigung oder Phänomen der 'langen Dauer?' " *Utopie kreativ*, no. 105 (July 1999): 59.

2. Ibid., p. 52.

3. Ibid., p. 58.

4. Christine Ostrowski and Ronald Weckesser, "Brief aus Sachsen. Für einen eigenen Weg statt 'links von der SPD,' " *Neues Deutschland* (8 May 1995).

5. Helmut Zessin, Edwin Schwertner, and Frank Schumann, *Chronik der PDS 1989 bis 1997* (Berlin: Dietz, 1998), p. 62.

6. Friedrich Hora, "Diskriminierung eines ganzen Berufsstandes—Berufsverbot für DDR-Pädagogen," in *Weissbuch 3: Bildungswesen und Pädagogik im Beitrittsgebiet*, ed. Gerd Buddin, Hans Dahlke, and Alfred Kossakowski (Berlin: KOLOG, 1994), p. 11.

7. Ibid., p. 22.

8. Ibid., p. 25.

9. Patrick Moreau and Jürgen Peter Lang, *Linksextremismus: Eine unterschätzte Gefahr* (Bonn: Bouvier Verlag, 1996), pp. 146–148 (about Komitees für Gerechtigkeit); Ostdeutschers Kuratorium der Verbände, *Mitteilungen Nr. 1* (Berlin: GBM, 1993) (about Kuratorium).

10. Moreau and Lang, *Linksextremismus*, pp. 141–143.

11. Ostdeutschers Kuratorium Verbände. *Mitteilungen, Nr. 2* (Berlin: GBM, 1994).

12. Manfred Gerner, *Partei ohne Zukunft? Von der SED zur PDS* (Munich: Tilsner, 1994), p. 234.

13. PDS, *Partei des Demokratischen Sozialismus: Programm und Statut* (Berlin: PDS, 1998), p. 23.

14. Ibid., p. 24.

15. Gerner, *Partei ohne Zukunft?* p. 236.

16. PDS, *Programm und Statut*, p. 24.

17. Gerner, *Partei ohne Zukunft?* p. 236.

18. Ibid.

19. Ibid., p. 243.

20. Ibid., p. 244.

21. PDS, *Programm und Statut*, p. 2.

22. Ibid., p. 8.

23. Sahra Wagenknecht, *Antisozialistische Strategien im Zeitalter der Systemauseinandersetzung. Zwei Taktiken im Kampf gegen die sozialistische Welt* (Bonn: Pahl-Rugenstein Nachfolger, 1995); Historische Kommission beim Parteivorstand der PDS, "Zur Geschichtsdiskussion in der PDS (1993)," in *Die PDS—Herkunft und Selbstver-*

ständnis. Eine politisch-historische Debatte, ed. Lothar Bisky et al. (Berlin: Dietz, 1996), pp. 375, 377.

24. For example, in the report by the parliamentary commission of inquiry, "Über-windung der Folgen der SED-Diktatur im Prozeß der deutschen Einheit" (Berlin: Deutscher Bundestag, 17 June 1998).

25. Christoph Kleßman and Martin Sabrow, "Zeitgeschichte in Deutschland nach 1989," *Aus Politik und Zeitgeschichte*, B 39 (1996): 9–10.

26. Patrick Moreau, "Transnationale Vergleiche," in *The Party of Democratic Socialism in Germany: Modern Post-Communism or Nostalgic Populism?* ed. Peter Barker (Amsterdam: Rodopi, 1998), p. 137.

27. Historische Kommission beim Parteivorstand der PDS, eds., *Der Stalinismus in der KPD und SED—Wurzeln, Wirkungen, Folgen. Materialien der Konferenz der Historischen Kommission beim Parteivorstand der PDS am 17./18. November 1990* (Berlin: PDS, 1991); Gregor Gysi et al., eds., *Zweigeteilt. Über dem Umgang mit der SED-Vergangenheit* (Hamburg: VSA, 1992); Lothar Bisky et al., eds., *Rücksichten. Politische und juristische Aspekte der DDR-Geschichte* (Hamburg: VSA, 1993); Lothar Bisky et al., eds., *"Unrechtsstaat"? Politische Justiz und die Aufarbeitung der DDR-Vergangenheit* (Hamburg: VSA, 1994).

28. The contributions to all 11 volumes are listed in Ludwig Elm, Dietmar Keller, and Reinhard Mocek, eds., *Ansichten zur Geschichte der DDR* (Bonn and Berlin: Bundestagsgruppe der PDS, 1998), 11:456–463.

29. Historische Kommission beim Parteivorstand der PDS, "Zur Geschichtsdiskussion in der PDS (1993)," p. 374.

30. Uwe-Jens Heuer, *Marxismus und Demokratie* (Baden-Baden: Nomos, 1990); also Uwe-Jens Heuer, "Zur Demokratiefrage und heutigen Aufgaben der PDS, zugleich zum Verhältnis von Demokratie und Diktatur," in *Gegenmacht Demokratie. Demokratisierung gegen Macht*, ed. Uwe-Jens Heuer and Harald Werner (Berlin: Grundsatzkommission beim Parteivorstand der PDS, 1994), p. 7.

31. Uwe-Jens Heuer, "Rechtsstaat und Unrechtsstaat. Zur PDS-Debatte," in *Die PDS—Herkunft und Selbstverständnis*, ed. Lothar Bisky et al. (Berlin: Dietz, 1996), p. 97.

32. Michael Schumann, "Zur Auseinandersetzung der PDS mit dem Stalinistischen Erbe," *UTOPIE kreativ*, nos. 81–82 (July–August 1997): 164–168.

33. André Brie, "Der zweigeteilte Parteitag. Versuch eines Beitrags gegen neue Legenden," in *Die PDS—Herkunft und Selbstverständnis*, ed. Lothar Bisky et al. (Berlin: Dietz, 1996), pp. 55–56.

34. "Rede von Bundespräsident Roman Herzog auf dem Bürgerrechtler-Kongress der Konrad-Adenauer-Stiftung am 23. Juni 1998 in Leipzig," *Pressemitteilung des Bundespräsidialamtes*, Berlin, 23 June 1998.

35. Richard von Weizsäcker, *Vier Zeiten. Erinnerungen* (Berlin: Siedler, 1997), p. 405.

36. Ibid., p. 410.

37. Ibid., pp. 406–407.

38. Gerner, *Partei ohne Zukunft?* p. 115.

39. Gero Neugebauer, "Hat die PDS bundesweit im Parteiensystem eine Chance?" in *Die PDS: Empirische Befunde and kontroverse Analysen*, ed. Michael Brie, Martin Herzig and Thomas Koch (Cologne: PapyRossa, 1995), p. 43.

40. Christine Ostrowski, *Im Streit* (Querfurt: Dingsda-Verlag, 1993), p. 200.

41. Patrick Moreau and Jürgen Peter Lang, *Was will die PDS?* (Berlin: Ullstein, 1994), pp. 104–117.

42. Social Democratic analyst Klaus-Jürgen Scherer also noted that PDS policies "looked like copied from social democratic debates of the seventies." "Die PDS und die PDS," in *The Party of Democratic Socialism in Germany: Modern Post-Communism or Nostalgic Populism?* ed. Peter Barker (Amsterdam: Rodopi, 1998), p. 185. The debates about "system-transcending reforms" are recapitulated in Christoph Butterwegge, *Jungsozialisten und SPD* (Hamburg: W. Runge, 1975), pp. 74–86, and in Norbert Gansel, "Die Strategie in der Diskussion der Jungsozialisten," in *Überwindet den Kapitalismus oder Was wollen die Jungsozialisten?* ed. N. Gansel (Reinbek: Rowohlt, 1971), pp. 79–100.

43. Moreau and Lang, *Linksextremismus*, pp. 446–450.

44. Moreau and Lang, *Was will die PDS?* p. 106.

45. Zessin, Schwertner, and Schumann, *Chronik*, pp. 129–130, 516.

46. Moreau and Lang, *Was will die PDS?* p. 90.

47. Ibid., p. 92.

48. Neugebauer, "Hat die PDS bundesweit im Parteiensystem eine Chance?" p. 48; Zessin, Schwertner, and Schumann, *Chronik*, p. 324.

49. Gregor Gysi, *Ingolstädter Manifest. Wir—mitten in Europa. Plädoyer für einen neuen Gesellschaftsvertrag* (Berlin: PDS, 1994).

50. PDS, *Opposition gegen Sozialabbau und Rechtsruck. Wahlprogramm der PDS 1994 (Entwurf)* (Berlin: PDS, December 1993), p. 6.

51. Patrick Moreau, "Das Wahljahr 1994 und die Strategie der PDS," *Aus Politik und Zeitgeschichte*, B1 (7 January 1994): 23; Hans-Georg Betz and Helga A. Welsh, "The PDS in the New German Party System," *German Politics* 4, no. 3 (1995): 92–111; Gerner, *Partei ohne Zukunft?* p. 226.

52. Kommunistische Plattform der PDS, "Beschluss der 5. Bundeskonferenz der Kommunistischen Plattform vom 8./9. 1994," *Pressedienst der PDS*, no. 8 (25 February 1994): 14.

53. Franz Oswald, "The Party of Democratic Socialism: Ex-Communists Entrenched as East German Regional Protest Party," *Journal of Communist Studies and Transition Politics* 12, no. 2 (1996): 184.

54. Zessin, Schwertner, and Schumann, *Chronik*, pp. 180–181.

55. Results of European elections and Bundestag elections documented in *Blätter für deutsche und internationale Politik* 40, no. 1 (January 1995): 124–128.

56. Zessin, Schwertner, and Schumann, *Chronik*, p. 531.

57. Gregor Gysi, *Das war's. Noch lange nicht!* (Düsseldorf: Econ Verlag, 1997), p. 264.

58. Ibid., pp. 274–276.

59. Ibid., p. 275.

60. Lothar Bisky, *Wut im Bauch. Kampf um die PDS: 29. November bis 7. Dezember 1994* (Berlin: Dietz, 1995), p. 10.

61. Weizsäcker, *Vier Zeiten*, p. 420.

62. Manfred Uschner, *Die roten Socken* (Berlin: Dietz Verlag, 1995), p. 197.

PART THREE

TRANSFORMING THE PARTY: "ARRIVING" IN THE NEW GERMANY, 1995–1998

5

PDS: Rethinking Its Opposition Role; SPD and Greens: Rethinking Their Exclusion Strategy, 1995–1997

SOCIAL DEMOCRATS BETWEEN TWO STRATEGIES: TO MARGINALIZE OR TO INTEGRATE THE PDS?

The initial strategy of marginalizing and eliminating the Party of Democratic Socialism was being questioned by 1994, and an integration strategy was discussed more often among Social Democrats and Greens. For the center-right Christian Democrats, the PDS had remained an extremist party to be isolated. This position was modified only for tactical reasons in 1990 when the CDU appreciated the temporary nuisance value of the PDS subtracting a small share of the left vote from the SPD. By 1994, however, the CDU intensified its campaign against the party labeled "red-lacquered fascists" by Chancellor Helmut Kohl. It was only in 1996 that East German CDU politicians such as Berndt Seite and Eckhard Rehberg began to question the utility of these all-out attacks on the PDS and on all former SED members.[1]

In the SPD, the hostility toward the Party of Democratic Socialism was initially as intensive as in the CDU, but by 1994 strategies of partial cooperation with the PDS were being considered. While the exclusion strategy was premised on a portrayal of the entire PDS as extremist or Stalinist, the advocates of integration strategies presented the PDS as more acceptable. They acknowledged that PDS leaders were reform socialists, while the party's local councillors and Land parliamentarians were pragmatically pursuing regional interests. An integration strategy could strengthen these reformers and pragmatists, bringing them closer to the SPD. This strategy accepted "a stabilisation of the PDS in the medium term, independently of the strategy developed . . . by the SPD." Yet, one could still expect the PDS to "lose its magic"[2] as it would be tied into government responsibilities and no longer able to act as populist opposition. Making use of the internal "divisions of the PDS into reformers and fundamentalists,"[3] this strategy of partial cooperation could also foster a split resulting in the absorption of PDS reformers into the SPD.

The strategy of weakening the PDS through partial cooperation could follow the French precedent[4] of the 1970s and 1980s when the Socialist Party formed a coalition with the French communists. The PCF (French Communist Party) had to share government responsibilities as well as the blame for shortcomings while it was losing its appealing role as vocal opposition. Similarly, the SPD could integrate and weaken the PDS.

The first example of partial cooperation between the SPD and PDS, the Magdeburg model of "toleration" of mid-1994, was not the result of strategic choice but the outcome of opportunity. Nevertheless, the portrayal of the PDS as conditionally acceptable made partial cooperation at least conceivable.

The advocates of marginalization were still stronger in the SPD than the proponents of partial cooperation. SPD leader Rudolf Scharping's Dresden Declaration of 11 August 1994[5] signaled strong resistance to any replication of the Magdeburg model in other East German regions, especially in Mecklenburg–West Pommerania and Thuringia, where regional leaders appeared to be tempted to cooperate with the PDS.

The Dresden Declaration also served to minimize any damage the Magdeburg model could cause in the forthcoming national elections of October 1994. Social Democrat leaders were very much aware of the unpopularity of the PDS among West German voters. While East German voters would not understand further exclusion of the PDS, West Germans might punish any cooperation with a party still widely perceived as "extremist."

The preferred approach was still elimination by exclusion, although the strategy of weakening by partial cooperation had found advocates and had been implemented in one case, the "toleration" arrangement of Saxony-Anhalt. However, the Dresden Declaration had clearly stated the firm intention of SPD leader Scharping to ensure that the Magdeburg model remained an exception, not a model for other SPD branches to follow.

MAGDEBURG MODEL OF "TOLERATION": PDS HALF ACCEPTABLE IN EAST

Five months before the Landtag elections of 26 June 1994 in Saxony-Anhalt, one of the five East German Länder, the PDS offered support for a future minority government of Social Democrats and Alliance 90/Greens. This offer made it conceivable for the SPD to replace its role as junior partner of the Christian Democrats with a leading role in a coalition with the Alliance 90/Greens, supported in parliament by the PDS. For the latter this proposal was another step toward demarginalization. Election platforms and broad left candidate selection had positioned the party closer to SPD and Greens, and now the PDS indicated that it was willing to support a center-left government without demanding ministerial positions. This presupposed that the PDS appreciated the difference between center-right CDU and center-left SPD although the policies of Social Democrats and Greens would be falling short of PDS demands. Thus the PDS was signaling a pragmatic approach to political compromise, a readiness to treat politics as the art of the possible.

The offer of support by the PDS had been rejected during the election campaign by Social Democrat leaders hoping to become the senior partner in a continued coalition with the Christian Democrats. Although the PDS was the third biggest party in the Landtag, the SPD still preferred the frustrations of a "grand coalition" with the CDU to any cooperation with the PDS. Yet eventually the election result made it impossible for the SPD to overtake the CDU, which had retained 37 seats to the SPD's 36. Thus the Social Democrats faced the choice of either remaining the CDU's junior partner or forming a minority government with Alliance 90/Greens (6 seats) depending on PDS support (21 seats).

This opportunity induced SPD leaders to break the taboo against cooperation with the PDS. The chance to lead a Land government and to implement social democratic policies was so attractive to SPD leader Höppner, compared to another term as junior partner of the CDU, that the PDS began to appear in a much friendlier light. The party as a whole and especially its left wing were still not acceptable for any cooperation, but the PDS parliamentarians in Saxony-Anhalt were now perceived as rather pragmatic representatives of local interests rather than dogmatic socialists. The minority government also made an effort to play down its dependence on "toleration" by the PDS. Höppner claimed that the coalition of SPD and Alliance 90/Greens was open to support from the CDU on the right and from the PDS on the left. Christian Democrats, however, regarded the new arrangement as "a de-facto coalition"[6] of SPD and PDS, a view confirmed by the regular practice of negotiating important legislation and the annual budget in meetings between parliamentary leaders of SPD, Alliance 90/ Greens, and PDS.

The "toleration" arrangement was justified by Social Democrats' leader Höppner as a new, more inclusive political style and as a contribution toward reconciliation of the divisions within East German society. At the same time, cooperation with the PDS was also presented as a method of making the PDS superfluous. For the CDU, on the other hand, the de facto coalition of SPD and PDS signified the breaking of a taboo. It was "the dissolution of the democratic basic consensus of the Federal Republic of Germany"[7] consisting in the exclusion of extremists from any cooperation while the democratic parties of center-right and center-left would compete and cooperate only with one another. In this logic, the CDU/CSU agreed not to enter alliances with the extremist far right (Republikaner, NPD, DVU), while the SPD excluded the far left from any alliance. Indeed, the SPD had never cooperated with the DKP, the West German communists.

The de facto coalition of SPD and PDS in the Magdeburg model of "toleration" was only justifiable if the PDS was not an extremist party. From now on Social Democrats and Greens had to portray the PDS as acceptable for cooperation at least in some circumstances.

CDU analyst Christoph Bergner acknowledged that the Magdeburg model was not a vehicle for the PDS to implement socialist objectives. The most negative effect, in his opinion, was that the PDS could regard it "as evidence for its emancipation on the political stage and as an occasion for confidence which could not have been developed out of a real opposition role."[8] The CDU strategy to keep the German left divided between a democratic SPD and an extremist PDS had experienced a first setback.

Within the PDS, the decision to tolerate a minority government of SPD and Alliance 90/Greens remained controversial. By reform socialist leaders, it was assessed as positive, albeit with some reservations: "The toleration approach has preserved chances to organize alternatives to conservative hegemony but it also means participation in the administration of the status quo," possibly involving "a creeping process of accommodation" and a loss of identity for the PDS.[9] The party's youth wing and the Communist Platform demanded the party should concentrate on strengthening extraparliamentary movements instead of losing its identity in unrewarding deals. On the other hand, PDS leaders hoped the Magdeburg model would become the beginning of the end of the party's marginalization.

PAINFUL REPOSITIONING, 1995–1997

Controversies within the PDS over the redefinition of its opposition role began during the preparation of the fourth party congress scheduled for January 1995. After two years of consolidating the party organization, and after the success in the national elections of 1994, the survival of the PDS was guaranteed for another four years, until the 1998 elections. Thus the party could afford to enter identity and strategy debates continuing in 1995 and 1996. PDS leaders embarked on a strategy of positioning the party further away from the left margin, closer to the center-left Social Democrats and Greens. If the expected controversies over the redefined opposition role were sorted out in 1995 and 1996, the PDS could be ready by 1997 for a unified approach to the 1998 election campaigns and, perhaps, for a government role in one or two Eastern Land governments. The acceptance of the PDS by Social Democrats and Greens at the Land level could pave the road toward an end of marginalization at the national level. The debates over identity and strategy of 1995 and 1996 made possible the repositioning of the party in 1997 and 1998. Indeed, by January 1997 the Schwerin congress marked the end of the long controversy about the party's opposition role: The majority of PDS delegates agreed that the party should join government coalitions if conditions were right.

Parallel to these internal changes, relations to SPD and Greens changed as well as these parties began to accept that the PDS was likely to survive in the medium term. Thus partial cooperation with the PDS came to be regarded as inevitable and possibly useful, at least at the Land level in East Germany.

"TEN THESES" AND "FIVE POINTS": TO BECOME PART OF A REFORM MAJORITY

The debate about the future direction of the PDS was started by the "Ten Theses about the Way Ahead for the PDS"[10] of the party executive to be adopted at the party congress of January 1995. The Ten Theses set a radical reform agenda for the PDS, in opposition to the neoliberal, neoconservative Kohl government and in cooperation with the Social Democrats and Greens.

Although Thesis 10 affirmed the socialist character of the PDS, Theses 1 through 9 left out any socialist objective, focusing instead on "change of policy" and the formation of a "reform majority" (Thesis 2). The objective of the required "reform initiative" was "to arrive at a new social contract" (Thesis 4). The latter term had appeared first in the "Ingolstadt Manifesto" of early 1994, which referred to F.D. Roosevelt's "New Deal" and to the "social market economy" of Western Europe. After the Great Depression and after World War II, a class compromise between labor and capital had moderated capitalism by introducing welfare state and interventionist policies. This compromise was now being rolled back by neoliberal economics since Reagan and Thatcher, closely followed by the Kohl government in Germany. Altogether, the Ten Theses demanded a reform effort to achieve a new compromise between labor and capital more acceptable than the Kohl government's dismantling of the welfare state.

The "new social contract" was a rather modest objective compared to ending capitalism altogether. The corresponding strategy was also much more pragmatic than a role as principled opposition remaining outside the system. The Ten Theses envisaged the party as "consistent left opposition" forming part of a "reform majority" (Thesis 2), that is, as an ally of Social Democrats and Greens, against CDU/CSU and FDP. Thesis 9 repeated the PDS slogan "Change begins with opposition"; however, the term "opposition" did not mean an outsider role abstaining from the limited reforms that were possible now. "The objectives of our opposition politics are democratic, social, ecological, and feminist changes."

Thesis 8 also created controversies by reaffirming the "basic consensus" of the foundation period of the PDS: "the break with the centralist, antidemocratic politics of the SED, with Stalinism. For us, there will not be a return to the political structures of the GDR."

The most vocal criticism of the Ten Theses came from the Communist Platform. Although it was of limited relevance for the party as a whole, its arguments illustrated in a concentrated form the concerns held more widely, in a diluted form, among PDS members wondering whether the leadership was transforming a left-socialist party into another social democratic party. The Ten Theses were rejected by the Communist Platform as preparations for an attack on the PDS program of 1993 to be replaced by a new program shaped by the "modern socialism" conceptualized by Michael Brie. In this context, the function of the Ten Theses was to prepare programmatic change and personnel replacement: "the programmatic 'ballast' hindering the acceptance of the PDS by the system-conformist parties SPD and Alliance 90/Greens was to be thrown over board. . . . The Stalinism-debate . . . was the lever to throw over board annoying 'ballast' among party personnel."[11]

For the Communist Platform, the Ten Theses meant abandoning the socialist identity of the PDS for the purpose of being accepted by Social Democrats and Greens. The Ten Theses were regarded as a response to the SPD's strategy shift, from marginalizing the PDS toward partial cooperation and integration. Sahra Wagenknecht argued that the Ten Theses deviated "from the existing basic consensus of our party; . . . the core of the theses is the renunciation of the programmatic compromise in the PDS and the replacement of the 'unclear' programmatic situation by a clearly social democratic one."[12] The most intensive dispute was provoked by two themes in the Ten Theses: the suggestions of class compromise through a "social contract" and the proposed extent of distancing from the GDR.

As resistance against the Ten Theses extended well beyond the Communist Platform, the party leadership replaced them a short time before the party congress by a new paper: the Five Points.[13] The differences between the Ten Theses and the Five Points illustrated in which respects the leadership had to accommodate concerns among members. There was no longer any mention of a "Social Contract." Instead, the first of the Five Points affirmed the "socialist character of the PDS," which had been mentioned as an afterthought in Thesis 10 in the earlier document. The new document also asserted that capitalism could not solve the great issues challenging humankind.

The second of the Five Points emphasized the "oppositional character of the PDS," affirming that "the PDS stood in principled opposition to the dominant societal relations in the Federal Republic of Germany." This formulation was more acceptable to many party members than the proposal in the second of the Ten Theses proposing that the PDS join a "reform majority." Nevertheless, the willingness of PDS leaders to cooperate more closely with Social Democrats and Greens was evident in both the Ten Theses and the Five Points. This was interpreted by the Communist Platform as giving a "green light . . . for the participation of the PDS in bourgeois governments."[14]

A controversy arose over the third of the Five Points. It reaffirmed the ideological pluralism within the PDS but stated also that "Stalinist views," just like "nationalist, chauvinistic, racist, antisemitic views," were not compatible with membership in the PDS. This point triggered heated debates between those who felt a need to reaffirmation the party's anti-Stalinist foundation consensus and others fearing a removal of the communist minority and other left positions from the PDS was being prepared.

In the end the congress adopted a formulation that declared Stalinist views incompatible with party membership. At the same time it stated explicitly that the PDS was "not anticommunist" but open to "democratic-communist positions." This formulation implied that there were undemocratic communist positions to be excluded from PDS pluralism.

The Communist Platform regarded the congress of January 1995 as a threat to the identity of the PDS. "It was a further serious step in the direction towards 'coalition ability' of the PDS, i.e., its integration into the system of established parties. In this pursuit the party leaders concede ground step by step to the demands of the rulers, among which the marginalisation of communists is a priority."[15]

One significant symbolic outcome of the congress was that Wagenknecht was not reelected as member of the wider party executive. She was the most visible member of a small neo-Stalinist grouping around the tiny journal *Weißenseer Blätter* attacking the revisionism that had, in their opinion, undermined the Soviet Union since Khrushchev. That Wagenknecht was supported in her bid for reelection by about a third of the delegates did not mean they agreed with the Communist Platform. Many delegates merely felt that she had been unfairly singled out by party leaders Gregor Gysi and André Brie.

The weakness of the Communist Platform became obvious within a few months after the congress of January 1995. In late 1994, political scientist Jürgen Raschke had predicted the emergence of a "centrist tendency" positioned "between reformers and the orthodox," which he expected to become more important than the KPF.[16] Indeed, by mid-1995 the KPF had been replaced as the most relevant voice of opposition to the Gysi-Bisky-Brie leadership by the Marxist Forum. The latter included, besides a number of Marxist intellectuals, a few KPF members to whom the label "democratic communist" might be applicable. On the other hand, defenders of the Stalin period such as Wagenknecht, Kurt Gossweiler, or Hanns-Heinz Holz were absent from the MF. This new constellation indicated that the Communist Platform as a whole had been completely marginalized since the PDS congress of January 1995.

The main outcome of this congress was that the PDS had started a process of redefinition. From 1990 to 1992, it had struggled against apparently terminal decline. From 1993 to 1994, the party had succeeded to survive and to consolidate. Once the issue of survival had been solved or, at least, deferred for the medium term, the role of this party in the German party system appeared on the agenda. The PDS asked itself whether its role as "societal opposition" meant priority for extraparliamentary movements and a permanent opposition role in all parliaments or whether "societal opposition" against the predominance of the profit motive was compatible with participation in government coalitions. This redefinition included a restatement of the anti-Stalinist basic consensus, a further marginalization of the Communist Platform, a turn toward acceptance of closer cooperation with Social Democrats and Greens, and a reduction of the fear of being integrated and absorbed by a hostile system.

The tense atmosphere at the congress did not indicate a comeback of nostalgic positions or a majority for Stalinist positions. With hindsight it can be interpreted as resistance against the speed of change initiated by Gysi, Bisky, and Brie. Two years later the change was completed. By 1997, this process of transformation had largely succeeded: A clear majority of the PDS had accepted a changed role for the party—no longer an outside critic but a participant willing to adopt opposition or government roles quite flexibly and pragmatically.

DEBATES ABOUT STRATEGY AND IDENTITY, 1995–1997

Soon after the congress of January 1995, a strategy paper by Lothar Bisky and André Brie[17] moved the strategy debate ahead. Well before the election campaigns of 1998 the party had to clarify its future role in the German party system. The Gysi-Bisky-Brie leadership envisaged a left-socialist party for the whole of Germany, to the left of SPD and Greens but close enough to these center-left parties to be able to enter into alliances with them. The main purpose of this broad left alliance was the removal of the conservative-neoliberal coalition from government and to embark on social and ecological reforms.

This concept was opposed from two different perspectives. Firstly, the Communist Platform and, later, the Marxist Forum suggested that the party should concentrate on a role as societal opposition, criticizing the capitalist system and working in society to achieve majorities for thorough change. This approach implied greater distance from Social Democrats and Greens. Second, regionalist pragmatists suggested that the PDS remain an East German people's party. Therefore, the party should not move into West Germany, nor should it position itself to the left of SPD and Greens. Instead of conducting programmatic and strategic debates, it should focus on practical East German politics in local government and in Land parliaments.

The controversies outlined in the following sections were all related to these three basic options. The debate about Stalinism and the debate about the foundation of the SED in 1946 had the function to clarify the relation of the Democratic Socialists to the history of East Germany and of the Soviet Union. The greater the distance of the PDS to its historical predecessor SED, the greater the proximity to its potential center-left allies. On the other hand, a total rejection of the history of GDR and SED would have deprived the Democratic Socialists of any tradition and identity to distinguish the party from Social Democrats. This total rejection would also have alienated many members and supporters who had brought their East German biographies into the new reality of united Germany. The debate about the "Letter from Saxony" clarified the question whether the PDS should adopt an exclusively East German, regionalist role or whether it should search for a nationwide role that implied a position to the left of the Social Democrats.

The strategy debate about the party's opposition role had implications for its relations to Social Democrats and Greens. Here the Democratic Socialists reenacted the tensions evident in socialist parties since the nineteenth century:

Should they remain a clear voice of opposition to an unfair social system, or should they prioritize reforms possible in the more immediate future by adopting a more pragmatic vision? From 1990 to 1993, the PDS was limited by other parties to a role as outsider opposition, adopted voluntarily as much as involuntarily. However, since 1994, the formation of coalitions was at least conceivable. Thus the PDS had to evaluate these options.

Finally, the PDS had to reposition itself through programmatic debates. Its programs of 1990 and 1993 had established a clear distance from the SED and from the "real socialism" of the GDR. However, the program of 1993 still left its role in the new reality of united Germany rather undefined. In early 1997, the party leadership launched a commentary to the party program of 1993. This did not amount to a replacement of the 1993 program, but it was an effort to guide the interpretation of the party program in the direction of "modern socialism."

The semiofficial *Kommentar*[18] as well as the strategy debates pointed in the direction of a party pursuing a radical reform agenda of social justice, feminism, pacifism, environmentalism, and East German regionalism in close alliance with Social Democrats and Greens. This approach differed not only from the narrow "Marxist-Leninist" tradition of the SED but also from the Marxist tradition in German social democracy, which had emphasized class conflict between labor and capital as well as the "property question." The opposition to the direction taken by Gysi, Bisky, and Brie came not only from the Communist Platform but also from those identifying with noncommunist Marxist traditions. In this context, the emergence of the Marxist Forum in 1995 was an important symptom of the ideological climate in the PDS.

The result of these debates was clear by January 1997 when the party congress of Schwerin adopted a strategy for the elections of 1998 and 1999. The debate advanced by party strategist André Brie and by leaders Gysi and Bisky since late 1994 had transformed the PDS. A vast majority in the PDS were ready for a role of the party as ally of center-left governments of SPD and Greens, possibly even ready to join a government coalition with the SPD. Societal opposition, as defined by the PDS, could be exercised even from the government benches.

DID STALINISM END IN 1953? HISTORY DEBATES AS FACTIONAL POWER STRUGGLE

During the Stalinism debates of the mid-1990s, the neo-Stalinist defenders of the Soviet system under Stalin were an insignificant minority in the PDS. The main line of conflict concerned the interpretation of the party's anti-Stalinist foundation consensus. The dominant reform socialists adopted an extensive notion of Stalinism, including the period of "real socialism" after Stalin's death in 1953. This version of anti-Stalinism implied a highly critical attitude to the history of East Germany from 1953 to 1989, still characterized by Stalinist

structures. On the other hand, those adopting a narrower notion limiting Stalinism to the period of Stalin's rule until 1953 defended a less negative evaluation
of East German history. While criticizing the GDR system as "centralist-
bureaucratic socialism" they attempted a qualified defense of the socialist experiment. The latter version of anti-Stalinism could be called "Stalinist" only if
the period after 1953 was also classified as Stalinism.

The debate about Stalinism and Stalinist positions, alleged and real, held by
PDS members, was reignited in late 1994, although the foundation congress of
December 1989 had pronounced a clear break with Stalinism and although this
anti-Stalinist consensus had been confirmed by the party program of 1993. When
a statement declaring Stalinist positions incompatible with party membership
was adopted by the party congress of January 1995, this did not end controversies.

In these debates, the reform socialists were "defending . . . their political-
intellectual hegemony in the PDS."[19] The debates were driven by factional ri-
valry as much as by the need to come to terms with history. It was acknowledged
by leading reform socialist Michail Nelken that "the Stalinism debate in the
PDS had primarily ideological character and a political function."[20] On the other
hand, Harry Nick, a member of the Marxist Forum, regarded it as "macabre"
that Nelken as "the head of the constitutional commission of a left-wing party
declared openly that he needed the Stalinism debate as a means of political
cleansing." Pressure from outside the PDS, Nick alleged, was translated into
attacks on minorities within the party.[21]

The affirmation of anti-Stalinist consensus by "modern socialists" was directed not only against a small number of PDS members who "blamed the
decline of socialism on the victory of revisionism and opportunism in 1956."
Two different groups of opponents were targeted: "The rejection of the post-
Stalinist historical revisionism of Gossweiler, Wagenknecht, or Holz . . . was
only one of the objectives. The more important intention . . . was the consolidation of the political-programmatic hegemony of reform-socialist 'Realpoli-
tik' " through an attack on "the conservative-legitimatory wing of the PDS."[22]

There were, indeed, two lines of conflict in this debate of 1994–1995. First,
there was the readily identifiable conflict between a small number of individuals
defending Stalinist positions and, on the other hand, PDS leaders such as Gysi
and Brie declaring their views incompatible with party membership. Second,
there was the much more important battle between those using a wider definition
of Stalinism encompassing not only the Stalin period until 1953 but also "real
socialism" after 1953 and those proposing a narrower concept of Stalinism,
limiting its use to the period of Stalin's rule and of mass terror until 1953. The
latter preferred the label "centralist-bureaucratic socialism" for the post-1953
period, a label that still expressed critical distance from post-1953 "real socialism" but made it possible to put forward a qualified, limited defense of the
socialist experiment in East Germany. This second debate was not one between
anti- and pro-Stalinists but between those emphasizing that the period after 1953

was still characterized by many Stalinist structures and those insisting that the end of mass terror also meant the end of Stalinism proper. Effectively, the debate was about the extent and degree of rejection of post-Stalin "real socialism." This more precise distinction was often hardly noticeable behind the attacks on a comeback of "Stalinist" positions in the PDS and the counterattacks claiming that an undifferentiated labeling of opponents as Stalinists was used as an instrument to shift the entire party in a more social democratic direction.

There was a need to reassert the party's anti-Stalinist foundation consensus, according to reform socialist Nelken. From the foundation congress in December 1989 to the conference about Stalinism on 17–18 November 1990, the PDS had critically analyzed the past and adopted strong and clear positions. However, during 1991 and 1992 the PDS had taken a "nostalgic" and "restorative turn" as "traditionalist, orthodox positions," which had initially been inaudible, were expressed once more. These found support among PDS members disappointed by the experience of postunification Germany. The resulting "ambivalent GDR nostalgia" could be used by "orthodox-communist" positions for attacks on the PDS majority. According to this view, the earlier highly critical evaluation of GDR history was being revised by 1991–1992.[23] In a defensive response to the experience of "colonization" from West Germany, PDS members began to defend their individual and collective past. This revival of "orthodox" positions was the background to the debate about Stalinism in 1993 and 1994.

The 1993 party program had adopted a narrow definition of Stalinism as the period of Stalin's rule until 1953. This avoided a wholesale rejection of post-1953 East German socialism. While reform socialists such as Nelken regarded this as part of a restorative shift in PDS discourse since 1992,[24] the 1993 party program was defended during the Stalinism debates of 1994 and 1995 by the opponents of the modern socialists. The debate calmed down in late 1993 because the imminent campaigns for the 1994 elections required party unity. However, as soon as the elections were over, debates were reignited in the preparation for the January 1995 party congress through the drafting of the Ten Theses, followed by the Five Points demanding clear distancing from Stalinist positions.

Nelken admitted that the "neo-Stalinist historical revisionism" articulated by Gossweiler, Holz, or Wagenknecht was a "marginal . . . extreme position" but claimed nevertheless that "their open appearance was symptomatic for a shift in the political-intellectual climate of the PDS"[25] that allowed views to be articulated in 1991 to 1993 that had been quiet in 1990. While Nelken was not exaggerating the strength of support for these marginal, extreme positions, he overstated their relevance as indicators for shifts within the PDS. In reality, the years 1991–1993 had seen a reassertion of GDR identity, a reassertion of the legitimacy of socialism as a historical answer in the late 1940s, an answer to the Great Depression, to World War I and World War II, and to fascism. This qualified defense of GDR history still involved a critical distance and should be distinguished from uncritical neo-Stalinist positions.

According to modern socialists, the foundation consensus of the PDS was based on an extensive concept of Stalinism, referring not only to "personality cult, show trials, terror and mass murder in the Soviet Union but to the collapsing system of the GDR, to bureaucratism, centralism, administrative methods, arbitrariness, to lack of democracy and rule of law." This consensus, according to Nelken, was threatened by reappearing "orthodox" positions and a variety of attitudes to Stalinism. This amounted to "a turning point in the debate on Stalinism" in mid-1991 after which "only the 'innovators' demanded more anti-Stalinism and deplored the 'neo-Stalinist restoration' of the PDS."[26]

Arguing for this wider concept of Stalinism, Brie claimed that the party's early anti-Stalinist consensus "included the assessment that the society of the GDR was ultimately structured in a Stalinist and post-Stalinist way" and opposed the "reduction of Stalinism . . . to the period of Stalin's rule, of the personality cult and of mass terror" that ignored "the comprehensive societal and ongoing character of Stalinism in political and economic structures." Brie acknowledged that "the end of mass terror was, of course, a result that cannot be valued too highly, and the fact that it did not happen in this form in the GDR constituted a significant difference." Nevertheless, he opposed any "attempt to deny the essential continuity between Soviet Stalinism and GDR post-Stalinism."[27]

On the other hand, Uwe-Jens Heuer, a representative of the Marxist Forum, applied "Stalinism" only for the period up to Stalin's death, preferring the term "bureaucratic-centralist socialism" for the post-1953 period. In this view, the continued existence of certain Stalinist structures did not justify the label "Stalinism" for the GDR because of the absence of mass terror, the central characteristic of Stalinism.[28] This approach implied a rejection of Stalinism until 1953 as well as a critical distance from "real socialism" after 1953. However, the label "bureaucratic-centralist socialism" suggested a much more qualified critique and even allowed a selective defense of aspects of GDR history, in contrast to their outright rejection as a late phase of Stalinism. The Marxist Forum defended itself against the allegation that it avoided using the term "Stalinism" altogether; it merely rejected its application to the post-1953 period.

The outcome of the Stalinism debate before and after the party congress of January 1995 was a new balance of the different currents in the PDS. The Communist Platform was divided and weakened, resulting in a "marginalization and self-destruction of the KPF during the conflict about GDR history and Stalinism."[29] Although the Platform presented an image of unity at the January 1995 congress, differences became visible between the neo-Stalinist positions of Wagenknecht and Gossweiler, on the one hand, and the position taken by Benjamin, on the other hand.

This weakness of the Communist Platform left space for the emergence of a new focus of opposition within the PDS, the Marxist Forum. Whereas the KPF had been hampered in these history debates because it included the defenders of indefensible neo-Stalinist positions, the MF had a more defensible position.

Its representatives argued for a narrow concept of Stalinism that implied a total rejection of the period of mass terror up to Stalin's death in 1953 but facilitated a differentiated assessment of the post-1953 period. Where the modern socialists rejected post-1953 socialism as Stalinist because it was still permeated by Stalinist structures even after the end of Stalinist mass terror, the Marxist Forum criticized the post-1953 period under the somewhat milder label of "centralist-bureaucratic socialism."

By mid-1995, the most visible line of ideological conflict in the PDS was no longer that between the Communist Platform and the reform socialist leaders backed by modern socialist intellectuals but the conflict between party leaders and the Marxist Forum.

THE MARXIST FORUM: "IN GREAT SORROW"

In mid-1995, a new type of opposition to the course of PDS leaders Gysi, Bisky, and Brie emerged. The marginal Communist Platform was replaced by the more centrist Marxist Forum as the most vocal opposition group. The congress of January 1995 had begun to move the PDS toward closer cooperation with the SPD and Greens, toward a reform strategy deemphasizing an anticapitalist, socialist vision and toward a softening of the opposition role of the PDS. The reform socialist leadership (Gysi, Bisky, A. Brie) and the modern socialist intellectuals (Klein, M. Brie, and others) consolidated their hegemony. The Communist Platform had resisted these changes, but the party congress had highlighted its numerical weakness further compounded by a lack of intellectual stature, organizational weakness, and marginality within the PDS.

In this situation a new opposition grouping emerged in the Marxist Forum. Its foundation was preceded by an appeal published in May 1995 under the title "In Great Sorrow." The 38 signatories warned that the identity of the PDS was under threat by a leadership intent on giving in to external demands for adaptation. They claimed that "the basic consensus of the party was being abandoned on three issues. First, the party's opposition was diluted as party leaders dismissed class struggle, bracketed out the property question, and promoted a social contract. Second, party leaders demanded a total rejection of the history of SED and GDR in the form of a verdict against Stalinism. Third, the party's internal pluralism was under threat.[30]

The Marxist Forum defended the party program against a leadership increasingly uncomfortable with the programmatic compromises of 1993, whereas reform socialists deplored that "the formulations of the programs could . . . become a legitimate line of retreat of . . . the Marxist Forum and others."[31] The modern socialists and the reform socialist leaders could not openly oppose the 1993 program but attempted to redirect party discourse in preparation for future programmatic change.

The ideological positions defended by the Marxist Forum were reminiscent of the Marxist tradition within German Social Democracy since August Bebel and Karl Kautsky. The argument that class struggle existed and that the property question was central to the strategy of a socialist party was not a symptom of Stalinism but, more precisely, a symptom of adherence to much wider socialist traditions.

Compared to the Communist Platform, the MF had more intellectual substance. It included professors, jurists, past state officials, and other members of the former GDR elites. The Communist Platform, on the other hand, gathered a mixture of a few intellectuals, party activists, and grassroots members, especially of the older generation who had been communists all their lives and could not understand how their struggle for justice and a better society could have been all wrong.

In spite of these differences, the Marxist Forum defended the right of the Communist Platform to remain within the PDS, arguing that the party should not sacrifice its left wing in order to accommodate outside pressure. The MF argued for party unity because the PDS could "only as a whole . . . be a problem for the rulers,"[32] whereas the expulsion or marginalization of the Communist Platform would facilitate further shifts of the PDS away from socialist positions.

Regarding GDR history, the Marxist Forum attempted a balancing act between critically rejecting Stalinism and defending the legitimacy of the historical attempt to build a different society. Pointing to the deficits of "real socialism" regarding civic and political rights, MF intellectuals concluded that the heritage of bourgeois liberalism, especially democracy and rule of law, had to be positively inherited rather than rejected.[33] Their articles even acknowledged the need to modify Marx's critique of commodity production. Harry Nick, for example, concluded that the abolition of commodity production was not desirable because a socialist society ought to be a commodity-producing society.[34] Before 1989, Western commentators would have described such arguments as critical and undogmatic; in the GDR or the USSR they would have been attacked as revisionist. Yet, a decade later, in united Germany, many analysts portrayed the MF as unreformed, nostalgic, and dogmatic.

The Marxist Forum insisted on socialist tenets such as class analysis, the property question, the relevance of a socialist objective, and the idea of a society beyond capitalism not as an immediate objective but as guidance to practical reform efforts.[35] Here the MF differed from modern socialists willing to discard or minimize any discourse of property and class. For the MF, class and property structures were still important, although not to the exclusion of gender issues or ecological issues. For the modern socialists, on the other hand, classes might perhaps exist, but they were certainly not relevant political agents. For them, the core objective of the PDS was not to overcome the dominance of capitalist property but only the dominance of the capitalist profit motive. This could conceivably be achieved by political pressure producing a legal-political framework curbing the absolute power of capitalist property.[36]

The Marxist Forum was more effective as opposition to the modern socialists than the Communist Platform, which was largely excluded from the leading bodies of the party, barely able to sustain a network of activists in the local and regional party branches. The MF had minority representation in parliamentary caucuses and in leading party bodies. It also had strong networks in East German interest groups such as the Gesellschaft zum Schutz von Bürgerrecht und Menschenwürde (GBM), the Kuratorium, and the Committees for Justice. The Communist Platform could be marginalized, whereas the MF represented a more significant component of the PDS.

On the one hand, the Marxist Forum was more successful in slowing down the repositioning of the PDS undertaken by the modern socialists. On the other, it was effective in bringing reluctant PDS members along in the party's new direction, albeit at a slower pace. To some extent, the MF performed a task of integrating hesitant parts of the PDS. The party as a whole integrated a large part of the East German population into the parliamentary democracy of united Germany. On a smaller scale, the MF integrated a significant minority of the PDS membership into the PDS. By 1995, the Communist Platform had become almost negligible for the whole of the PDS. The MF, on the other hand, signaled to PDS leaders a stress line that they could not afford to break.

STRATEGY DEBATE AT THE 1996 MAGDEBURG PARTY CONGRESS: "SOCIETAL OPPOSITION" MAY JOIN GOVERNMENT

In 1996, the debates about the opposition role of the PDS, which had been triggered by the Magdeburg model of "toleration" in 1994, reached a new level of intensity. "Opposition" had been the first and the last word in election platform for the 1994 elections, drafted in December 1993. On page 1, the PDS defined its task as "opposition against social demontage and shift to the right," asserting that Germany needed "a strong left opposition." And the platform ended with the catchphrase "Change begins with Opposition."[37] This opposition role was identified with an emphasis on extraparliamentary political work, accompanied by a role as opposition in parliament.

Earlier, in late 1989 and early 1990, PDS members had to come to terms with the loss of a role as permanent government of the GDR, which the SED had enjoyed. Even before its defeat in the Volkskammer elections of March 1990, the PDS began to discover that opposition can be a meaningful role for a party. The PDS had no choice anyhow, as it was marginalized by all other parties. This ascribed role as opposition was also positively adopted: A socialist party in a capitalist society had to be "societal opposition."

By 1994, however, the situation had changed. During 1992 and 1993, the PDS had gained some strength in local councils and Land parliaments in the East. At the local level, PDS mayors and local councillors had taken on executive responsibilities in local government. At this level of government, the multitude of day-to-day practical issues diluted ideological divisions between parties and softened the marginalization of the PDS by all other parties. By 1994, the

PDS was ready to modify its opposition stance, and at the same time, Social Democrats and Greens had begun to change from a strategy of exclusion and elimination toward a strategy of integrating the PDS. The Magdeburg model of toleration was the result of change on both sides. For the first time, the PDS had influenced the formation of a government executive, albeit only at the Land level.

After the 1994 national elections, which strengthened the representation of the PDS in the Bundestag, leaders began to prepare the party for government responsibility. At the congresses of 1995, 1996, and 1997, the consensus of the PDS was shifted toward an acceptance of government responsibility, toward a redefinition of "opposition." In the end, the party still defined itself as "societal opposition"; its 1993 party program still defined the PDS as an anticapitalist party with an emphasis on extraparliamentary campaigning. However, by 1997 it was majority consensus that a role as societal opposition was compatible with a variety of roles in parliament, either as parliamentary opposition or in a "toleration" arrangement as in Magdeburg or as part of a governing coalition, should the conditions be right.

At the Magdeburg congress (27–28 January 1996) delegates met for the first time outside the PDS strongholds of East Berlin. It had been in Magdeburg that the party had for the first time overcome its isolation when a minority government of Social Democrats and Alliance 90/Greens gained office due to "toleration" by PDS parliamentarians. Magdeburg was chosen as venue for the 1996 congress to signal a clear intention: PDS leaders wanted to adopt a strategy of cooperation with Social Democrats and Greens, possibly including the formation of government coalitions at the Land level.

The redefinition of the party's role as societal opposition was at the center of all debates. Hans Modrow,[38] honorary president of the PDS and integration figure for many older members, reminded the delegates of the principle "change begins with opposition" and questioned all talk about the "ability to govern." This expressed the feelings of many older members, of the left wing of the party (MF, KPF), of many West German members, and of the Youth Wing.

All other leaders, however, argued for a more flexible understanding of "opposition" making "toleration" and "coalition" at least conceivable for some time in the future. Party President Lothar Bisky, for example, argued for a case-by-case approach: "Our approach to politics is not guided abstractly by opposition, toleration, or coalition, but by contents: What can and has to be changed?" He wanted to leave the question open for decision by the relevant PDS branches when the choice would be relevant.[39] This conciliatory position of Bisky was, effectively, the preparation for a shift toward accepting coalitions. Federal parliamentary leader Gysi also began his speech with a reference to the decision of the party congress of January 1995 defining the PDS "as societal opposition."[40] Nevertheless, this basic position did not preclude flexible roles in parliament. At the national level, forming coalitions was not an issue at this stage. In the parliaments of the Eastern Länder, however, the situation was different.

There Bisky's preference was for a toleration model. The condition for eventual coalitions in Eastern Länder would be a decision of the relevant PDS branch assessing whether relevant change could be achieved.

Roland Claus, PDS chairman of Saxony-Anhalt, gave a positive evaluation of the experience with the toleration model in his Land. Should a toleration model not be possible, arithmetically, then the PDS should break its taboo against entering coalitions if this could prevent a government including the Christian Democrats.[41]

Party leaders wanted to add the weight of the PDS to a broad center-left coalition against the conservative-neoliberal government: "The political objective of the PDS consists . . . in making a contribution towards pushing back and overcoming the conservative hegemony in society. To form majorities this side of the CDU/CSU, the PDS searches for common points with other forces, movements and parties."[42] This strategy committed the PDS to a reform strategy for limited achievable objectives: to replace the government of Christian Democrats and Free Democrats by a government of Social Democrats and Greens, possibly relying on PDS support.

Altogether the conflicts within the PDS were much less intensive at the 1996 congress than in January 1995, observers such as Heinrich Bortfeldt still expected an imminent split into reformers and communists, while Gerner wrote of irreconcilable differences.[43]

Taken together, the three party congresses of January 1995 (Berlin), January 1996 (Magdeburg), and January 1997 (Schwerin) showed that internal differences about strategy were substantial but not irreconcilable. The opposition to government participation by Marxist Forum representatives was not fundamental but conditional. Uwe-Jens Heuer, Eckehard Lieberam, and Gregor Schirmer, for example, objected to the ease with which the Gysi/Bisky/Brie leadership wanted to enter into coalitions. Instead, they demanded that the condition for joining governments should be the existence of a real chance to implement reform policies.[44] In the end, the resolution moved by the party leadership set a much more modest objective: the replacement of the conservative coalition of CDU/CSU and FDP.

The result of this prolonged strategy debate was a broad majority consensus in favor of a flexible strategy, open for all options including opposition, toleration, or government coalition. This consensus was possible because the rank-and-file membership was not, contrary to Gerner's claims, attached to Communist Platform positions. At the end of the discussion process, the limited relevance of the Communist Platform was evident, whereas the skepticism of many PDS members regarding joining coalitions had been overcome in patient discourse over a two-year period.

At the end of the Magdeburg congress, the decision about opposition, toleration, or coalition had been kept open. This alone constituted significant change compared to the strong identification with an opposition role during the years 1990 to 1995. The party leadership had managed to shift party discourse to this open position. PDS chairman Bisky pointed out that in the East German Länder broad left majorities against the CDU could be possible after the next set of elections. "Then one has to decide: for a strong opposition against a Grand Coalition in which conservatives crack the whip, for a toleration model as in Magdeburg, or for strong left wing influence in a joint government." Bisky suggested that this decision be made dependent on regional circumstances, while parliamentary leader Gregor Gysi argued that the decision about opposition, toleration, or coalition be made in the relevant PDS branch after democratic discussion.[45]

The delegates were getting used, gradually, to the fact that the PDS had choices in the new party system and was able to exercise options other than remaining in opposition as a critical outsider. Klaus Höpcke reminded the delegates of the slogan "Change begins with opposition." However, in a new interpretation, he argued "that change, which begins with opposition, does not exhaust itself in opposition."[46] This gentle persuasion came from a member of the Marxist Forum, which, evidently, was not a "fundamental opposition."

Communist Platform representative Sahra Wagenknecht warned that the partial cooperation offered by SPD and Greens was a strategy to weaken and eliminate the PDS in the medium term. Party leader Gregor Gysi, on the other hand, interpreted the new situation as opportunity: "We have emerged stronger out of the time in which we were almost completely marginalised, when we were judged only by what we had been and where we had come from. And those who now believe that we could not get through a time of dialogue, perhaps even of a few embraces and political controversies, they are wrong again."[47]

Indeed, the strategy suggested to Social Democrats and Greens by political analysts Jürgen Raschke and Manfred Gerner was ambivalent. Partial cooperation in order to weaken and divide the PDS was, in the first instance, cooperation. It was an opportunity for the PDS to have political impact, provided it could avoid the risk of losing its identity and of being divided, transformed, or absorbed by the larger SPD.

"LETTER FROM SAXONY": PDS TO REMAIN EASTERN REGIONALIST PARTY?

Opposition to the strategy of the Gysi-Brie leadership also came from some of the pragmatic PDS representatives in East German local councils and Land parliaments. Their views were articulated in the "Letter from Saxony" criticizing the Gysi-Brie strategy of building a nationwide left-socialist party. Instead of wasting time and energy on a futile expansion into West Germany, the PDS should concentrate on what it did best: to represent East German regional interests neglected by the economic and political elites of West Germany.

In their "Letter from Saxony," published on 7 May 1996, Christine Ostrowski, president of the Dresden city organization of the PDS, and Roland Weckesser, leader of the PDS city councillors in Dresden, recommended that the PDS should be an "East German people's party."[48] This appeal was symptomatic of a current among East German PDS members whose priority was the representation of the interests of their fellow East Germans in local government, in Land parliaments, and in the Bundestag. For them the frustrating long-term effort of building the PDS in West Germany was nothing but a costly distraction from regional interests.

Local political activists such as Ostrowski and Weckesser had been the backbone of the party's credibility in the districts of major cities and in the towns of East Germany. They had taken up issues concerning every East German as inhabitant of a local area, as tenant coming to terms with housing problems and local government services. These local activists could easily have been members of the Social Democratic Party if they only had been born in West Germany. It was only the accidents of history and geography that had placed them into the PDS subculture.

These pragmatic politicians envisaged a regionalist role for the PDS: representing the grievances of millions of East Germans. The implication of this role was to abandon the ambition of building a nationwide left-socialist party. This reorientation would have made the coexistence of the PDS with the SPD relatively unproblematic as the PDS would have settled into a role as a regionally based alternate version of the SPD.

This would still have created some discomfort for the Social Democrats insofar as about half of the left vote in the East would have supported another party. However, if this regionalist PDS had become no more than a regional version of the SPD under another name, the future relation between SPD and PDS could have been similar to the relation between CDU and CSU. Like the Bavarian CSU, the PDS would have been a regional junior partner of its major nationwide partner, differing only in its regional identity, not in its ideological orientation.

The response to the "Letter from Saxony" in the PDS was overwhelmingly negative. Not only the left wing of the PDS (Marxist Forum, Communist Platform, and the West German branches) insisted on a socialist identity. The party's leadership also intended to continue the balancing act of appealing to East German interests, to the secular-socialist subculture in the East, and to a small minority in the West attracted to a left-socialist party.

Besides the political inclinations of individual leaders, there was also the strategic consideration that the PDS could only be relevant and have a chance to retain representation in the Bundestag if it held together its diverse clientele: East German regionalists, East German socialists, and the West German left-socialist potential.

Thus the PDS operated as a cluster of alternating and interlocking alliances. For the purposes of leading the PDS closer to the center-left SPD and Greens, the reform-socialist PDS leadership and the modern socialists found allies among the pragmatic, regionalist local politicians against the socialist left of the party. On the other hand, for the purpose of developing the PDS into a nationally

relevant left-socialist party, the reform-socialist PDS leaders were supported by
the left of the party against local pragmatists preferring a regionalist East
German future for the PDS.

The positions adopted by PDS leaders in these strategy debates corresponded
to opportunity structures. Regional differences between the southern and northern parts of East Germany contributed to this diversity of preferences. In the
south of the East, in Saxony especially, the PDS was divided between regionalist
pragmatists and more traditionalist socialists close to the Marxist Forum. The
PDS had little hope of entering a regional government because Christian Democrats had a clear majority in Saxony, while the Social Democrats of Saxony
were more averse to cooperation with the PDS than in any other Eastern region.
Thus the PDS was restricted to pragmatic local government politics or to as-
sertions of socialist identity. In the northern parts of the East, the opportunity
structure was different. The PDS had a chance of enjoying some influence on
Land politics. In Brandenburg the party could exercise influence through parliamentary committees; in Saxony-Anhalt it was "tolerating" a minority government of SPD and Greens; and in Mecklenburg–West Pommerania the option of
forming a government coalition with Social Democrats was seriously negotiated
in April 1996 and became reality in 1998. These opportunity structures had
substantial impact on the plausibility and attractiveness of strategic options.

For PDS members in the West, the only rationale for the existence of the
party was to build a nationwide left-socialist party relying on the Eastern
branches to lend a helping hand. For PDS members in the south of the East,
the plausible options were either pragmatic East German regionalism focusing
on local government issues or principled socialist identity politics. For PDS
members in the north of the East, and for the leadership of the party, the most
promising option was to build a socialist party to the left of the SPD while
positioning their party close enough to Social Democrats and Greens to overcome the isolation of the PDS and to become a part of a broad left reform
majority. The juggling act of uniting these divergent perspectives was possible
because the exclusion strategy adopted by all other parties held the PDS together. The different components of the party had nowhere else to go, and they
could only hope to gain some political relevance by staying together.

THE ANNIVERSARY OF THE 1946 MERGER OF KPD AND
SPD

Relations between Social Democrats and PDS were strained in 1996 by the
fiftieth anniversary of the merger of the KPD and SPD to form the Socialist
Unity Party of Germany (SED) in the Soviet Occupied Zone. For the opponents
of any cooperation between the SPD and PDS, the anniversary of the *Zwangsvereinigung* (coercive merger) served as a reminder of the negative experience
of Social Democrats in cooperation with communists. Even those in the SPD
opting for partial and conditional cooperation with the PDS made it a prereq-

uisite that the PDS distance itself clearly from the 1946 merger. In the PDS, the interpretation of the 1946 merger was crucial for its attempt to find an identity different from its predecessor SED and from its present competitor, the SPD. The anniversary was an opportunity to search for legitimate traditions, to discuss the identity of the party, and to define its relations to the SPD.

While most approaches to the history of 1946 were colored by highly partisan perspectives, the West German historian Hermann Weber provided an interpretation of 1946 that did not simplify the past for the sake of retrospective projection of partisan ideals. He emphasized that the unity party did not result from a voluntary unification between equals[49] but acknowledged nevertheless that Social Democrats in 1946 had reasons other than coercion for joining the SED and that until 1948 the SED "was not a cadre party in the Leninist sense, but a . . . socialist mass party" (p. 11). It was not a bolshevist party "in its ideology (German road to socialism) and in its structure (mass party in which former Social Democrats still had parity in all executive committees). In 1948 the party underwent its first decisive change" (p. 13). By then "many former Social Democrats were in opposition to the party leadership as was a considerable number of disappointed old communists" (p. 14).

A differentiated approach such as Weber's did not have a chance during the Cold War. From the 1950s to the 1970s, there were two dominant interpretations of 1946. In East Germany, the ruling SED's historiography celebrated the party's foundation in 1946 as the historic achievement of unity of the working class. In West Germany, Social Democrats rejected the merger as *Zwangsvereinigung*, as a coercive merger during which the KPD destroyed the East German SPD. For a short time in the mid-1980s, there was hope for a more differentiated interpretation of 1946 while SPD and SED engaged in an East-West dialogue between political parties. Then GDR historians were beginning to acknowledge contradictions connected with the merger, while West German historians were no longer denying the widespread desire for a unity party immediately after World War II.

However, in the year of German unification, the merger of 1946 had once more become a topic of polarized controversy. Social Democrat Werner Müller, in an article subtitled "Plea for the Concept 'Coercive Merger,' "[50] insisted that East German Social Democrats had been forced by the Soviet Military Administration and by the KPD to join the SED. In 1990, the SPD had to be wary of interpretations of 1946 that would allow conservatives to portray the party as naively procommunist. This was the objective of a publication by the CDU/ CSU parliamentary organization in 1990 highlighting the voluntary participation of many Social Democrats in the 1946 merger and suggesting that the SPD had to share some responsibility for four decades of SED dictatorship. Conservative commentators Friedrich Bohl and Rudolf Kraus argued that the term "coercive merger" served to disguise the Social Democrats' "share of responsibility for the party merger and to portray the SPD as a party of martyrs."[51]

By 1996, the discussion about 1946 occurred in a slightly different context.

In 1990, the PDS had been completely marginalized, and reminders of 1946 could only serve to confirm this exclusion. However, when the PDS had achieved a degree of acceptability in the East German electorate by 1994, partial cooperation between Social Democrats and PDS became conceivable and, in the Magdeburg model of "toleration," even reality. Thus clarification of the shared history of 1946 became a precondition for further improvements in the relations between the two parties.

For the PDS, the interpretation of 1946 became a difficult balancing act. On the one hand, it had to distance itself from the failed and discredited tradition of the SED under Ulbricht and Honecker. On the other, it had to remain different from the social democratic tradition of Kurt Schumacher leading to the Godesberg Program of 1959. Without political space between these two interpretations of history, the very existence of the PDS could not be justified.

Before 1990, East German historiography had treated the 1946 merger as a step toward a Leninist party. "Interpretations dominated which did not ascribe to the SPD an autonomous role and portrayed it as . . . 'wavering' partner adopting strategy and tactics formulated by the KPD thus showing acceptance of 'historical necessity.' "[52] The SED of 1946 was interpreted as "not yet" a Leninist party: "Already at the time of the foundation of the SED it was clear that the great task of unification would only be completed . . . if the SED was to become a party which had reached the heights of Marxist-Leninist science and acted according to the principles of the party of the new type."[53] The coercive elements of the merger were denied and rejected as slander: "Kurt Schumacher maligned the foundation of the SED as 'coercive merger.' "[54] In this perspective, the transformation of the unity party by 1949 into a communist party modeled on the CPSU was the desirable and inevitable outcome intended in 1946.

Social Democratic historians, on the other hand, restated their views of the 1946 merger in 1996 at a forum organized by the Historical Commission of the SPD in Berlin (14–15 March 1996). Two aspects of this forum are important here: First, the interpretation of 1946 as "coercive merger" was restated; second, the processes of 1946 were interpreted from the perspective of the post-1959 SPD. Historian Helga Grebing presented the SPD of 1946 as if it had already moved close to the party it was to become by 1959, the year of the Godesberg Program. She claimed that there was already in the first postwar years "a consensus . . . about . . . a widening of the *class party* anchored above all in the industrial working class towards a *people's party* encompassing bourgeois strata as well." Grebing saw the post-1959 catch-all party already emerging in the 1940s as the SPD "endeavoured to extend those programmatic elements already prefigured in Weimar, leading ultimately to the statements of the later Godesberg Program of 1959."[55]

While SED historians had projected their ideal of a Marxist-Leninist party retrospectively onto the 1946 merger, SPD historian Grebing projected her ideal of a left-of-center catch-all party back onto the Social Democrats of 1946. The

SPD approach tended to deny the existence of left social democratic currents more interested in unity of the working class than in a shift from class party to catch-all party.

The approach to the 1946 merger taken by PDS historians highlighted the positions that had failed in 1946: the early attempts to form a united party without working through KPD and SPD; the "special German road to socialism"; the hope that the merger of the parties would change the Stalinist structures of the KPD. The 1997 *Kommentar* described the SED as "object of Stalinization from outside but also from inside."[56] This presupposed that the SED had not been Stalinist from the outset. The *Kommentar* pointed to social democrats and reform communists opposed to "Ulbricht's power apparatus." For example, Erich Gniffke, a former East German SPD leader, claimed that in 1946 several communists had asked his cooperation to prevent a dominance of the old KPD apparatus in the merged party. Ackermann's German Road to Socialism "expressed the hopes of many social democrats as well as the expectations of 'independent minded, critical communists' (Leonhardt) directed to the emerging SED."[57]

The SED of 1946 was not the Stalinist party it became from 1948 on. Its statements on socialism were reminiscent of the Erfurt Program of the SPD of 1891, and the party constitution was without the structural characteristics of communist parties such as candidate member period, purges, party control commission, Politburo, or Secretary General.[58] Although the Stalinization of the SED had been foreshadowed since its foundation, as key positions in the party were held by Comintern officials and "Soviet emigrants," the changes of 1948 were, nevertheless, a clear break in the development of the SED.

With hindsight, PDS historians questioned whether the unity party had been the best option in 1946, although they showed empathy with those social democrats and communists who had hoped for a united party beyond KPD and SPD. Günter Benser, for example, argued that the unity of action of two separate working-class parties would have been preferable to the 1946 merger.[59]

This interpretation of the 1946 merger contributed to the formation of a distinct PDS identity. It established distance from its SED predecessor without denying continuity; it discovered a tradition supportive of a left-socialist identity distinct from communist traditions and from the social democratic tradition leading to the Godesberg Program. It provided the PDS with acceptable predecessors whose hopes had turned out to be illusionary. Yet their existence could be taken as evidence of a left-socialist potential different from KPD and SPD.

The PDS did not accept the interpretation of 1946 as *Zwangsvereinigung* which Social Democrats had demanded as prerequisite for cooperation in 1996. Nevertheless, the reevaluation of 1946 during the anniversary year 1996 helped to reduce the distance between the two parties. At the end of 1996 several East German SPD leaders declared regional cooperation with the PDS to be inevitable.

MAPPING OUT A NEW STRATEGY: CAN THE
INTERNALLY DIVIDED PDS BE SPLIT?

The failure of the strategy of marginalizing and eliminating the PDS was evident by late 1995. Political analyst Manfred Gerner even claimed that the portrayal of the PDS as an entirely left-extremist party had "contributed significantly to the electoral success of the PDS in the East of the republic."[60] Instead, Gerner described the PDS as "a party of irreconcilable contradictions" (p. 228) that was "predominantly ruled by reform forces professing democratic socialism" (p. 238), by "a social democratic wing" confronting the Communist Platform that "represented without doubt an orthodox-Marxist line" (p. 230). Although Gerner was aware of the numerical weakness of the Communist Platform (itself claiming 3,000 to 4,000 members, while opponents estimated only 1,000; Gerner, p. 234), he assumed it had widespread influence among PDS members: "Ideologically the majority of the old rank and file are close to the 'Communist Platform.' " Gerner predicted that "in case of a split of the party into 'Communist Platform' and the rest of the PDS, it would have to be expected that a least a qualified minority of the party rank and file would follow the 'Communist Platform' " (p. 239).

Instead of the failed exclusion strategy, Gerner's portrayal of the PDS as internally divided into a social democratic wing and a communist wing suggested to other parties a strategy of partial cooperation capable of accentuating the internal tensions within the PDS. "The breaking up of the apparent cohesiveness of the PDS could weaken the party decisively and threaten its existence in the long run" (p. 239). Therefore, other parties should deny the Democratic Socialists their comfortable role as vocal opposition: "As soon as the PDS is taken into responsibility, one can assume that tension and conflicts will emerge within the party, which will cause it to break apart" (p. 239).

Gerner's approach confirmed what Jürgen Raschke had recommended two years earlier.[61] While conservative analysts such as Patrick Moreau still provided the Christian Democrats with a portrayal of the PDS as an extremist party to be marginalized and eliminated, more precise analysts such as Raschke and Gerner acknowledged the medium-term survival of the PDS and distinguished between acceptable and unacceptable components of the party. This approach acknowledged the short-term failure of the exclusion strategy. Instead, a strategy of partial cooperation capable of weakening the PDS in the long run was suggested.

The feasibility of this strategy depended on the depth of the internal divisions within the PDS. In this respect, Gerner overestimated the role of the Communist Platform. He claimed quite rightly that many rank-and-file members of the PDS were "still attached to the old thinking in terms of class struggle."[62] However, this did not mean they were crypto-communists. The emphasis on class struggle has been shared by a variety of currents in the working-class movements, not only communists but also social democrats or labor supporters. The insistence of the Marxist Forum on concepts such as "class struggle" or "property question" merely proved the survival of a social democratic tradition going back to Bebel and Kautsky, not to Lenin or Stalin.

The test for Gerner's diagnosis occurred in 1998. The PDS eventually joined a state government as junior partner of the SPD, in Mecklenburg–West Pommerania. The fact that the PDS was not torn apart by this step showed that the conflicts within the party were not as deep as Gerner claimed. This implied that most of the rank and file did not share the Communist Platform's opposition against joining "bourgeois coalitions."

Gerner conceptualized the divisions within the PDS in terms of social democratic versus communist. This dichotomy did not allow more precise distinctions. In the PDS the dominant current of modern socialists pursued a New Left agenda mixing social justice themes with pacifist, environmentalist, feminist, and radical democratic issues. This was opposed by parts of the membership identifying with "old labor," old social democratic ideas, perhaps Marxist in a Kautskyian sense. The Communist Platform created the misperception, believed by outside observers, that it was the speaker of these members. In reality, the role of the Communist Platform was much more limited.

In spite of these flaws, the portrayals of the PDS offered by Raschke and Gerner were far more accurate than those provided by Moreau and other "extremism experts." They also offered new strategies ready to replace the failed marginalization and elimination approach.

For the PDS, the pressures of the exclusion strategy had contributed to its consolidation but had also quarantined it in an outsider role. The new strategy of partial cooperation showed a different type of ambiguity. On the one hand, the pull effect of cooperation and integration could affect its left-socialist identity; it could weaken and divide the party. On the other hand, partial cooperation could increase the acceptance of the PDS among voters, especially in West Germany. It could allow the party to add its weight to a broad left coalition capable of replacing the government of Christian Democrats and Free Democrats.

SOCIAL DEMOCRATS OPT FOR INTEGRATION STRATEGY

By late 1996, the debate among Social Democrats about the costs and benefits of cooperation with the PDS had reached a new stage. In 1990, the SPD had been as hostile to the PDS as all other parties. By 1994, the SPD had accepted "toleration" by the PDS for a minority government of Social Democrats and Greens in Saxony-Anhalt, but SPD leader Rudolf Scharping had reaffirmed his party's distance from the PDS in the Dresden Declaration. The Magdeburg model of toleration was to remain an exception not to be replicated in other East German Länder such as Mecklenburg–West Pommerania or Thuringia where regional SPD leaders considered cooperation with the PDS. In 1994 marginalization was still preferred to the strategy of partial cooperation, aimed at integrating and weakening the PDS.

However, when Scharping was replaced as SPD chairman at the Mannheim congress in November 1995 by Oskar Lafontaine, East German SPD leaders felt encouraged to pursue the option of governing with the PDS. During a coalition crisis between Christian Democrats and Social Democrats in April 1996, Harald Ringstorff, SPD leader in Mecklenburg-Vorpommern, entered into preliminary negotiations with the PDS. National SPD leader Lafontaine opposed this, not in principle but only because the Alliance 90/Greens were not represented in the Schwerin parliament.[63] In other words, direct cooperation of Social Democrats and PDS, without Alliance 90/Greens as primary partners, was still too controversial.

In 1996, vocal opponents of cooperation between the Social Democrats and PDS, such as Stephen Hilsberg, a Bundestag parliamentarian from Brandenburg, still argued that the PDS in its present form was unacceptable. Even if the PDS were to "social-democratize" itself, it would be superfluous as there was already the SPD. Therefore, the SPD should isolate the PDS to foster a split into an unacceptable communist wing and a social democratic wing to be absorbed by the SPD.[64] On the other hand, by December 1996 SPD Vicechairman Wolfgang Thierse and the chairmen of the SPD branches in four of the five East German Länder declared, in the "Thierse-paper," that Social Democrats could not avoid cooperation with the PDS in the East, although it should be excluded on the national level.[65]

The willingness among Social Democrats to be associated with the PDS increased for several reasons: First, the survival and regained regional relevance of the PDS in the East made a strategy of marginalization and elimination futile; second, growing acceptance of the PDS among East German voters made hostility toward the PDS more costly, and a less negative image in the West made cooperation less problematic; third, the changes within the PDS, especially its adaptation to a role as participant in a competitive party system, made cooperation feasible; and fourth, the emerging three-party system in the Eastern Länder, which reduced the options for forming government without the PDS, made cooperation with the PDS one of the few possible options for forming government majorities. The only remaining significant parties were the CDU, SPD, and PDS, as FDP and Greens lost representation in Eastern parliaments. CDU and SPD could possibly govern with one another, if they could not govern on their own. The only other option was an SPD government supported by the PDS, either through toleration (since 1994 Magdeburg) or coalition (for the first time in 1998, Schwerin). Thus, facts, perceptions, and political options changed.

In this situation, it was in the interest of the CDU/CSU and FDP to strengthen the taboo against the PDS, as this would narrow the options of the center-left SPD and Greens, not only in the East German Länder but also at the national level. At the end of 1996 and at the beginning of 1997, significant decisions were made about the strategies of all parties for the elections of 1998. Which combinations of political parties would be possible if the Kohl government of CDU/CSU and FDP was to lose its majority? One possible outcome was a government coalition of Social Democrats and Greens, which had been practiced at the regional level in Hesse, North Rhine-Westphalia, and Hamburg. However, if SPD and Greens could not achieve a majority on their own, would the SPD form a "grand coalition" with the CDU, or would SPD and Greens form a minority government relying on "toleration" by the PDS? The "productivist" right of the trade union movement rejected the Greens as a threat to jobs in industry and preferred a "grand coalition" with the CDU/CSU. Most SPD party members, however, preferred a coalition of Social Democrats and Greens. This would require a large swing to these parties. It also depended on the PDS not detracting too many voters from SPD and Greens.

ERFURT DECLARATION VERSUS WÖRLITZ DECLARATION: NO ALLIANCE FOR 1998 ELECTIONS

An "alliance for social democracy" including the SPD, Greens, and PDS was suggested in the Erfurt Declaration by trade union officials, intellectuals, and Protestant clerics of 9 January 1997.[66] Here the PDS was to be accepted not merely as an arithmetic necessity but as a genuine part of a left majority. Although the Erfurt Declaration still criticized the PDS as being insufficiently reformed, it signaled some positive acceptance of the party beyond coalition arithmetic. The Erfurt Declaration expressed the views of a social democratic minority considering the PDS as ally. This minority in the SPD was far more significant than the few social democratic unionists and students contemplating cooperation with West German communists (DKP) in the 1970s or 1980s.

Although the Erfurt Declaration did not decide Social Democratic strategies for the 1998 elections, the fact that this position could be articulated and find support indicated, nevertheless, that the PDS had managed to reduce its isolation further by achieving a higher degree of acceptance among social democratic trade union officials and intellectuals.

Most of the initial signatories of the Erfurt Declaration were members of the SPD. They included the writers Günter Grass and Gerhard Zwerenz as well as leading trade union officials from the IG Metall, IG Medien, IG Holz, and HBV. Later signatories included prominent SPD politician Egon Bahr, in the early 1970s foreign affairs adviser of Chancellor Willy Brandt.

The Christian Democrats influenced the discussion about the acceptability of the PDS in two ways: They portrayed the PDS as an extremist party that had to be observed, perhaps banned, by the authorities, and they arranged well-timed defections of Green and Social Democratic politicians highlighting that former anticommunist GDR dissidents could no longer feel at home in parties contemplating cooperation with the PDS. Vera Lengsfeld, a member of the Bundestag for Alliance 90/Greens, was the most prominent Green to join the CDU.

This was indicative of the divisions among East German dissidents who, in

1989, had been united in their opposition against SED rule in the GDR. By 1996, however, this was no longer sufficient to hold the Alliance 90 together. For Vera Lengsfeld and others, the fight against the SED was still the central motive in their political life, and this implied unconditional rejection of the PDS as SED successor. As the stance of Social Democrats and Greens toward the PDS softened, it was only logical for them to join the CDU as most consistent opponent of the PDS. On the other hand, former dissident Hans-Jochen Tschiche rejected this perpetual struggle against an SED that no longer existed. For him social and ecological policy objectives were more important than past struggles.[67] Therefore Tschiche advocated cooperation between Alliance 90/Greens, the Social Democrats, and the PDS.

The dispute among Social Democrats, expressed in the Thierse-paper, the Kunckel-Schwanitz statement, and the Erfurt Declaration, found a parallel in the Green party. Green Bundestag parliamentarians distanced themselves from the PDS in the Wörlitz Declaration (10 January 1997) stating that they aimed for a majority of Social Democrats and Greens in the Bundestag elections of 1998. "In this respect we exclude any cooperation with the PDS—be it in a coalition or in the form of toleration." While acknowledging that "the PDS (was) no longer the SED," they still demanded more change. Their four criteria expected from the PDS, first, a clearer position toward GDR history and its own "historical guilt as SED successor"; second, a recognition of democracy and the rule of law together with a greater distance "from the ideological and financial heritage of the SED"; third, a clearer position regarding the Stasi entanglement of PDS members; and fourth, "separation from old and post-Stalinists."[68]

These responses by Social Democrats and Alliance 90/Greens persuaded the initiators of the Erfurt Declaration to modify their stance. In October 1997, a congress of the supporters of the Erfurt Declaration no longer insisted on their demand for including the PDS in an alliance for social democracy. Nevertheless, their proposal to step out of the "spectators' democracy" by mobilizing for social democratic policies, for a rejection of neoliberal attacks on the welfare state and workers' rights, implied that the center-right Christian Democrats were political enemies, whereas the PDS was a potential ally.

DISTANCING FROM THE 1993 PROGRAM: THE *KOMMENTAR* OF 1997

The programmatic discussion within the PDS was stimulated by the publication in January 1997 of the volume *Zur Programmatik des Partei des Demokratischen Sozialismus. Ein Kommentar*. The *Kommentar* was not really a commentary on the 1993 party program but rather an explication of programmatic thinking possibly leading beyond the 1993 program. The distance of the authors, including party strategist André Brie and a group of "modern socialist" intellectuals, from the 1993 program was noticeable although for some commentators, this distance was not sufficient. Eva Sturm and Eberhard Schmidt, for example, argued that the *Kommentar* had been too much of a tactical concession to the backward-oriented parts of the party. It was much more a didactic effort than a development of new thoughts. These critics claimed that the PDS had avoided programmatic debates since 1993 and was only now getting around to it. They deplored that it was the pedagogical intention of the *Kommentar* to achieve "the persuasion of forces . . . who come from an orthodox concept of socialism."[69]

Commentators linked to the Marxist Forum, on the other hand, regarded the *Kommentar* as an attack on the party program of 1993, endorsed by the party leadership as an attempt to shift party consensus further in the direction of "modern socialism," undertaking a de facto correction of the program.[70]

Four issues were characteristic of the modern socialist approach taken in the *Kommentar*: (1) the positive evaluation of the "civilizing achievements of capitalist modernity"; (2) the low priority given to any considerations of class and working class; (3) the relative weighting of parliamentary and extraparliamentary action; and (4) the shift away from the "property question" toward the question of the "predominance of the profit motive."

1. Since 1989, modern socialists in the PDS had emphasized that "real socialism" had failed because it could not match the modernity that capitalism had achieved over centuries. The *Kommentar* highlighted this dual characterization of bourgeois society as both capitalist and modern: "The society of the Federal Republic is *capitalist*. For its development is dominated by capitalist property and profit. Furthermore this society is *modern* in the sense that it has at its disposal institutions characterized by the potential of development or evolution. This provides it with the characteristics of an open society, capable of development and reform. . . . In this sense we talk about *capitalist modernity*" (*Kommentar*, p. 135).

The basic institutions of capitalist modernity constituting its evolutionary potential were the market, pluralist democracy, and the Rechtsstaat (rule of law) (p. 143). The *Kommentar* did not include capitalist property in this list of basic institutions. It is not clarified whether capitalist property was not a basic institution at all, or whether it was one without evolutionary potential.

Modern socialists were not the only PDS current to recognize the achievements of capitalist modernity. Representatives of the Marxist Forum also acknowledged the value of bourgeois democracy, criticizing Marx's assumption that "the specifically political question" of democracy could be replaced by "the question of the social revolution." Here Uwe-Jens Heuer rejected the Marxist tenet that a specific quest for political democracy "was not possible before the revolution and not necessary after the revolution."[71] Heuer also regarded democratic institutions as "important civilizing achievements" and insisted on the value of the *Rechtsstaat* in spite of the objection that it could not solve problems such as unemployment.[72]

The difference between modern socialists and the Marxist Forum concerned the extent to which these civilizing achievements of bourgeois society were a

reality in Germany. MF member Klaus Höpcke conceded that for decades the
SED had erred in underestimating the evolutionary potential of capitalism, but
he queried whether the PDS had swung into the opposite error of overestimating
it. He emphasized that "classic bourgeois democratic theories had to be turned
against contemporary bourgeois antidemocratic practices."[73]

For modern socialists, the appreciation of capitalist modernity amounted to
more than an appreciation of the liberal-democratic heritage. Their discussion
of modernity as subsystem autonomy and as evolutionary potential underpinned
a reform strategy that did not require a socialist objective beyond the evolutionary potential of capitalist modernity. It was only necessary to make the
political effort to direct this evolutionary potential away from the predominance
of the profit motive.

2. The approach to class issues taken by the *Kommentar* was influenced by
André Gorz' "good-bye to the proletariat" and by Ulrich Beck's claim that
individualization and diversification of life situations and lifestyles had reduced
the relevance of class and stratification models (*Kommentar*, p. 219). "In contrast
to the Communist Manifesto, in which the class contradiction was of central
significance, the class concept is completely avoided in the program of the PDS"
(pp. 196–197). This omission resulted from disagreements between different
wings of the party in 1993, but also from the view of modern socialists who
queried whether class conflict "existed at all in modern societies" and whether
it had "any relevance for societal development, or had . . . been contained or
thoroughly relativised by a network of other conflicts" (p. 201).

As class conflict was regarded as rather unimportant, the working class was
not a revolutionary subject: "In this century there have occurred . . . considerable
differentiations among wage and salary earners . . . which together had the effect
that presently class action (working class as subject) cannot be noted" (p. 231).

Drawing strategic conclusions from this analysis of social structure, the *Kommentar* opposed a "revolutionary scenario" requiring a societal subject for a
"historical mission" and the "formation of a revolutionary class" (p. 236). Instead, the commentary suggested a scenario of "evolutionary change" aiming
for "evolutionary self-change of existing society." This strategy implied that
"ultimately all societal forces will be involved" and "[p]ossibly very diverse
social subjects could become the agents of partial steps and particular developments" (p. 237). This scenario "abolishes the traditional exclusivity of con-
necting the socialist project to the social interests of one particular class"
(p. 238).

The centrality of class struggle was thus rejected by modern socialists, and,
instead, pacifist, environmentalist, and feminist themes were emphasized. To
some extent, even the Marxist Forum supported this shift. While still insisting
on the existence of class struggle, they acknowledged the importance of global
issues concerning all of humankind such as disarmament and ecologically sus-
tainable production.

3. "Extraparliamentary struggle for social change" had been regarded by the

PDS Program of 1993 as "decisive." The party's role as "societal opposition" included, at the same time, a striving for "parliamentary strength." It was "willing to accept political responsibility for radical social and ecological change."[74] Between 1993 and 1994 the debates about this opposition intensified, as the PDS consolidated its parliamentary positions.

The *Kommentar* indicated that the PDS, in principle, was open to join coalitions or to offer support to left-of-center minority governments, "depending on political constellations" (p. 317). The Federal Executive of the PDS had, on 10 June 1996, adopted the objective of "overcoming conservative hegemony in the Federal Republic" including "the replacement or prevention of governmental power of CDU and CSU federally and in the Länder" (p. 319).

In spite of the variety of interpretations of the party's opposition role, there was an underlying consensus that the PDS had overcome the antiparliamentarianism of the communist movement of the past. "Parliamentary democracy is regarded by the PDS not as a political institution to be rejected but as a civilizing achievement whose obvious crisis has to find a constructive solution" (*Kommentar*, p. 319). Even members of the Communist Platform acknowledged the value of "parliamentary democracy" and rejected the term "dictatorship of the proletariat" as "not adequate for the characterization of the political system of a socialist society."[75]

4. The central strategic objective of the PDS was not to put an end to capitalist property structures but "to overcome the predominance of the profit motive as the basic criterion of all things" (*Kommentar*, p. 123). This rather general formula was capable of a range of interpretations, ranging from social democratic corrections of a capitalist economy to an abolition of capitalist property altogether. This variety of opinions was compatible with a party constitution welcoming those "who want to resist capitalist society and reject the existing conditions in principle" as well as those intending to "change existing conditions step by step."[76]

Overcoming the predominance of the profit motive was not aimed against the market per se. Instead, the market as a method of economic interaction was recognized as civilizatory achievement, as a basic institution of modernity (*Kommentar*, p. 143). Nor did overcoming the predominance of profit imply the abolition of capitalist property. The "transition to a better society capable of solving contemporary problems of humankind" was "not to be equated with the desire for one great act of abolishing capitalist property of economic means." Instead, "the subordination of extra-economic social spheres under capital valorization has to be overcome gradually." The subordination of everyday life under the imperatives of economy and state had to be reduced. Here the PDS was much closer to Habermas's critique of the "colonisation of the life world" than to Marxian anticapitalism.

The power of capital owners was to be restricted but not their property rights as such: "In all cases in which property of capital avoids the social obligations expressed in the Basic Law and does not acknowledge the need to preserve nature, wherever it leads to enterprise decisions which oppose social, ecological and antipatriarchal progress, those negatively affected are challenged to put into place institutional changes which achieve a reduction of the dispositional rights of owners" (p. 130).

The *Kommentar* favored a plurality of property forms, "a retention of municipally owned enterprises . . . the continuation of public-law institutions such as the banks of the Länder. . . . In the sphere of infrastructure the significance of public property is widely recognized because necessary infrastructural investments are frequently not profitable in the short and medium term" (p. 132). Overcoming the predominance of the profit motive would lead, according to the *Kommentar*, to a mixed economy in which the profit motive of private enterprise could be harnessed to serve politically defined social and ecological objectives.

The *Kommentar* emphasized "modernity" rather than "capitalism" while distancing itself from any discourse of "class." It emphasized parliamentary politics while distancing itself from traditional socialist challenges to capitalist property. Thus the *Kommentar* signaled that PDS leaders and modern socialists, and perhaps the entire PDS, were close to social democratic reform strategies and willing to support the reform politics of a left-of-center government of SPD and Greens.

NOTES

1. Gregor Gysi, *Das war's. Noch lange nicht!* (Düsseldorf: Econ Verlag, 1997), p. 264; Berndt Seite, "Die PDS im Bonner Machtkalkül," *Die politische Meinung*, 41, no. 323 (October 1996): 5–7.

2. Jürgen Raschke, "SPD und PDS: Selbstblockade oder Opposition?" *Blätter für deutsche und internationale Politik* 39, no. 12 (December 1994): 1463.

3. Manfred Gerner, "Entscheidung vertagt. Die 2. Tagung des 4. Bundesparteitags der PDS." *Deutschland-Archiv* 29, no. 2 (March–April 1996): 177.

4. Raschke, "SPD und PDS," p. 1461.

5. Rudolf Scharping et al., "Dresdner Erklärung der SPD vom 11. August 1994," *Blätter für deutsche und internationale Politik* 40, no. 1 (January 1995): 119–120.

6. Christoph Bergner, "Das Magdeburger Experiment," *Die politische Meinung* 41, no. 315 (February 1996): 15.

7. Ibid., p. 17.

8. Ibid.

9. André Brie et al., eds., *Zur Programmatik der Partei des Demokratischen Sozialismus. Ein Kommentar* (Berlin: Dietz Verlag, 1997), p. 318.

10. "10 Thesen zum weiteren Weg der PDS" (28 November 1994). Documented in Heinz Beinert, ed., *Die PDS—Phönix oder Asche? Eine Partei auf dem Prüfstand* (Berlin: Aufbau-Verlag, 1995), pp. 207–220.

11. Sahra Wagenknecht, "Wir müssen aus der Defensivstellung herauskommen," *Kommunisten in der PDS. Sonderheft der Mitteilungen der Kommunistischen Plattform der PDS* (June 1995): 34.

12. Ibid., pp. 32–33.

13. "Fünf Punkte: Sozialismus ist Weg, Methode, Wertorientierung und Ziel." Documented in Beinert, *Die PDS—Phönix oder Asche?* pp. 221–226.

14. Wagenknecht, "Wir müssen," p. 33.

15. Motion adopted at the second session of the sixth Federal Conference of the KPF, 26 February 1995, reprinted in *Sonderheft der Mitteilungen der KPF* (June 1995): 36.

16. Raschke, "SPD und PDS," pp. 1462–1463.

17. Lothar Bisky and André Brie, "Deutschland braucht eine neosozialistische Alternative," *Neues Deutschland* (21 February 1995).

18. Brie et al., *Zur Programmatik der Partei des Demokratischen Sozialismus.*

19. Michail Nelken, "Schwierigkeiten einer Emanzipation. Zur Stalinismusdebatte in der PDS," in *Die PDS—Herkunft und Selbstverständnis. Eine politisch-historische Debatte,* ed. Lothar Bisky et al. (Berlin: Dietz, 1996), p. 69.

20. Ibid., p. 66.

21. Harry Nick, "Sozialistisches Ziel und praktische Politik," *Marxistisches Forum,* no. 10 (November 1996): 7.

22. Nelken, "Schwierigkeiten," pp. 72, 74.

23. Ibid., p. 69.

24. Ibid., p. 72.

25. Ibid.

26. Ibid., pp. 67, 70.

27. André Brie, "Der zweigeteilte Parteitag. Versuch eines Beitrags gegen neue Legenden," in Bisky et al., *Die PDS—Herkunft und Selbstverständnis,* p. 55.

28. Uwe-Jens Heuer, "Rechtsstaat und Unrechtsstaat. Zur PDS-Debatte," in Bisky et al., *Die PDS—Herkunft und Selbstverständnis,* p. 97.

29. Nelken, "Schwierigkeiten," p. 75.

30. "In großer Sorge," in Beinert, *Die PDS—Phönix oder Asche?* pp. 227–228.

31. Nelken, "Schwierigkeiten," p. 72.

32. "Unsere Sorgen sind nicht geringer geworden" (Statement by the Marxist Forum of 14 October 1996), *Marxistisches Forum,* no. 10 (November 1996: 1.

33. Ingo Wagner, "Moderner Sozialismus als sozialistische Moderne," *Marxistisches Forum,* nos. 17–18 (February 1998): 29.

34. Harry Nick, "Die Marxsche Lehre im Lichte des sozialistischen Disasters," *Marxistisches Forum,* nos. 15–16 (December 1997): 8.

35. Wagner "Moderner Sozialismus," p. 26.

36. Dietmar Wittich, "Wer kann etwas verändern?" in Brie et al., *Zur Programmatik der Partei des Demokratischen Sozialismus,* pp. 193–242, especially the section on "Class theory—possibilities and limits," pp. 225–233.

37. PDS, *Opposition gegen Sozialabbau und Rechtsruck. Wahlprogramm der PDS 1994 (Entwurf)* (Berlin: PDS, December 1993), pp. 1, 11.

38. Hans Modrow, "PDS am Beginn einer komplizierten Wegstrecke," *DISPUT,* no. 2 (1996): 4.

39. Lothar Bisky, "Kommunen stärken—Gesellschaft von unten verändern: Zur politischen Situation und zur Strategie der PDS bis 1998," *DISPUT,* no. 2 (1996): 7–8.

40. Gregor Gysi. "Die Oppositionspolitik der PDS im Deutschen Bundestag," *DISPUT,* no. 2 (1996): 13.

41. Axel Hildebrandt, "Eine Debatte zu drei Fragen," *DISPUT,* no. 2 (1996): 20.

42. "Politische Aufgaben der PDS 1996 bis 1998. Beschluss der 2. Tagung des 4. Parteitages der PDS," *DISPUT,* no. 2 (1996): 22.

43. Heinrich Bortfeldt, "Pyrrhussieg der Reformer," *Deutschland-Archiv*, no. 3 (1995): 228–230; Gerner, "Entscheidung vertagt," p. 173.

44. Uwe-Jens Heuer, Eckehard Lieberam, and Gregor Schirmer, "Zur Regierungsbeteiligung der PDS," *DISPUT*, no. 8 (1996): 7–8.

45. Bisky, "Kommunen stärken," p. 7; Gysi, "Die Oppositionspolitik," p. 15.

46. Axel Hildebrandt, "Eine Debatte zu drei Fragen," *DISPUT*, no. 2 (1996): 20.

47. Gysi, "Die Oppositionspolitik," p. 17.

48. Christine Ostrowski and Ronald Weckesser, "Brief aus Sachsen. Für einen eigenen Weg statt 'links von der SPD,' " *Neues Deutschland* (8 May 1995).

49. Hermann Weber, *Die Sozialistische Einheitspartei Deutschlands 1946–1971* (Hanover: Verlag für Literatur und Zeitgeschehen, 1971), p. 7.

50. Werner Müller, "SED-Gründung unter Zwang—Ein Streit ohne Ende? Plädoyer für den Begriff 'Zwangsvereinigung,' " *Deutschland-Archiv* 24, no. 1 (January 1991): 52–58.

51. Friedrich Bohl and Rudolf Kraus, eds., *SPD und SED. Die politischen Verstrickungen der SPD in die SED-Diktatur* (Bonn: CDU/CSU-Fraktion im Deutschen Bundestag, 1990), p. 3.

52. Andreas Malycha, *Auf dem Weg zur SED. Die Sozialdemokratie und die Bildung der Einheitspartei in den Ländern der SBZ. Eine Quellenedition* (Bonn: J.H.W. Dietz Nachfolger, 1995), p. xi.

53. Institut für Marxismus-Leninismus beim Zentralkomitee der SED, *Geschichte der deutschen Arbeiterbewegung in 15 Kapiteln. Kapitel XII. Periode von Mai 1945 bis 1949* (Berlin: Dietz, 1968), p. 267.

54. Ibid., p. 158.

55. Helga Grebing, "Probleme einer Neubestimmung demokratisch-sozialistischer Politik nach 1945," in *Zwangsvereinigung?* ed. J. Klotz (Heilbronn: Distel Verlag, 1996), pp. 27–29.

56. Brie et al., *Zur Programmatik der Partei des Demokratischen Sozialismus*, p. 25.

57. Ibid., pp. 257–8.

58. Ibid., pp. 390–391.

59. Günter Benser, "Zusammenschluß von KPD und SPD 1946: Erklärungsversuche jenseits von Jubel und Verdammnis," *Hefte zur DDR-Geschichte*, no. 27 (Berlin: Forscher- und Diskussionskreis DDR-Geschichte, 1995), p. 30.

60. Manfred Gerner, "Antagonismen der PDS: Zum Pluralismus der SED-Nachfolgepartei," *Deutschland-Archiv* 29, no. 2 (March-April 1996): 227.

61. Jürgen Raschke, "SPD und PDS: Selbstblockade oder Opposition?" *Blätter für deutsche und internationale Politik* 39, no. 12 (December 1994): 1453–1464.

62. Gerner, "Antagonismen der PDS," p. 239.

63. *Der Spiegel*, no. 50 (1996): 17.

64. Stephan Hilsberg, "Strategien gegen die PDS," *Neue Gesellschaft/Frankfurter Hefte* 43, no. 1 (January 1996): 921–925.

65. Wolfgang Thierse, "Strategiepapier 'Gesichtspunkte für eine Verständigung der ostdeutschen Sozialdemokraten zum Thema Umgang mit der PDS,' " *Frankfurter Rundschau* (19 December 1996). Detailed discussion in Axel Brückom, "Jenseits des 'Magdeburger Modells,' " in *Jahrbuch Extremismus und Demokratie*, ed. Uwe Backes and Eckhard Jesse (Baden-Baden: Nomos, 1997), 9: 181–185.

66. "Erfurter Erklärung," documented in *Blätter für deutsche und internationale Politik* 42, no. 2 (February 1997): 251–254.

67. "Grüne Unschuld verloren," *Der Spiegel,* no. 2 (6 January 1997): 44–47; Vera Lengsfeld, "Kein Pardon für die PDS," *Die politische Meinung* 45, no. 365 (April 2000): 70–72.

68. "Wörlitzer Erklärung," *Blätter für deutsche und internationale Politik* 42, no. 2 (February 1997): 254.

69. Eva Sturm and Eberhard Schmidt, "Ein Kommentar zur Programmatik der PDS oder das Problem der Diskursunfähigkeit," *UTOPIE kreativ,* no. 84 (October 1997): 81–82.

70. Wagner, "Moderner Sozialismus," p. 32.

71. Uwe-Jens Heuer, "Zur Demokratiefrage und heutigen Aufgaben der PDS," in Uwe-Jens Heuer and Harald Werner, *Gegenmacht Demokratie—Demokratisierung gegen Macht* (Berlin: Grundsatzkommission der PDS, 1994), p. 7.

72. Ibid., p. 13.

73. Klaus Höpcke, *Geordnete Verhältnisse* (Schkeuditz: GNN, 1996), pp. 140–141, 176.

74. PDS, *Partei des Demokratischen Sozialismus. Programm und Statut* (Berlin: PDS, 1998), p. 25.

75. Michael Benjamin, "Was wollen die Kommunisten heute?" (unpublished manuscript), 1996, pp. 3–4, quoted in Brie et al., *Zur Programmatik der Partei des Demokratischen Sozialismus,* p. 320.

76. PDS, *Programm und Statut,* p. 25.

6

Junior Partner in Regional Government: Almost a Normal Party Now, 1998

SCHWERIN CONGRESS 1997: READY FOR COALITION WITH SOCIAL DEMOCRATS AND GREENS

Consensus within the PDS had clearly shifted further toward accepting participation in government coalitions. The party congress of January 1997 brought closure to strategy debates that had started after the 1994 German elections. Then, in January 1995, the controversies over the party's role as "societal opposition" had been so heated that some observers expected an imminent split.[1] Two years later, broad consensus about strategy had been achieved without breaking the party apart.

As Social Democrats signaled greater willingness to cooperation with the PDS, the Schwerin congress reciprocated by positioning the PDS another step closer toward SPD and Greens. Party leaders Gysi, Bisky, and Brie argued that the PDS had to help bring down the conservative government of Christian Democrats and Free Democrats. This would require cooperation with Social Democrats and Greens. Whether the PDS would opt for opposition, toleration, or coalition was to depend on negotiations about policies.

The debate about the party's role as "societal opposition" highlighted the relative positions of the different factions. The reform socialist leaders and their modern socialist intellectual backers were ready to move the PDS closer to Social Democrats and Greens in order to add the weight of the PDS to a center-left alliance. The Marxist Forum was concerned about the socialist, anticapitalist identity of the PDS but was also ready to support center-left reform efforts within capitalism. The Communist Platforms and its allies in West German branches were most skeptical about the potential for reform under capitalist conditions, most cautious about the danger of losing a socialist identity through integration into the system, and most insistent on change through extraparliamentary opposition. These strategic preferences were premised on different theoretical positions regarding the possibility of significant reforms under capitalist conditions.

There were few fundamental objections to the PDS leaders' strategies. The Marxist Forum gave conditional support to joining government coalitions but pointed out that such coalitions posed the risk of integrating the PDS into the ruling party cartel. There was the danger that PDS ministers would have to participate in "social demontage and repression." Altogether, accommodating outside demands could endanger the party's "socialist, pluralist character."[2]

A total rejection of government participation came only from the Communist Platforms and from the Hamburg branch of the PDS. The latter wanted to confine the role of the PDS to the exercise of outside pressure on governments, perhaps extending support by "toleration" to a center-left reform government. Joining coalitions, however, was regarded as unacceptable: "Were the PDS to join a government under the given societal conditions, it would have to abandon its socialist claims and would thereby lose its legitimation." In a similar vein, a motion by the Communist Platform rejected coalitions under given conditions. "Under the present balance of power, our party would exhaust itself through participation in government." Participation in coalitions was acceptable only if the PDS would not be tied to antisocial and antidemocratic politics. "Any weakening of the effort as extraparliamentary opposition . . . would be integration into bourgeois parliamentary business."[3]

The positioning of the PDS closer to Social Democrats and Greens was underlined by a decision distancing the party even more from the German Communist Party. An amendment to the party constitution now excluded any dual party membership.[4] This affected especially the Communist Platform, as it was now impossible for its members to remain within the PDS, while holding membership in the DKP at the same time. The congress also decided that, in future elections, members of other parties could no longer stand on the tickets of the PDS although the tickets would still be open to individuals who were not members of any party.

Only on one issue did congress delegates vote against the leadership. The executive had proposed to change the system of allocating numbers of congress delegates, to be elected by branches and platforms. Only local branches and issue-based platforms (for example, the ecological platform) should have delegates whereas "ideological platforms" such as the Communist Platform would no longer have the right to elect their own delegates. This entitlement had been introduced in the first party constitution in order to strengthen the pluralist character of the party. Now party leaders were arguing that members of "ideological platforms" should just be entitled to vote through the party branches in which they were members. A majority of congress members, however, preferred the existing rule. Thus the Communist Platform remained entitled to elect a few congress delegates. Although the KPF had been clearly outvoted on all substantive issues, it benefited from the fact that delegates wanted to confirm the structural guarantee of pluralism in the PDS constitution.

After the Schwerin congress the PDS entered another relatively quiet period in order to concentrate on the coming elections of 1998 and 1999. Four years earlier, the heated debates of 1991–1992 had subsided in late 1993 in the run-up to the 1994 national elections. From late 1994 on the debates had intensified again, resulting in the broad consensus of the Schwerin party congress of January 1997. Since late 1994, party strategist André Brie had pushed the party toward the ability to act politically (*Politikfähigkeit*), toward arriving (Ankommen) in the social and political reality of united Germany. By January 1997, this adjustment had been achieved to a great extent. The PDS was ready to campaign throughout 1997 and 1998 without being hindered by major internal disunity.

POSITIONING FOR THE 1998 ELECTIONS: THE ROSTOCK CONGRESS

The Party of Democratic Socialism had positioned itself for the 1998 Bundestag elections since after the 1994 Bundestag elections. It had redefined its role in the party system: "societal opposition" did not have to mean parliamentary opposition but was compatible with flexible adoption of roles, either as opposition, as part of toleration arrangements, or as part of a government coalition. It had redefined its strategic priorities: The difference between the neoliberal-neoconservative Kohl government and a possible SPD-Green government was relevant enough to warrant PDS support for Social Democrats and Greens. It had "arrived in the Federal Republic": This was a requirement often expounded by party strategist André Brie, parliamentary leader Gregor Gysi and party chairman Lothar Bisky.

The party congresses of January 1995 (Berlin), January 1996 (Magdeburg), and January 1997 (Schwerin) had been landmarks in this process of transforming the PDS. Earlier, from 1990 to 1994, the priority had been survival and consolidation. While the PDS had been marginalized by others, it was not a crucial issue whether its self-ascribed opposition role amounted to self-marginalization. However, when the successes in the 1994 Bundestag elections and several Eastern Landtag elections confirmed that the PDS had survived, Social Democrats and Greens were forced to rethink their strategy of exclusion and elimination. In this situation it was becoming relevant that the PDS was also ending its self-marginalization.

The party had positioned itself closer to Social Democrats and Greens in several respects:

• From the beginning the PDS had defined itself as a noncommunist party. Over time the relevance of communist positions within the party, whether neo-Stalinist or not, had diminished. As early as 1990, PDS leaders had adopted a distance from the (West) German Communist Party. Subsequently they had gradually marginalized the Communist Platform within the PDS, first, by marginalizing neo-Stalinist individuals such as Sahra Wagenknecht who had been voted out of the wider party executive in January 1995; second, by renewing Stalinism debates that forced some members of the Communist Platform to distance themselves from others; and third, by changing the party constitution to exclude dual party membership, which affected especially some members of the Communist Platform in the PDS who were also members of the DKP.[5]

• The programmatic and strategic discourse of the PDS had shifted. In 1993, the party adopted a program still including Marxist perspectives of a different, socialist society. By 1997, the party leaders published the *Kommentar*, replacing a critique of capitalism with a critique of the dominance of the profit motive. To overcome the latter was the focus of PDS strategy. The property question, so central to traditional socialist discourse, was replaced by the issue of "dispositional power." The latter could be modified even while private capitalist property remained. In many respects, the 1997 PDS *Kommentar* sounded less radical than the 1989 Berlin Program of the Social Democrats.

• The PDS had shown its reliability as alliance partner in the toleration arrangement in Magdeburg since 1994. The PDS parliamentarians in the Landtag of Saxony-Anhalt had accepted frustrating compromises and had voted for budgets and policies that must have been disappointing to themselves, their party members, and their voters.

• The PDS had critically distanced itself from the history of the SED and of the GDR. That this distance was sufficient could still be denied by those opposed to any cooperation with the PDS, but it could also be acknowledged by those favoring cooperation.

• Reform socialist leaders, together with pragmatic city councillors and Land parliamentarians, had dominated PDS party congresses in 1995, 1996, and 1997 to an increasing extent. It had become very difficult to portray the PDS as an extremist party.

Thus the Rostock congress of 1998 had the function of consolidating and confirming the new position of the PDS resulting from the controversies of the preceding years. This enabled party chairman Bisky to state that "the PDS was ready, under today's conditions, to support the formation of a government carried by SPD and Alliance 90/Greens."[6] Two or three years earlier, some delegates had still argued that the PDS could not support or join any government under capitalist conditions. Others had demanded that the PDS could only join or support a government if there was a realistic prospect that social, economic, and ecological policies of a new government would match PDS policies. By 1997, however, it had become PDS consensus that the dismissal of the Kohl government of CDU/CSU and FDP would be a relevant success even if the policies of a government of Social Democrats and Greens were quite unpredictable.

This willingness of the PDS to appreciate the differences between a moderate center-left coalition of SPD and Greens, on the one hand, and a conservative-neoliberal coalition of CDU/CSU and FDP, on the other, demonstrated new political realism. In the 1920s and early 1930s, Communists had often regarded Social Democrats as traitors, more or less as despicable as conservative parties.

The ultimate example of this approach had been the "social fascism thesis" of the 6th Comintern Congress that denied the differences between social democrats, bourgeois liberals, and fascists. By 1994, and even more clearly by 1998, the PDS had learned to appreciate finer differences. It had realized that it was possible to retain a left-socialist identity while offering to add the party's weight to a center-left alliance.

The PDS presented itself as a more consistent social democratic party than the SPD and as more consistently pacifist and environmentalist than the Alliance 90/Greens. In his speech at the end of the Rostock party congress, Gregor Gysi indicated that the PDS would put pressure on a possible government of SPD and Greens by reminding them of their own policies.[7] Anticipating that SPD and Greens would abandon their own policies once in government, he suggested the PDS could move motions originally proposed by these parties while in opposition. Similarly, the election platform of the PDS contained policies acceptable to most Social Democrats and Greens, focusing on issues such as work, social justice, a critique of the methods of introducing the common European currency, nondiscrimination, alternative policies for East Germany, and proposals for democratization.

The conspicuous presence of environmental, feminist, and pacifist themes in PDS statements was interpreted by Gerner as borrowings from SPD and Greens amounting to "plagiarism." Conservative analysts Moreau and Lang found a more sinister meaning, claiming that these themes were adopted merely to disguise "classical communist methods of subversion." Betz and Welsh, on the other hand, regarded the PDS as an almost left-libertarian party similar to the West German Greens of the 1980s.[8] In any case, the presence of these nonclass themes indicated a significant shift, signaling a modification of socialist traditions in the case of the Marxist Forum and a departure from socialist traditions in the case of the "modern socialists."

In its selection of candidates, the PDS demonstrated once more its openness toward social democratic and Green positions. The most prominent former Social Democrat on the PDS ticket was Fred Gebhardt, who stood for the PDS in Frankfurt where he had for many years been a prominent member of the SPD's left wing. After the election, Gebhardt was to be the oldest member of the Bundestag, entitled to open the first session and to give the first speech.

The response by Social Democrats and Greens to all overtures by the PDS was negative. Social Democrats had debated about two coalition options: either a Grand Coalition with the CDU/CSU or to govern with the Greens. The Grand Coalition of the two major parties, the center-right Christian Democrats and the center-left Social Democrats, was the preferred choice for the right wing of the SPD; however, in the end the Social Democrats opted for the riskier center-left coalition with Alliance 90/Greens. This was courageous enough. To include the PDS would have stretched the SPD consensus too far and might have backfired among the West German electorate. Throughout the election campaign, both Social Democrats and Greens argued that the removal of the Kohl government would require a majority of SPD and Greens on their own. A vote for the PDS, according to this argument, effectively meant a vote for the CDU because this vote would be denied to SPD and Greens.

Four years earlier, in the Land elections of Saxony-Anhalt, the SPD had also rejected the offer of support by the PDS during the election campaign, hoping to be strong enough to govern alone. After the election, however, the SPD was still not as strong as the CDU, and in this situation it announced that it was ready to govern with PDS support. On the national level, however, the Magdeburg model of a minority government of Social Democrats and Greens, supported by PDS parliamentarians, was still inconceivable.

"PILOT PROJECT EAST"/ROSTOCK MANIFESTO: EASTERN SOLUTIONS TO HELP WEST

Could the Party of Democratic Socialism maximize its appeal as representative of East German interests while developing into a nationwide socialist party acceptable to West Germans as well? This strategic dilemma had to be solved again in preparation for the 1998 elections. A solution was suggested in the Rostock Manifesto, a policy paper presented to the delegates of the party congress on 5 April 1998. In this document the PDS called for a "Pilot Project East," a special effort by the German government to develop disadvantaged East German regions. The Rostock Manifesto was introduced by Christa Luft, economics minister in the second last East German government under Prime Minister Modrow from December 1989 to March 1990. She argued that defending the specific interests of the East was also in the interest of average West Germans threatened by neoliberal policies.[9] Both East and West Germans would benefit from rejecting neoliberal economic policies while turning to social and ecological reform.

Commentators interpreted this emphasis on East German problems as the end of the party's effort to gain a foothold in the West, as resigned acceptance of a role as regionalist Eastern party. The exclusive reliance on its strength in the East had indeed been advocated in the "Letter from Saxony" of May 1996, in which Ostrowski and Weckesser had expressed the feelings of many party members.[10] However, this approach was rejected by the leadership of the party and the modern socialists, supported, on this issue, by the Marxist Forum and the Communist Platform. Instead, the continued focus on Eastern interests and the resulting regional strength of the PDS were to be made compatible with growing acceptance in West Germany.

Linking its strategies for the East and for the West had always been difficult for the PDS. In 1992, PDS leaders had hoped that the Committees for Justice could become the vehicle for broad popular mobilization in the East while also stimulating the formation of activist groups in the West. The Committees for Justice, however, achieved no more than a consolidation of the network of East German interest groups allied to the PDS. In 1994, the party had run different election campaigns in East and West Germany. In the East, it could rely on its numerous local activists, city councillors, and Land parliamentarians. It could connect local and regional issues with the national and European elections of 1994. In the West, on the other hand, the PDS had to rely predominantly on its role in national parliament and its ambition as a nationwide party, without close connections to local and regional issues. In the West, the party was present through its publicity much more than through its minuscule membership. In 1998, the PDS once more decided to maximize its support in the East, without quite neglecting its opportunities in the West.

The Pilot Project East demanded new economic policies in order to make social and ecological reforms possible. Such economic, social, and ecological reforms, it was argued, were necessary for all of Germany; they were merely more urgent in the East. Since 1990, the East had been Kohl's field of experimentation for neoliberal attacks on the welfare state and on employees' rights. The Pilot Project East was meant to reverse this by turning the East into the front runner for reforms beneficial for the West as well. The West was to benefit in two ways: First, if the Eastern economy could be stabilized, the West would not be affected by the costs resulting from the deindustrialization of the East; second, the social and ecological reforms to be tried out in the East could also be implemented in the West.[11]

RESULT OF 1998 ELECTIONS: SOCIAL DEMOCRATS AND GREENS DON'T NEED PDS

In the elections of 27 September 1998, the Party of Democratic Socialism regained representation in the Bundestag with an improved result compared to 1994. Overall, its share of the vote increased to 5.1 percent (1994: 4.4 percent). For the first time, the PDS qualified by overcoming the 5 percent threshold, not just by winning three or more direct mandates. In the East, its share of the vote had risen to 21.6 percent (1994: 19.8 percent), in the West to 1.2 percent (1994: 1.0). The bulk of the party's votes still came from the East (2,054,773 votes; 1994: 1,697,224 votes). However, the 1.2 percent in the West still amounted to a considerable absolute number of voters: 460,681 votes in 1998, compared to 368,952 votes in 1994. Thus PDS support in the West had grown beyond the circa 100,000 votes of 1990 and contributed significantly to the national total of 2,515,454 votes (1994: 2,066,176 votes).[12]

For the first time, the PDS had sufficient votes and seats to qualify for *Fraktion* status, as a full parliamentary party, whereas it had been just a *Gruppe*, a group of parliamentarians, after the 1990 and 1994 elections. The *Fraktion* status increased the party's entitlements to parliamentary finance, to allocated speaking times, and to representation on parliamentary committees. It also gave the PDS one of the positions as deputy president of the Bundestag.

The most controversial question regarding the PDS could be left unanswered due to the outcome of the election. Hypothetically, it was conceivable before the elections that the governing coalition of CDU/CSU and FDP would lose its majority, while the gains of Social Democrats and Greens would be insufficient to form a majority government as PDS parliamentarians would hold the balance of power. Would Social Democrats grasp the opportunity to form a minority government together with the Greens even if it depended on the support of the PDS? Or would the anti-PDS taboo force the SPD to forgo this opportunity, turning instead to a coalition with the other major party, the CDU/CSU?

During the election campaign, SPD and Greens had firmly excluded any cooperation with the PDS at the national level, arguing that any vote for the PDS would detract from support for their center-left alliance. In spite of these statements, it had still been conceivable that SPD and Greens could change their mind, should the opportunity arise, just as they had done in Saxony-Anhalt, after the 1994 Landtag elections.

Eventually the overall outcome of the election allowed the SPD and Greens to avoid the issue of cooperation with the PDS. Substantial losses of CDU/CSU and FDP resulted in a majority for Social Democrats and Greens not requiring any support from the PDS. This outcome avoided the sensitive question whether the PDS was acceptable enough to become part of a "toleration" arrangement as in Magdeburg 1994.

Whether the PDS had become a sufficiently "normal" and acceptable party at the national level—this question could be deferred for at least another four years. At the Land level, however, the SPD and PDS were ready to move beyond the toleration arrangements of Magdeburg 1994, forming a government coalition in Mecklenburg—West Pommerania.

SPD AND PDS FORM GOVERNMENT IN MECKLENBURG– WEST POMMERANIA

The social democratic strategy of integrating the PDS was put to a first serious test in late 1998. Cooperation between Social Democrats and the PDS went beyond the Magdeburg model of toleration after the elections to the Landtag of Mecklenburg–West Pommerania of 27 September 1998. SPD leader Ringstorff expressed once more, as in 1994, his preference for a coalition of SPD and PDS. This time, after four more years of strained relations in a coalition with the Christian Democrats, there was majority support in the SPD[13] for an alliance with the PDS, leading to the formation of a coalition government on 3 November. In the government the SPD held five ministerial positions, including Premier Ringstorff, while the PDS held three portfolios, including Deputy Premier Helmut Holter.[14] For the PDS, entering the Schwerin coalition was another step toward acceptance as a normal party playing all roles in a parliamentary democracy, albeit only at the local and regional levels, so far.

Not only the PDS had to change to make the Magdeburg model of 1994 and the Schwerin model of 1998 possible. The benefits for Social Democrats of governing in the Eastern Länder with support of the PDS had to be greater than the resistance of SPD members with memories of the fate of their party in East Germany after 1946. Without broad acceptance by most East German voters of the PDS as a normal party, Social Democrats could have continued the earlier strategy of marginalizing the PDS. Moreover, without a reduction of the aversion against the PDS among West German voters, any cooperation of the SPD and PDS would have created a costly electoral backlash in the larger West. It was only after the national elections of September 1998 that Social Democrats could openly opt for a coalition with the PDS in Mecklenburg–West Pommerania.

The PDS congresses of 1996 and 1997 had paved the way by accepting that, in principle, the party could opt for opposition, toleration, or coalition in Land governments. The decision was left to the relevant Land branches of the PDS. In the Mecklenburg–West Pommerania branch the attitudes to joining coalitions had changed considerably. The controversial debates of 1994–1997 had given way to an overwhelming consensus that joining coalitions was welcome.[15] Even a modest reform agenda, pursued together with the SPD, was preferable to a continuation of CDU-led governments.

The formation of the SPD-PDS coalition in Schwerin was another step for the PDS in its transformation from marginalized postcommunist party toward an accepted left-socialist component of the party system. For the SPD, on the other hand, Mecklenburg–West Pommerania was the ideal place to pursue its ambivalent strategy toward the PDS. The left wing of the SPD may have regarded the Schwerin coalition as an example of the left majorities possible in Germany by uniting SPD, Greens, and PDS. However, for centrist SPD strategists, Mecklenburg–West Pommerania was a good place to integrate and tame the PDS. It was, after all, one of the smallest and, financially, perhaps the weakest Land in the Federal Republic. There the PDS would have to learn to live within budget limits and to tone down the vocal demands made while in opposition. PDS ministers would have to explain to party members and supporters the disappointing outcomes of governing a small and weak part of the federation. The PDS gained respectability and ministerial positions, but it would have to share the burden of responsibility under unrewarding circumstances.

ELECTIONS FOR EASTERN REGIONAL PARLIAMENTS, 1998–2000

The elections of the year 1999 consolidated, but have not further changed, the position of the PDS in the party system. It managed to strengthen its parliamentary representation in the East, but its integration into the party system did not proceed beyond the precedents of Magdeburg 1994 and Schwerin 1998. Nevertheless, the strong position of the PDS in the East, as third party in a three-party system, has made its inclusion in a government coalition a conceivable option for the SPD, depending on future election outcomes in Brandenburg, Saxony, and Thuringia.

The Magdeburg model of toleration of 1994 and the Schwerin coalition of

1998 were possible because the PDS had become one of the three major parties in the Eastern Land parliaments, not only in Saxony-Anhalt and Mecklenburg–West Pommerania but also in Brandenburg, Saxony, and Thuringia. On the other hand, Alliance 90/Greens and the FDP were losing representation in Eastern parliaments. The arithmetic possibility of forming governments including the PDS and the disappearance of FDP and Alliance 90/Greens from Eastern Land parliaments changed the political scenery, which left Christian Democrats and Social Democrats with few options.

The presence of the PDS as third biggest party in East German parliaments provided Social Democrats with the choice of leaving coalition governments led by the CDU. Instead, the SPD could consider forming coalitions with the PDS in which the SPD would be undisputed leader. Other options diminished as Free Democrats and Alliance 90/Greens lost representation in several Land parliaments. Some of the remaining options were arithmetically feasible but politically impossible, for example, a coalition of CDU and PDS or an alliance of CDU and the extreme right DVU. This opportunity structure made the arguments for cooperation with the PDS rather convincing among East German SPD leaders.

The Magdeburg model of toleration of 1994 was put to a test in the Landtag elections of Saxony-Anhalt on 26 April 1998. Of the two partners in the minority government tolerated by the PDS, the SPD managed to increase its share of the vote, whereas the Alliance 90/Greens were reduced to less than 5 percent. The SPD became the strongest party in the Landtag, whereas the Greens were no longer represented. This demise of the Greens was not due to the particular constellation of Magdeburg but confirmed the general decline of Alliance 90/Greens in all Eastern regions. The PDS lost support but only marginally, declining from 19.9 percent in 1994 to 19.6 percent.

This result signaled neither clear approval nor rejection of the partial cooperation between the SPD and PDS. The SPD, this time without the Alliance 90/Greens, once more formed a minority government tolerated by the PDS. The alternative of forming a coalition with the CDU, as from 1990 to 1994, was unattractive for the SPD, especially since the CDU had lost one-third of its support, declining from 34.4 to 22.0 percent. Most of these losses went to the right extremist DVU (12.9 percent).[16]

Thus the Magdeburg model of toleration was continued, as it seemed to benefit the Social Democrats, although some of their success must be explained through the appeal of national SPD leader Gerhard Schröder, government leader in the neighboring state of Lower Saxony. The slight losses of the PDS could encourage those who saw in the integration strategy a method of depriving the party of its comfortable role as populist opposition without political responsibility.

The 1999 elections in Brandenburg, Thuringia, and Saxony brought improvements in support for the PDS, but neither the Magdeburg toleration nor the Schwerin coalition was replicated. In Brandenburg (5 September 1999) the PDS won 23.3 percent. The SPD lost its absolute majority but remained the strongest party. After negotiations with the PDS, the Social Democrats formed a coalition with the CDU. In Thuringia (12 September 1999), the PDS improved to 21.3 percent. However, as SPD support sank to 18.5 percent the CDU won a majority of 51 percent and was able to govern alone, no longer requiring the SPD as junior partner. In Saxony, support for the PDS rose to 22.2 percent (19 September 1999).[17] The CDU defended its absolute majority and continued to govern alone. Thus the Christian Democrats were able to consolidate in the south of East Germany the successes they had achieved immediately after unification, whereas the SPD fell behind the PDS in Thuringia and Saxony.

The main reason for SPD losses in these three elections was widespread disappointment about the federal government elected in September 1998. It was less likely that voters were responding against the Land governments formed by the SPD with PDS support in Schwerin and Magdeburg.

ELECTIONS FOR EUROPEAN PARLIAMENT, 1999

The PDS continued its series of relative successes by gaining 5.8 percent in the election of the European Parliament on 13 June 1999.[18] The six MEPs elected on the PDS ticket joined the European Left/Nordic Green Left grouping, together with MEPs from France, Italy, Sweden, Greece, and so on. This grouping included Northern European parties that had developed away from communist traditions after 1956, Southern European former Eurocommunist parties, as well as the left-socialist PDS.

BUILDING THE PDS IN THE WEST: FEW MEMBERS BUT TRADE UNION EXPERTISE

The development of the PDS in West Germany was not a complete failure but rather a mixture of disappointments and modest success. PDS membership in the West had grown at a snail's pace, from circa 600 in late 1990, via 1,180 in 1993, to 2,326 in 1994.[19] West Germany provided the PDS with only about one-fortieth of its membership. The network of local and state branches remained fragile, prone to internal bickering and to conflicts with the national leadership. The Western PDS branches depended for their electoral campaigns on funds, personnel, and credibility provided by the national organization. In elections, the PDS campaigns attracted voters far beyond its own membership; however, after elections the party organization was not able to reach these voters and to translate their support into more permanent involvement.

Electoral support in the West had grown to a nonnegligible quantity, from 125,947 votes (0.3 percent) in the national elections of 1990 to 368,952 votes (1.0 percent) in 1994, and 460,681 votes (1.2 percent) in 1998.[20] This was still a very modest level, but nevertheless the West provided the PDS with almost one-fifth of its vote. This Western contribution was important because even 20 percent in the East (circa 2 million votes) would not be enough, on their own, for the PDS to reach a nationwide total of 5 percent. Compared to 1994 there had been a regional redistribution of PDS support in the West. Some West German strongholds in major cities with universities had seen PDS voters drift back to the Greens. On the other hand, PDS support in 1998 was more widespread in the West than before.

In Western regional parliaments the PDS was still not represented at all. The closest it had come to overcome the 5 percent threshold was in Bremen (14 May 1995: 2.4 percent; 6 June 1999: 2.9 percent). The results in Hamburg regional elections had been even more disappointing when the PDS achieved only 0.7 percent on 21 September 1997, compared to 2.2 percent at the national elections of 1994. Here the Hamburg branch had decided to stand against the advice of the PDS national leadership.[21]

The PDS had gained a few isolated footholds in local councils, beginning with a handful of Green town councillors in Heimbach (North Rhine–Westphalia) who defected to join the PDS on 31 May 1996. After that PDS councillors were elected in Lower Saxony (15 September 1996) when the PDS gained one seat each in Hannover, in Oldenburg, and in three shire councils. In Hesse (2 March 1997) the PDS gained four council seats in the traditionally left university town of Marburg.[22] This contrasted starkly with the East German situation where the PDS was represented in local government by several thousands of local councillors and 100 to 200 mayors.

The one field in which the West PDS contributed more than the Eastern branches was expertise about and influence in the trade union movement. Three factors explained the weakness of the East PDS among workers and trade unionists. First, due to the deindustrialization of the East after unification the numbers of blue-collar workers had diminished, and many PDS members were unemployed after 1990. Second, the loyalty to socialist ideals after the collapse of the GDR was greater among white-collar employees. It was the "service class" of the GDR that provided members and voters for the PDS. Third, the unions in the GDR did not have much practice in representing the interests of the producers against management. The unions had a welfare function but rarely entered into any conflict with GDR managers. It was assumed that the overall identity of interests between the working class as owner of all nationalized means of production and the working class as workers in these enterprises had made industrial conflicts superfluous. Therefore, the potential of union militancy was minimal after the collapse of the GDR. The PDS had become a left-socialist party without a trade union and working-class base.

As East German unions had collapsed during unification in 1990, the West German trade union federation (DGB—Deutscher Gewerkschaftsbund) moved into the East, rebuilt unions, and imported officials from the West. Quite a few of these Western organizers were left-social democrats with some sympathy for the PDS. It was quite ironic that the PDS established itself as an electoral party to the left of the SPD, whereas in East German workplaces and in trade unions left-social democrats coming in from the West did much of the organizational work, leaving it to the PDS to play the part of the well-meaning outsider, accompanying industrial conflicts with sympathetic comments from its local party branches and politicians.

This did not mean that the PDS remained isolated from unionism. By 1994, the PDS had a foothold in the trade union movement as Manfred Müller[23] (HBV [Handel, Banken und Versicherungen] = commerce, banks, and insurance employees' union) and other union officials stood for parliament on the "open tickets" of the PDS, without becoming party members. Since 1994, the PDS has been invited as guest to the congresses of trade unions.

Another connection to trade unionism was provided through a number of trade union activists and experts who had been members of the (West) German Communist Party (DKP). In 1990, the PDS had clearly distanced itself from the DKP, attracting instead members of other leftist groups originating in 1960s student radicalism. The latter had little connection with unionism. However, a few years later a growing number of former DKP unionists joined the PDS.

The surprising distance from trade unionism of many East German PDS politicians can be illustrated by a 1997 debate in Dresden between representatives of small East German business and speakers for the PDS trade union subcommittee. At that time trade unions were campaigning to raise East German wages to West German levels. They argued that employers should not be allowed to use lower East German wages to drag down West German incomes, that East German workers deserved the same wages for the same work, and that local purchasing power in the East could be strengthened by these wage increases.

The PDS congress of January 1997 had just adopted a motion that public sector contracts should be given only to private companies paying award wages to their workers. This met with resistance by representatives of the party's small business wing. For example, Ronald Weckesser criticized that "eighty percent of all union officials in Saxony spoke Swabian dialect"[24] and were incapable of understanding the problems of East German enterprises. Other PDS politicians supported Weckesser's arguments, for example, Ralf Eißler, a regional leader of Offener Wirtschaftsverband für Kleine und mittelständische Unternehmen (OWUS), a small business association close to the PDS. He claimed that paying award wages would ruin East German small and medium enterprises. From their point of view, the PDS as an East German regionalist party had to look after East German small and medium business.

For these regionalist PDS members, union officials from the West (speaking Swabian dialect) were colonizers just like Western big business: The PDS as regionalist party had to resist both. It was left to a Westerner, Harald Werner, an expert on trade unions working for the PDS parliamentary party, to explain party policy on paying award wages to the irate business wing of the Dresden PDS.

After a decade of sustained effort, the PDS had achieved a modest level of success in the West, enough to contribute to the party's improved representation in national parliament since 1998. The political culture within the PDS was still divided between East and West. Nevertheless, as the governing Social Democrats and Greens were shifting to the centre, more political space on the left was likely to become available to the PDS, even in West Germany.

NOTES

1. For example, Heinrich Bortfeldt, "Pyrrhussieg der Reformer," *Deutschland-Archiv*, no. 3 (1995): 228–230.

2. Marxistisches Forum der PDS, "Änderungsantrag zum Leitantrag des Bundesvorstandes," *Pressedienst PDS*, nos. 50–51 (13 December 1996): 5.

3. Landesverband Hamburg, "Grundsätze und Ziele der PDS bei den Wahlen 1997–1999," *Pressedienst PDS*, nos. 50–51 (13 December 1996): 9; Kommunistische Plattform, "Änderung Ziffer 7/7," ibid., p. 10.

4. Statutenkommission der PDS, "Änderungen des Statuts," ibid., p. 34.

5. Ibid.

6. Lothar Bisky, "Für eine gerechte Verteilung von Arbeit und Reichtum," *DISPUT*, no. 4 (1998): 13.

7. Gregor Gysi, "Die PDS—Herausforderung von links," *DISPUT*, no. 4 (1998): 54.

8. Manfred Gerner, *Partei ohne Zukunft? Von der SED zur PDS* (Munich: Tilsner, 1994), p. 241; Patrick Moreau and Jürgen Peter Lang, *Was will die PDS?* (Berlin: Ullstein, 1994), p. 168; Hans-Georg Betz and Helga A. Welsh, "The PDS in the New German Party System," *German Politics* 4, no. 3 (1995): 103.

9. Christa Luft, "Endlich den Osten als Chance begreifen," *DISPUT*, no. 4 (1998): 26–28.

10. Christine Ostrowski and Ronald Weckesser, "Brief aus Sachsen. Für einen eigenen Weg statt 'links von der SPD,' " *Neues Deutschland* (8 May 1995).

11. Bisky, "Für eine gerechte Verteilung," p. 10.

12. "Wahlen 1994 (I)," *Blätter für deutsche und internationale Politik* 40, no. 1 (January 1995): 124–128; "Wahlen 1998 (II)," *Blätter für deutsche und internationale Politik* 44, no. 2 (February 1999): 253–256.

13. Jörg Schulze, "Ganz in Rot: SPD-Parteitag in Güstrow," *Freitag* (6 November 1998): 6.

14. "Innerparteilich ist einiges zu klären" (interview with Helmut Holter), *Frankfurter Rundschau* (14 October 2000): 5.

15. Kathrin Valtin, "Das erste Mal: PDS-Parteitag in Parchim," *Freitag* (6 November 1998): 6.

16. "Wahlen 1998 (I)," *Blätter für deutsche und internationale Politik* 44, no. 1 (January 1999): 127.

17. "Wahlen 1999 (II)," *Blätter für deutsche und internationale Politik* 45, no. 2 (February 2000): 253–256.

18. "Wahlen 1999 (I)," *Blätter für deutsche und internationale Politik* 45, no. 1 (January 2000): 127–128.

19. Patrick Moreau and Jürgen Peter Lang, *Linksextremismus. Eine unterschätzte Gefahr* (Bonn: Bouvier Verlag, 1996), p. 41.

20. "Wahlen 1990 (III)," *Blätter für deutsche und internationale Politik* 36, no. 4 (April 1991): 508–511; "Wahlen 1994 (I)," *Blätter für deutsche und internationale Politik*, 40, no. 1 (January 1995): 124–128; "Wahlen 1998 (II)," *Blätter für deutsche und internationale Politik* 44, no. 2 (February 1999): 253–256.

21. Helmut Zessin, Edwin Schwertner, and Frank Schumann, *Chronik der PDS 1989 bis 1997* (Berlin: Dietz, 1998), p. 256; "Wahlen 1999 (II)," p. 254; Zessin, Schwertner, and Schumann, *Chronik*, p. 516.

22. Zessin, Schwertner, and Schumann, *Chronik*, pp. 374, 409, 462.

23. Franz Oswald, "The Party of Democratic Socialism: Ex-Communists Entrenched as East German Regional Protest Party," *Journal of Communist Studies and Transition Politics* 12, no. 2 (1996): 190.

24. Marcel Braumann, "PDS weit weg. Sachsens Sozialisten streiten über Tariflöhne," *Neues Deutschland* (4 February 1997): 8.

7

The Place of the PDS in the Party System

In the first years after unification, the deep divisions that had separated the two Germanies during the Cold War period were still visible in the party system. The PDS, the successor of the SED, East Germany's ruling party, was an outsider marginalized by all other parties, perceived as "extremist" and "totalitarian." A decade later, the effect of Cold War patterns of perception has receded, and the assessment of the PDS has become more factual and more precise. The discontinuities between the SED and PDS were already significant in 1990; however, by 1998 they were obvious to all analysts except those still insisting on counterfactual claims as to the unreformed communist and nostalgic nature of the PDS. In reality it had become a left-socialist party positioned close enough to the SPD and Alliance 90/Greens to be acceptable as a coalition partner in or outside support of center-left government at the Land level but still not a possible participant in federal government. There was enough common ground between the SPD, Alliance 90/Greens, and PDS regarding economic and social policies to make government coalitions at least conceivable in the Eastern regions of Germany where the PDS was a major party. However, the distance between the PDS and all other parties was still too great in foreign and security policy to imagine PDS participation in federal government in the near future.

Beginning with an example illustrating newer relatively positive portrayals of the PDS by political scientists informed by modernization theory, this concluding chapter will discuss changes within the PDS, the place of the PDS in the German party system, and the change of the party system resulting from the inclusion of the East German electorate and the survival of the PDS.

INTEGRATING POSTUNIFICATION GERMANY: THE
CONTRIBUTION OF THE PDS

By 1997 a new, more positive evaluation of the PDS had appeared among
social scientists: "The PDS as a post-communist regional party, rooted socio-
structurally in the milieu of the former East German service class, provides
contributions to the mastery of the transformation process which other parties
cannot provide."[1] This was the central thesis of Sigrid Koch-Baumgarten's assessment of the PDS. She followed the modernization theoretical approach of
Stöss, Neugebauer, and Raschke, acknowledging that the PDS fulfilled a temporary function of integrating East Germans in a transitional situation. In the
long term, this would still leave the PDS superfluous once the integration of
East Germans into the society of united Germany was completed.

Without the integrative function of the PDS, the disappointments of many
East Germans since unification could have turned into alienation from society
and from the constitutional order, into support for violent protest or for the
xenophobic nationalism that the neo-Nazi NPD and DVP were spreading among
unemployed East German youths.

This relatively positive portrayal of the PDS differed from earlier approaches.
In the early 1990s, the party was regarded by many observers as a "party without
future" (Gerner), close to its "certain demise" (Moreau).[2] Analysts and strategists
could treat the PDS as a short-term problem. The perceived weakness of the
PDS made a strategy of elimination by marginalization appear feasible. This
exclusion strategy was also justified by a characterization of the entire PDS as
a left extremist party with totalitarian views that had to be excluded from the
consensus of democrats, just like the right extremists of the DVU or NPD.

This blunt exclusion strategy had not achieved the party's speedy demise but
only served to stabilize PDS support. A new, more flexible strategy was developed in response to the continuing presence of the PDS in East German Land
parliaments. This approach acknowledged the fact that the PDS was to survive
for some time, and it characterized the PDS as somewhat more acceptable,
distinguishing between unacceptable unreformed communists and possibly acceptable social democrats within the PDS. This characterization justified a strategy of partial cooperation that could weaken or split the PDS, by integrating
PDS moderates while isolating traditionalists. Here the exclusion strategy was
to be applied only to parts of the PDS. Jürgen Raschke and Manfred Gerner are
examples of this approach emphasizing the internal divisions of the PDS.[3] Since
the relative success of the PDS in the elections of 1994, the discussion "circling
around the two action options of exclusion and inclusion" (Koch-Baumgarten,
1997, p. 866) had to come to terms with the stabilization of the PDS. Between
1994 and 1998, SPD strategies toward the PDS shifted more toward an emphasis
on partial cooperation leading to an integration of the PDS, whereas the long-
term objective of eliminating the PDS was either deferred or abandoned.

Later a third approach emerged that discovered and emphasized the relative merits of the PDS. Modernization theory was the guiding framework replacing concepts such as "extremism" or "totalitarianism." According to this approach, the PDS had a function in the Eastern regions of Germany undergoing a catch-up modernization. On the other hand, the PDS remained irrelevant in the West, which was not undergoing the same transformation.

Thus the PDS could be regarded as a symptom of the "limited integrative capacity of the established West German parties" (Koch-Baumgarten, p. 864) and could be ascribed a useful function in the party system and in the whole political system. While the "extremism experts" (Jesse, Lang, Moreau, and Neu) regarded the PDS as a dysfunctional disturbance, the modernization theorists Raschke, Neugebauer, and Stöss acknowledged "signal functions" of the PDS contributing to the party system's functions of representation and integration (Koch-Baumgarten, p. 865).

The PDS was best described by the "identity thesis" according to which it represented a premodern East German milieu (p. 867). It was sustained by a "diffuse GDR identity" and anchored in the milieu of the GDR service class (p. 871). This approach could justify partial cooperation with the PDS, during its transient existence as representative of a premodern subculture during catch-up modernization of East Germany.

Other possible explanations for the existence of the PDS were rejected by Koch-Baumgarten. First, the PDS was not a protest party, as it had survived longer than expected under this approach. Its members and voters were not disadvantaged groups of "unification losers" (p. 867); its electoral support showed stable identification, not "fluctuating protest voters" (p. 868). Second, Koch-Baumgarten rejected the "regional interest thesis," which compared the PDS to the BHE (League of Expellees and Dispossessed), a short-lived party representing economically disadvantaged refugees in the 1950s. The PDS did "not at all represent the material interests of socially disadvantaged unification losers" (p. 869). Third, she rejected a portrayal of the PDS as "modern socialist reform party," as this view was held only by commentators close to the PDS. For Koch-Baumgarten, the PDS's emphasis on the social question could not be relevant in West Germany considering the growing relevance of new cleavage lines such as "materialist versus postmaterialist and libertarian versus authoritarian" (p. 870). In this respect, the PDS was a premodern party, preserving remnants of Marxist-Leninist essentials together with "old left social democratic models of socialism" (p. 871).

The portrayal of the PDS as a left extremist, antisystem party (p. 867) was also rejected by Koch-Baumgarten. Authors such as Moreau, Lang, Pfahl-Traughber, or Zitelmann wanted to see the PDS excluded from the "anti-totalitarian consensus" of all democrats. They all advocated an exclusion strategy, although there were minor differences between these authors. Moreau advocated banning the PDS as anticonstitutional and extremist. Pfahl-Traughber, on the other hand, opposed banning the PDS because this would produce solidarization in the East. These "extremism experts" ignored, according to

Koch-Baumgarten, the existence of wings in the PDS, the learning process taking place, and the fact that even the traditionalist veterans were not hostile to the democratic system (p. 874).

More differentiated assessments of the PDS had become possible over time. Social scientists shifted one step further toward declaring the PDS an acceptable normal party. For conservative "extremism experts" such as Moreau, the entire PDS was unacceptable. Gerner distinguished between an acceptable reform socialist leadership and an unacceptable Communist Platform, probably supported by a silent majority of nostalgic and tradition-bound PDS members. In Koch-Baumgarten's diagnosis, not only reform socialist PDS leaders were acceptable, but even "traditionalist veterans" among the members were, more or less, bearable. This approach reduced the unacceptable components of the PDS to the Communist Platform but did not claim that the silent majority of PDS members shared the views of this minority. In this perspective, the unacceptable component of the PDS was much smaller, whereas the "traditionalist veterans" were considered capable of being integrated by the reform socialist leadership of the PDS.

Koch-Baumgarten's diagnosis goes further in suggesting an integration strategy than earlier arguments by Gerner and Raschke hoping that cooperation could split the PDS. In Koch-Baumgarten's approach, the reform socialist leadership as well as the "traditionalist veterans" could be integrated. If the party was representative of an East German premodern subculture, then it could have useful functions in a transition situation, and partial cooperation would be, for the time being, justified. The PDS could "take on functions in the party system as a transitional phenomenon" as it had a "function of representation" (p. 875), especially since Western parties excluded all former SED members. It had an "integration function" as young PDS members found avenues for participation in local and Land politics and administration, while older PDS members found a political home in the PDS milieu (p. 876). There was also a "legitimation function" (p. 876) as the party "channeled discontent" and helped to legitimize the political system by mobilizing voters to participate (p. 877). Thus the PDS was and would remain an Eastern regional party remaining "marginalized permanently" in the West (p. 875).

While this analysis justified temporary and partial cooperation with the PDS, as advocated by many leaders of the SPD and of the Greens, it did not, however, justify a positive inclusion of the PDS in an alliance for change. Consequently, Koch-Baumgarten distanced herself from the Erfurt Declaration of January 1997 that advocated including the PDS, together with the SPD and Greens, in an "alliance for social democracy."

The strategic conclusion of the portrayal of the party as representative of a premodern East German subculture was that cooperation with the PDS on the national level would neither be acceptable to other parties nor feasible without massive loss of votes in West Germany. In the East, on the other hand, an exclusion strategy would only favor the Christian Democrats while it would imply a renunciation of power for the SPD. Continuing an exclusion stategy would stabilize the PDS, whereas a strategy of inclusion contributed "in the medium term, to an erosion of the PDS' electoral camp" (p. 878).

Thus, between 1993 and 1997, the voices for an inclusion strategy among political scientists had grown somewhat stronger, not only willing to include the PDS out of sheer strategic necessity but because the PDS had a useful function for a transition period. The advocates of exclusion and elimination, on the other hand, were no longer as dominant as in the early 1990s. Fewer were advocating a ban of the PDS as anticonstitutional—the party might still deserve a ban, but there were pragmatic political reasons against it.

According to Koch-Baumgarten, the PDS was viable in the medium term as long as it had the function of integrating East Germans in a transitional phase of catch-up modernization. In the long term, however, it would be superfluous because of its emphasis on social justice issues. This continuation of the "social question" of the nineteenth century was outdated, compared to new lines of conflict ("postmaterialist versus materialist" and "libertarian versus authoritarian").

This argument raises interesting issues for political analysts comparing the success of the PDS and Greens over the next decade. The identity of the Greens was defined by postmaterialist and libertarian positions, to the exclusion of the "social question." The PDS, on the other hand, attempted to combine social justice issues with radical democratic, feminist, pacifist, and environmental themes. The relative success of Greens and PDS in the medium term should be a useful indicator as to whether the "social question" was outdated or not.

CHANGE WITHIN PDS: SUMMARIZING THE LEARNING PROCESS

A summary of the learning processes undertaken by different components of the PDS can support the claim of Koch-Baumgarten that the PDS has served to integrate many East Germans into the society of united Germany. What has the PDS learned from the pre-1990 past and from its decade in united Germany? If we believe Moreau and other "extremism experts," the PDS has remained a left-totalitarian party that has learned from the past only insofar as it has developed better disguises. Moreau's denial of real change by interpreting it as changing camouflage had to rely increasingly on counterfactual arguments as the PDS developed contrary to his analyses and prognoses. As late as August 2000, Viola Neu claimed the PDS had still retained the old objectives of the SED: "The goal of a socialist society in the colours of the GDR stands firmly." And Wilfried Schulz misunderstood PDS demands for regulatory state intervention in the economy: "We have had that previously in the GDR."[4]

Other analysts argued that the leading reform socialist minority had been able and willing to learn from the past, whereas a less visible, rather silent majority of nostalgics and traditionalists was hindering the implementation of that learning. This approach postulated a simple dichotomy of modernizers and hardliners, a leftover of Cold War classifications in good social democrats and bad communists. It had a useful function in supporting a strategy of partial cooperation, conditional upon further changes in the PDS. It could also justify cooperation with the intention of splitting the PDS, integrating its social democratic wing and isolating the communist wing.

An inability to learn was ascribed to the PDS by Gerner arguing that the division between the minority of leading reformers and the silent nostalgic majority was bound to paralyze the party. Yet with hindsight the ability of the PDS to redefine itself had to be acknowledged: "In the last ten years there were always large majorities for a politically realistic reform strategy."[5]

Polemical statements by one wing of the PDS about another also made it difficult to assess the learning process within the party. On the one hand, the "modern socialists" used a very extensive notion of Stalinism in order to delegitimize not only real neo-Stalinists but also a wider range of Marxist traditionalists. On the other, the Communist Platform claimed the reform socialists were intent on turning the entire PDS into a social democratic party in order to advance their parliamentary careers. Here the PDS appeared to be torn between nostalgics unable to arrive in the reality of the Federal Republic and careerists accused of selling out rather easily in order to "arrive" in German society.

Beyond these polemical assessments, it is possible to show that there were learning processes in all ideological wings of the PDS, with very few exceptions. Reform socialist leaders and modern socialist intellectuals have left behind not only the Marxism-Leninism of the SED but also the broader Marxist traditions influential among Social Democrats since the nineteenth century. In a learning process that began in the late 1980s with Michael Brie's analyses of capitalist modernity and the reception of Western sociological theories, a framework was developed that influenced the strategies of Brie and Gysi, as well as programmatic thinking, guided by Klein, expressed in the *Kommentar* of 1997 and in the *ReformAlternative* volume of 2000.

The intellectuals gathered in the Marxist Forum also have left the Marxism-Leninism of the SED far behind. This learning process, too, began in the 1980s as illustrated in the works of Heuer. His arguments about the need to appropriate the heritage of bourgeois liberalism and democracy are strongly reminiscent of the Italian political scientist Norberto Bobbio, in this respect. Heuer, not unlike Bobbio, argued that "real socialism" failed because Marxists have focused one-sidedly on social and economic rights while neglecting political and legal rights altogether. The illusion that the state would wither away soon and that the replacement of capitalist power by working-class power would automatically provide socialist democracy led to the neglect of the question of democratization. Heuer criticized an approach in which "the question of democracy as a specifically political question is sidelined by the question of social revolution."[6] In Western political science, nobody would accuse Bobbio of hard-line Marxism-Leninism. In German polemics, however, exponents of the Marxist Forum such as Heuer were misunderstood as inflexible hard-liners. A closer reading of their texts suggests, however, that the MF was capable of using its Marxist framework for a critical analysis of Stalinism and post-Stalinist "real socialism." Its advocacy of a strategy combining reform politics with a socialist perspective was comparable to the SPD of the Erfurt Program of 1891.

The pragmatic PDS politicians elected to local councils and regional parliaments of East Germany realized that their administrative skills could also be applied usefully in united Germany, in a political system operating within a capitalist economic framework.

Large numbers of aging party members learned that bourgeois democracy in the Federal Republic allowed more political space for a left-socialist party than suggested by historical memories of the fate of the SPD in Wilhelmine Germany, of the KPD in the Weimar Republic, and of both parties under Hitler. The experience of working-class parties in Germany before 1918, between 1918 and 1933, and again from 1933 to 1945 came close to a confirmation of the simple thesis that bourgeois democracy was not democratic at all. Since 1990, however, even older PDS members learned to appreciate the benefits of bourgeois democracy. This was implied in the party's acceptance of a new place in the party system: no longer the marginalized opposition of the early 1990s but a party flexibly adopting different roles in the late 1990s.

Even those former East Germans who found themselves penalized and marginalized for their close involvement with the GDR, as party or state officials, as members of the armed forces or of the secret police, have undergone a process of adaptation and adjustment with the help of the PDS and networks of East German interest groups. When these officials found themselves unemployed, in early retirement on reduced pensions, in many instances also accused and penalized by the court system of united Germany, it was conceivable that this could have resulted in responses such as the formation of illegal networks. It was the merit of the GBM and other interest groups, together with the PDS, to have given these individuals legal support and an environment in which they could come to terms with the failure of the system they had served and also with their individual guilt—if they were directly or indirectly involved with human rights violations.

It is only in the Communist Platform that we have to observe a mixture of learning and nonlearning, perhaps best illustrated in a comparison of Benjamin and Wagenknecht. Benjamin exemplified a position of critical distance from Stalinism. While still defining himself as communist he acknowledged that there were fundamental flaws inherent in East European socialism, especially "that the deficit of democracy was an essential reason for the failure of the GDR." On the other hand, there was the neo-Stalinist position of Wagenknecht, Gossweiler, and Holz. Here the cause of the collapse of "real socialism" was not sought in the inherent flaws of Stalinist and post-Stalinist systems. Defeat was blamed on revisionist deviations from Stalin's course since Khrushchev, culminating in Gorbachev's sellout and on the strategies of imperialism against which revisionists failed to remain vigilant.[7]

Overall, the entire PDS has undergone massive processes of change and learning—the only exception being the neo-Stalinist minority within or close to the Communist Platform. Depending on the preferences of the observer, these learning processes may have gone just far enough or perhaps too far. Or the change may not have gone far enough, if one regarded the insistence of the Marxist Forum on class concepts and on property issues as unjustified traditionalism. Irrespective of these finer distinctions, it is clear that the articulated views of virtually the entire party, with the exception of a few marginal individuals, sustained an anti-Stalinist consensus, albeit differentiated between narrower or wider notions of Stalinism.

The strongest indicators of these learning processes were the structure and the constitution of the party. There was neither an obligatory ideology nor a compulsory view of history nor a structure based on workplace branches geared toward industrial conflicts. Instead, the PDS had a constitution and a program guaranteeing the opportunity to express minority views. And it had a structure based on locality branches geared toward participation in election campaigns.

Last and not least, an important indicator of learning is the presence of pacifist, radical democratic, ecologist, and feminist themes in the party's programs. The party has not only adopted a new position in the left-right spectrum. It has also recognized the importance of these new themes, not just as subordinate side issues next to the central theme of class struggle but as priorities in their own right.

Thus the PDS has become a left-socialist party that has taken a "postmaterialist" turn, very much like the Socialist Peoples Party of Denmark or the Swedish Party of the Left. As such it competes for political space with the left wing of the SPD and with the left wing of the Greens. This proximity signals not only competition but also the possibility of alliances.

TOWARD REPLACING THE 1993 PROGRAM

In January 1999, the PDS party congress resolved to initiate a programmatic debate and to appoint a program commission. Gero Neugebauer suggested that this debate was a response to the limitations of the party's electoral success in 1998. Although the PDS had increased its electoral support and was reelected to the Bundestag, "party strategists argued the PDS had to become open to themes relevant for the future in order to mobilize new voters."[8] Other reasons for the program debate were of less recent origin. The replacement of the 1993 party program by a new document became an issue as consensus within the PDS shifted toward a clearer dominance of "modern socialists" and pragmatic local politicians. In the transition from SED to PDS, in 1989 and 1990, the party had adopted a first program and a party constitution, both hastily stitched together in a situation when survival, distancing from the immediate past, and a rough orientation in a new direction were the priorities. In 1993, the PDS adopted a more permanent program circumscribing the left pluralism of the PDS in a compromise between modern socialists turning to reform strategies, Marxist traditionalists demanding that reform strategies be combined with socialist perspectives, and the Communist Platform emphasizing above all the socialist perspective.

Party leaders repeatedly assured members that there was no intention to replace the 1993 program. Nevertheless, from late 1994 to the party congress in January 1997 there had been a significant shift in PDS discourse and practice. The argument appeared that time had not stood still and that programmatic debate should not be locked into the 1993 situation.

The two most visible attempts to move the programmatic identity of the PDS into a new direction were the *Kommentar* of 1997 and the *ReformAlternative* of 2000.[9] For the modern socialists these two volumes were contributions to ongoing programmatic thinking. On the other hand, the Marxist Forum and the Communist Platform were concerned that party leaders and modern socialists were undermining the 1993 program. Especially the *Kommentar* of 1997 was understood by MF commentator Ingo Wagner as "an attempt . . . to modify de facto" the 1993 document in preparation for a new program. From a modern socialist perspective, however, the *Kommentar* was attacked for not being more critical of the 1993 program. An article by Eva Sturm and Eberhard Schmidt in 1997 deplored that the *Kommentar* still was too much of a compromise with traditionalist forces. For Sturm and Schmidt the *Kommentar* was an indicator of the unfortunate necessity to educate the backwards oriented, traditionalist party members very slowly.[10]

The majority of the program commission published, in November 1999, its "Theses towards a Programmatic Debate," while dissenting commission members presented their own "Vote to the Theses." The depth of the controversy affected the party congress of April 2000 in Münster. There delegates decided to extend the program debate beyond the mid-2000 time limit set by the Berlin congress of January 1999.

The majority theses restated the tenets of modern socialism together with the reform strategies derived from these. "Modernity," in this approach, was more than capitalism. "Modern bourgeois society" included achievements such as "pluralist democracy," the "market" as "inexpendible decentral selection mechanism," and the *Rechtsstaat* (rule of law). These core institutions were supplemented by characteristics such as "the differentiation of society into efficient subsystems," "internationalization of economy and society" as well as "individualization."[11] These aspects of present society made a reform strategy feasible that aimed to overcome the dominance of the profit motive, as discussed earlier in the *Kommentar* of January 1997.

The minority paper criticized the absence of a socialist objective aiming for a different society. The majority had defined socialism as a movement and as a set of values—an approach reminiscent of the 1959 Godesberg program, which had completed the transition of the West German SPD from a class party into a "catchall" or "people's" party. The emphasis by the majority of the PDS program commission on modernity was rejected by the minority as overly accepting of capitalism by exaggerating its positive features. Consequently the minority also queried the neglect of the property question. Indeed, the majority's objective of "overcoming the predominance of the profit motive" did not imply any expropriation, relying instead on restrictions and directives modifying the dispositional powers of owners.[12]

The majority's emphasis on positive aspects of capitalist modernity translated into a reform strategy and a willingness to join government coalitions with center-left parties. The left minority, on the other hand, insisted on a clearer opposition role. A further point of conflict was the evaluation of GDR history and "real socialism." The minority rejected the extent of criticism implied in the majority theses.

In a section on foreign policy the majority of the program commission signaled it was willing to accept German participation in armed interventions abroad provided they occurred under UN control, whereas NATO (North Atlantic Treaty Organization) interventions without UN approval were rejected. On the other hand, the minority rejected UN interventions as well because the dominance of the U.S. and other NATO powers in the UN Security Council would turn UN interventions into another instrument of U.S. and NATO policy.[13] This issue was to reemerge at the Münster party congress, where the left minority could mobilize widespread pacifist attitudes among delegates.

It became obvious that majorities were not (yet) willing to abandon the 1993 program. Nevertheless, the reformers in the PDS were continuing their arguments for a new program: "The entire program is permeated by the perspective of collapse, decline and persecution. It serves the purpose of . . . self-defence. . . . It communicates East German experiences."[14] According to this view, the 1993 program was shaped by an East German response to German unification, but it did not take account of the settled reality of a united Germany. Socialist traditionalists, on the other hand, suspected that the process of bringing the program up to date would also involve a significant ideological shift away from the socialist identity established in 1993.

After prolonged controversies, PDS president Gabi Zimmer presented a revised draft program to the party membership and to the public, on 27 April 2001. The debates continued along the lines indicated by "Theses" of the majority of the Program Commission of November 1999 and the "Vote to the Theses" of the Commission minority. It had been envisaged, when the first session of the sixth party congress in January 1999 initiated the program debate, that the adoption of a new program would renew the party's public profile in time for the federal elections of late 2002. However, this timetable had to be adjusted due to the intensity of the controversies. In order to preserve party unity in the year leading to the Bundestag elections the adoption of a new program was postponed to the year 2003.[15] This deferral enabled the PDS to approach the election campaign of 2002 with a degree of party unity.

THE EXPERIENCE OF GOVERNMENT PARTICIPATION: RESTRAINED BY TIGHT BUDGETS

The willingness to join government coalitions at the Land level was an outcome of the PDS strategy debates of 1995–1997. Since 3 November 1998, the party had the opportunity to put these new aspirations into practice in the Land government of Mecklenburg–West Pommerania as the party held three out of eight cabinet positions in Schwerin, in a coalition led by the SPD. A very optimistic conclusion from the experience in the SPD/PDS coalition was drawn by Helmut Holter, chairman of the PDS in Mecklenburg–West Pommerania and deputy premier of the Land government. He recommended a long-term "strategic partnership with the SPD." The way forward for the PDS was to acquire "competence" and to define itself as future party of government.[16]

Other commentators regarded the results of the first participation of PDS ministers in a government coalition as hardly inspiring. The coalition agreement between SPD and PDS had aimed for a change of policies in the direction of "more work, social justice and democracy as well as reconciliation."[17] This change of policy was, however, not implemented because "reform politics at the state level" had to accept financial restraints. Reforms "can today no longer be tackled by a policy of distributing financial surplus or by additional new debts but . . . only on the basis of . . . consolidated state finances."[18] In a summary trying to make the best of this experience, Frank Berg came to the conclusion that there had been few policy changes. Nevertheless, the SPD-PDS government had achieved a change in the style in which government dealt with the population and with interest groups.

The main achievement was, still, the participation of the PDS in government. Without substantially changing policy choices in Mecklenburg–West Pommerania, the PDS had reduced its marginality in the party system. Berg hoped that the SPD-PDS government could develop "a specific version of East German modernization," but for the time being, the main outcome was "the fact . . . that SPD and PDS had formed the first red-red coalition in Germany."[19]

The effect expected by SPD strategists that the PDS would suffer from being tied into government responsibility, thus losing its populist appeal as opposition, had arrived. PDS ministers faced the task of explaining to party members that being in government without achieving policy changes was a success.

FOREIGN AND SECURITY POLICY: THE LIMITS OF ACCOMMODATION: MÜNSTER, 2000

A severe setback to the PDS leaders' strategy of positioning the PDS closer to SPD and Greens occurred at the party congress in Münster (7–9 April 2000).

First, delegates rejected an important motion regarding foreign and security policy. Second, as party president Lothar Bisky and parliamentary leader Gregor Gysi announced their intention not to stand again for their positions at the subsequent congress in Cottbus, the PDS had to find a new generation of leaders to take over from those who had led the party since its foundation in 1989. And third, holding the party congress in Münster to get the attention of West German voters had limited success, as the PDS did not gain more than 1.1 percent in the regional elections of North Rhine–Westphalia.[20]

It became obvious that party leaders were not able to position the PDS close enough to Social Democrats and Greens in time for a possible alliance for the national elections in 2002. Party members resisted against the speed and the direction of change. After several years of slowly but successfully shifting party consensus toward a more pragmatic reform strategy, toward a more accommodating opposition role, and toward accepting the compromises necessary in coalitions with other parties, party leaders met with resistance on two issues: the replacement of the party program of 1993 and the acceptance of military interventions.

About two-thirds of delegates voted against a motion that the PDS could, possibly, in the future approve of armed interventions of German troops in other countries, provided it occurred under the auspices of the United Nations. Instead, delegates adopted a motion demanding "the dissolution of NATO," objecting to "the militarisation of the European Union," and rejecting "any intervention abroad" by the Bundeswehr including participation in "military interventions mandated by the UN based on Chapter VII of the UN Charter." The background to this debate was the participation of German combat troops in NATO actions against Serbia in 1999. These actions had been legitimized by government as humanitarian intervention, as measures required to stop human rights violations committed by the armed forces of the Serbian government.

The motion proposed by party leaders was also critical of the German government, which had agreed to participate in actions supported only by NATO consensus without any mandate of the UN Security Council.[21] This criticism was shared by all PDS delegates and was consistent with statements made during the armed conflicts of 1999.

However, this degree of distance from NATO interventions and government policy was not enough for the majority of delegates. It was criticized that the proposal gave PDS parliamentarians the option to approve, on a case-by-case basis, future armed interventions on humanitarian grounds, provided they were justified by a UN mandate. While the leaders' motion argued that the party should not "reject all military use of force without exception," delegates did exactly that.[22]

The resistance of delegates on this issue was significant beyond this particular motion. The process of repositioning the PDS closer to Social Democrats and Greens had been carefully managed since late 1994, demanding painful debates about identity and strategy in nonelection years, always keeping conflict intensity below the breaking point, and calming debates in time for election campaigns. However, in an attempt to make an alliance of the PDS with SPD and Greens possible at the national level in time for the 2002 elections, party leaders had gone beyond the pain threshold of delegates.

The defeat of PDS leaders in Münster was interpreted by conservatives such as Viola Neu as a victory of orthodox socialism over PDS reformers. On the other hand, Horst Kahrs argued that the vote did not reflect "the balance of strength between 'reformers' and 'traditionalists.' " Rather, "it was a victory of the logic of extraparliamentary action over the logic of parliamentary action."[23] Party activists had participated in campaigns against the NATO attacks on Serbia in 1999. Therefore, they found it difficult to follow the suggestions of party leaders that the PDS could approve of future military interventions under the right conditions.

In contrast to the PDS, it had been possible for Green leaders to distance their party from past demands for the dissolution of NATO. The shedding of radical-pacifist positions had made it possible for the Alliance 90/Greens to join national government in late 1998 and for Green leader Joschka Fischer to become foreign affairs minister. Green accommodation had made possible the acceptance of a Social Democratic and Green coalition government by Germany's NATO partners. On the other hand, the insistence on radical pacifist positions by the PDS congress majority in Münster signaled that the PDS was not ready to follow the Green example of softening pacifist positions.

NEW GENERATION OF PDS LEADERS REPLACES FOUNDERS: COTTBUS, 14–15 OCTOBER 2000

The party chairman of the PDS from its foundation until January 1993, its parliamentary leader in the Bundestag since 1990, Gregor Gysi stepped down at the Cottbus party congress as he had announced several months earlier in Münster. On previous occasions Gysi had threatened to step down in order to make congress delegates accept controversial decisions (of course, they did not want to lose the party's most appealing electoral asset); on other occasions, he had considered stepping down just to get out of politics. Together with Gysi, Lothar Bisky, party chairman since January 1993, also stepped down in order to concentrate on his future in the parliament of Brandenburg.

This signaled the transition to a new generation of leaders. Gysi and Bisky had been among those brought to the top of the party in the turmoil of late 1989. Everything happened in Berlin, everything was quite improvised, and those in the right location at the right time were catapulted into leadership positions, filling the vacuum left behind by the demise of the SED leadership around Secretary General Erich Honecker, followed by the speedy dismissal of his successor Erich Krenz.

In October 2000, the new generation of leadership contestants and eventual leaders consisted of a different group. They were somewhat younger than Gysi

and Bisky. They had gained power at the regional level of the PDS organizations, and their rise into the party leadership reflected the strength of the PDS
in the five Eastern Länder and in East Berlin. The contestants were either parliamentary leaders or party presidents from the Eastern regions, with the exception of one position of deputy party president reserved for a West German.

The witty and entertaining personality of Gysi could not be replaced. His
sharp tongue and gift of formulation gave him an entry to West German media
even at times when the PDS had been severely marginalized. He was a unique
electoral asset for the party as the only PDS politician with an impressive media
personality and significant appeal to West German voters. However, the party
had developed a number of competent potential successors risen through Land-
level politics.

The Cottbus congress elected Gabi Zimmer, deputy president since 1997, as
party president to succeed Lothar Bisky. Zimmer had been chairwoman of the
Thuringia PDS (1990–1998) and party leader in the Thuringia parliament (since
1998) during a time when it improved its electoral influence from 9.7 percent
in 1990 to 21.3 percent in 1999, replacing the SPD as second strongest party
in Thuringia. Petra Pau (chairwoman of the Berlin PDS) and Peter Porsch (chairman of the PDS in Saxony) were elected deputy presidents, together with the
West German Diether Dehm. PDS parliamentarians in the Bundestag elected
Roland Claus as leader to succeed Gregor Gysi. Claus had been chairman of
the party organization in Saxony-Anhalt, playing a leading role in the "toleration" model in which the PDS had been supporting minority governments led
by Social Democrats since 1994.[24]

The founder generation of PDS leaders had emerged during the turbulent
transition from SED to PDS. They had led the party through the period of
decline and weakness (1990–1992) and the consolidation phase of 1993–1994.
They had succeeded in leading the party out of total marginality to a degree of
relative acceptance. They had transformed the party, bringing it out of self-
marginalization into active participation in competitive party democracy. The
next generation of pragmatists had risen through regional politics and was ready
to reap the benefits of the efforts of Gysi, Bisky, and Modrow. Thus the PDS
had overcome, according to its new president Gabi Zimmer, the setbacks of the
Münster party congress. As the PDS continued its effort to find its position in
society, it was getting ready for success in the national elections of 2002.

THE PLACE OF THE PDS IN THE PARTY SYSTEM: AN
ALMOST NORMAL PARTY

The place of the Party of Democratic Socialism in the German party system,
its self-ascribed role, and the perception of the PDS by other parties have all
changed significantly in the decade since its foundation in 1989. From 1990 to
1994, the PDS was subject to marginalization, "placed in a state of quarantine"[25]
by other parties. This exclusion was only broken in 1994 with the Magdeburg

model when a minority government of SPD and Greens in Saxony-Anhalt accepted "toleration" by PDS parliamentarians.

Mirroring its treatment by other parties, the PDS itself initially adopted an opposition role on the margins of united Germany's party system. In 1994 elections, the PDS still campaigned under the slogan "change begins with opposition," but it also took one step closer to government responsibilities in the toleration arrangement of Magdeburg. During internal debates in 1995–1997, the PDS redefined its role as "societal opposition" to include the possible acceptance of executive responsibilities in local and regional government. Finally, in 1998, the PDS was for the first time included in a Land government, as junior partner of the SPD in Mecklenburg–Vorpommern. The SPD's strategy toward the PDS had shifted from marginalization to integration, and the PDS was for the first time willing to join a Land government. The PDS's role changed due to its unexpected survival, due to internal changes, and because its existence offered opportunities to the Social Democrats that made a reevaluation of the PDS by the SPD rewarding.

The "normalization" of the PDS was also confirmed by the decision of Germany's parliament to grant public finance for the political education and research programs of the Rosa Luxemburg Foundation for the second half of 1999.[26] The decision meant that the PDS received, for the first time, this form of indirect party finance from the state given to foundations connected to political parties with stable representation in the Bundestag. The PDS had been refused this support even after it had regained representation in 1994. Only after the 1998 elections, when the PDS had won more than 5 percent and a sufficient number of seats to qualify as a full parliamentary party (*Fraktion*), did the other parties in the Bundestag accept the claims of the PDS and the Rosa Luxemburg Foundation.

The new constellation in the German party system can only be obscured by the dichotomy of social democratic versus communist. This dichotomy was a useful tool of classification only for the period 1917 to 1991. "The Socialist People's Party of Denmark and the Party of the Left of Sweden have demonstrated for several decades . . . that it is possible . . . to develop politically effective parties beyond the social democratic and also beyond the communist type of party."[27] The PDS managed to occupy this space in the German party system: neither social democratic nor communist but left-socialist. It could function, in a way past communist parties (KPD, DKP) could not, as "strategic reserve"[28] of the SPD. Although the result of the 1998 elections gave SPD and Greens a majority in the Bundestag without the PDS, the new constellation in the party system makes future "Swedish majorities" possible in Germany, that is, minority governments of Social Democrats and Greens relying on parliamentary support by a left-socialist party.

The position of the PDS in the German party system has undergone significant change in three respects. First, there is the fact of its survival. The party was close to self-dissolution in December 1989 and early 1990. For several years, the "party without future"[29] was declared moribund by many observers. However, by 1994 the PDS had become a stable minor party nationwide and a major party in East Germany. Second, the PDS was far less marginal in the late 1990s than in 1990–1992. The party had managed "to overcome . . . the political ostracism to which the PDS was exposed."[30] It had gained acceptance in the East German electorate, in local government, and to a limited extent, as participant in Land-level government. And third, the PDS had found a role in the competitive party system in a parliamentary democracy. Its predecessor, the SED, had its role as permanently governing "leading party" guaranteed by the power structure and the constitution of the GDR. After the loss of this habitual role, the PDS found a new raison d'être by identifying with an opposition role—the only role other parties would allow the PDS but also the only role PDS members themselves could imagine in an alien political environment. However, within a few years the PDS made another massive adjustment: Closer acquaintance with the political system of the FRG made PDS members realize that it was possible to combine an identity as critical left-socialist party with a variety of roles in the political process, as opposition in parliament, as participant in "toleration" arrangements, even as participant in coalitions. The PDS learned to live within a multiparty system, as competitor, as participant. This was a break with the past in which its predecessors knew only two roles: either as outsider opposition, as long as capitalism lasted, or as permanently ruling party for the entire period of building socialism and communism.

Since 1994, and more clearly since 1998, the PDS had become a participant in a multiparty system. This certainly presupposed that most PDS members regarded a strategy of reforms as promising. For PDS leaders and for the "modern socialists," these reform efforts in themselves were the raison d'être of the PDS, serving to overcome "the predominance of the capitalist profit motive," counterbalancing economic power by democratic mobilization. For the Marxist Forum and other members, these reform efforts were sustained by the hope for an eventual transformation of capitalist property structures.

This role as participant in a multiparty system also implied that the PDS had overcome a traditional weakness of the radical left: its dismissive attitude to formal democracy, rule of law, and other aspects of "bourgeois democracy." The PDS has learned to appreciate bourgeois democracy, first, in its analysis of the shortcomings of socialism in the GDR and in the Soviet Union, and second, in the practice of its first decade in the FRG.

The PDS continued the heritage of the Old Left in so far as it still emphasized the theme of social justice. This was interpreted by Koch-Baumgarten as indicative of "traditional, premodern sets of attitudes centred especially around the social question," whereas the PDS neglected modern themes such as ecology, gender equality, and individual self-determination.[31] Here Koch-Baumgarten underestimated the extent to which the PDS had adopted themes such as feminism, pacifism, or democratization, which were of secondary importance for the Old

Left, compared to the central theme of class struggle. And it has adopted new themes, which the Old Left could not even think of, such as environmentalism.

The PDS has survived because it has managed to package several heterogeneous themes. It represented an East German sociocultural milieu of socialists and secularists. It expressed East German regional interests and identities. And it appealed to a dispersed West German socialist potential to the left of the SPD. Careful packaging and external circumstances have allowed the PDS to combine these themes to sustain a viable small party. Its continued existence remained a balancing act, trying to expand its left-socialist appeal in West Germany before its regionalist appeal to disadvantaged East Germans exhausted itself.

THE LIMITS OF INTEGRATION: "NOT (YET) GENERALLY ACCEPTED"

The PDS has become, in the words of Gero Neugebauer, a "not (yet) generally accepted coalition party."[32] The experiences of the Magdeburg model of toleration since 1994, the successes of the 1998 elections, and the example of the first government coalition of SPD and PDS in Mecklenburg-Vorpommern were not replicated. In 1999, Landtag elections in the East were relatively successful for the PDS but did not bring about majorities for SPD and PDS due to losses for the SPD. Thus the hopes of PDS strategists "to expand the role of the party at the Land level as well as at the federal level via cooperation with the SPD" were disappointed (p. 40).

Among leading Social Democrats, former SPD leader Oskar Lafontaine was among those most sympathetic to potential cooperation with the PDS. Yet even Lafontaine pointed to a lack of common policies as a major obstacle to the inclusion of the PDS in center-left governments: "Given the considerable support that it still enjoys in East Germany, I not only consider the PDS to be entitled to sit in the parliaments of the *Länder*, but I would also see no difficulty about including it in the federal government, if common policies could be agreed upon." Lafontaine identified three policy issues separating the SPD and PDS: "They rejected the euro, whereas the acceptance of European economic union and a single currency was a firm plank in our policy. Then they had a negative attitude towards NATO, whereas for us NATO was the basis of our defence policy. And their economic and social demands were purely and simply impossible to finance."[33]

Two of Lafontaine's three obstacles to cooperation could be overcome. The role of the PDS in the Land government of Mecklenburg-Vorpommern and its toleration of SPD minority governments in Saxony-Anhalt showed that the party was capable of adjusting its social and economic policies to the budget restraints of regional government. The criticism of the PDS regarding the European currency was directed against the policy of austerity connected with its introduction, not against the Euro per se.

This left the third obstacle that appears indeed to be insurmountable given the decisions of the PDS party congress of April 2000 in Münster. Not only the rejection of all military interventions abroad by the congress majority would preclude PDS participation in a federal government. Even the more accommodating stance of the party leadership to allow participation in interventions sanctioned by a UN mandate differs clearly from the position of the government. The coalition of SPD and Alliance 90/Greens approved participation of German combat troops in NATO's intervention in Kosovo without making it conditional on a mandate by the UN Security Council. PDS leaders such as André Brie were aware that this decisive difference in foreign and security policy made the desired "centre-left block at federal level" impossible. In this area "there is, at this moment, no common ground between the PDS, on the one hand, and SPD and Greens, on the other."[34]

A test case of "immense symbolic significance" was the level of acceptance in Berlin.[35] While the PDS had enjoyed its greatest support in its strongholds in East Berlin, the antipathy toward the party in West Berlin was intense as a result of the front-line role played by this city during the four decades of the Cold War. In the elections for the Chamber of Deputies of Berlin on 23 October 2001 the Democratic Socialists increased their share of the vote to 22.6 percent (1999: 17.9 percent). The PDS managed to extend its position as the strongest party in East Berlin (47.6 percent compared to 39.5 percent in 1999). At the same time, its support in West Berlin rose to 6.9 percent (1999: 4.2 percent).[36] For the first time, the PDS achieved more than 5 percent in any region outside the former GDR.

In spite of this electoral success the PDS remained initially excluded from the formation of Berlin's Land government. SPD leader Klaus Wowereit's decision to opt for a coalition with Alliance 90/Greens and the FDP followed advice from Chancellor Gerhard Schröder, the leader of Germany's government, to exclude the PDS because of its criticism of U.S. military intervention in Afghanistan. The party congress of the PDS (Dresden, 6–7 October 2001) had, like all other German parties, condemned the terrorist attacks on New York and Washington of 11 September. At the same time, the PDS congress had warned against the danger of a "spiral of violence" resulting from military actions against Afghanistan by the United States. This stance differed from the support of U.S. actions by the German government and made coalitions with the PDS unacceptable for Chancellor Schröder.[37]

However, after negotiations between SPD, Alliance 90/Greens and Free Democrats failed in December, a coalition between SPD and PDS was the only politically viable option. The coalition agreement of 8 January 2002 acknowledged the "dramatic financial situation" of the Berlin state government implying a "reduction of state activities" and "lowering of personnel costs." The SPD/PDS government was elected in the Berlin Chamber of Deputies on 17 January. Gregor Gysi, the foundation president of the PDS and its parliamentary leader in federal parliament from October 1990 to October 2000, now held one of the party's three ministerial positions, as deputy leader (Bürgermeister) and Senator for the Economy, Labor and Women's Issues.[38] As partner in a second state government the PDS gained acceptance. On the other hand, sharing the responsibility for public service cutbacks in this "dramatic financial situation" may negatively impact on the party's electoral prospects.

Through its positions in two Land governments (Mecklenburg–West Pommerania and Berlin) the PDS also gained some leverage to influence national politics. In Germany's federal system the second chamber of parliament is a states' house: The Bundesrat (Federal Council) consists of delegates from the 16 state governments. This chamber is rather evenly balanced between SPD–governed and CDU–governed states. If coalition partners in a state government disagree on proposed legislation, the state usually abstains from voting in the Bundesrat. Thus the passage of legislation in the second chamber may depend on support by PDS ministers in two state governments as the PDS could deprive the federal government of SPD and Alliance 90/Greens of the Bundesrat votes of Berlin and Mecklenburg–West Pommerania.

Although the intense antipathy among West Berliners against the PDS could be reduced, it will be much more difficult to overcome the cultural distance between the PDS entrenched in East German society and the majority of West Germans for whom the PDS remains very remote. While West Berlin regained its connections with its geographic surroundings, the continuing distance between West and East Germany resulted in a party system characterized by regionalized pluralism.

A NEW GERMAN PARTY SYSTEM: REGIONALIZED PLURALISM AND CENTER-LEFT HEGEMONY

Two misperceptions affected many analyses of the West German party system after unification. First, it was expected that the West German party system would be replicated on a larger scale after the absorption of East Germany into the Federal Republic. Second, it was feared that the unexpected survival of the PDS would contribute to polarized pluralism, dangerously destabilizing German democracy by increasing the antidemocratic potential on the left, mirroring right-wing extremist parties (DVU, Republikaner, NPD). Neither of these two scenarios eventuated. Instead, a form of "regionalized pluralism" emerged.[39]

Two different party systems are visible, at the regional level, in East and West Germany. In the West, there is still the four-party system of the pre-1990 FRG: CDU/CSU and SPD as major parties, as well as FDP and Greens as relevant minor parties whereas the PDS struggled to raise its support from 0.3 percent in 1990 to 1.2 percent in 1998. In the East, on the other hand, the PDS is one of the three major parties, besides CDU and SPD. In the East, the PDS had significant influence in regional parliaments. Since 1994, the SPD-led minority governments of Saxony-Anhalt have depended on support by PDS parliamentarians; since 1998 the PDS has been junior partner in a formal government coalition in Mecklenburg–West Pommerania, and as a result of the election of

23 October 2001, PDS parliamentarians had to be taken into account for the formation of the state government of Berlin.

At the national level, fragmentation increased as the PDS gained representation in the Bundestag. This fragmentation did not, however, amount to "polarized pluralism." If the PDS was an extremist party, as claimed by Moreau, Neu, or Jesse, and if the PDS had to be excluded from the consensus of democrats, then the 5 to 6 percent support for the PDS could be regarded as indicative of polarized pluralism, together with the combined support of 5 to 6 percent for the right-wing DVU, Republikaner and NPD. In this case, Germany would be facing "polarized pluralism," although not to any extent rendering stable majority governments difficult to form. On the other hand, as the PDS has become accepted as a potential coalition partner close to the SPD and Greens, its survival has not produced polarization but merely regional variety. The earlier strategy of marginalizing the PDS could have produced polarized pluralism, but the integration strategy emerging since 1994 has prevented such polarization.

In its self-image, the PDS appeared as a left-socialist corrective to the shift of Social Democrats and Greens to the "New Center" and the "Third Way" as defined by British Prime Minister Tony Blair and German Chancellor Gerhard Schröder.[40] However, in the larger scheme of things, the PDS has merely added its weight to the center left potential. Thus the survival of the PDS is likely to have the net effect of ending the long-term hegemony of the center-right CDU/CSU in the German party system, shifting the balance in the whole party system toward the center left.

From 1949 to 1998, the most likely government of the FRG was a center-right coalition led by the CDU/CSU. Since 1998, as the long-term effects of unification became visible, the most likely government of the FRG is a coalition including the SPD, either in a centrist coalition of SPD and CDU/CSU (or SPD with FDP) or in a center-left coalition of SPD and Greens, possibly relying on PDS support.

After the 1998 elections, Stephen Padgett argued that the "centre-left majority was situational in character" as the CDU defeat had been caused by short-term factors such as the growing unpopularity of long-serving Chancellor Kohl.[41] Richard Stöss and Oskar Niedermayer also characterized the outcome of the 1998 elections as exceptional, similar to that of 1972: These were the only time in the history of the FRG that the SPD could gain more support than the Christian Democrats. This approach suggested that the CDU/CSU was likely to regain and continue its hegemony, allocating to the SPD a "permanently second place,"[42] whereas Padgett's analysis acknowledged the weakening of CDU/CSU's hegemony without claiming its replacement by a center-left dominance.

The argument by Stöss and Niedermayer underestimated the impact of the inclusion of the East German electorate, which made any comparison between the West German election of 1972 and the 1998 election in united Germany questionable. It would be more precise to point out that short-term factors connected with German unification saved the CDU twice, in the elections of 1990 and 1994. The impact of changes in the composition of the German electorate due to unification was delayed by the popularity of Kohl as the "Chancellor of unification." It was not before 1998 that the inclusion of 16 million largely secularized East Germans, many of whom share "old labor" social justice values, ended the hegemony enjoyed by Christian Democrats since 1949 in a West German electorate including 45 percent Catholics.

Since the 1998 elections it has been obvious that the balance in the German party system has shifted toward the center-left as a result of unification. In Sweden, a government of Social Democrats and Greens, relying on left-socialist or Eurocommunist support in parliament, has been common for decades. In Germany, a government of Social Democrats and Greens, relying on PDS support, remained definitely very unlikely for the 2002 elections. Although the practice of the PDS in Mecklenburg-Vorpommern and in Saxony-Anhalt had shown that it could accept compromises regarding social and economic policy, the differences in foreign policy and security would make a center-left coalition including the PDS unworkable at the federal level. Yet by 2006 the normalization of the PDS could be sufficiently advanced to allow the formation of a "Swedish majority."

NOTES

1. Sigrid Koch-Baumgarten, "Postkommunismus im Spagat. Zur Funktion der PDS im Parteiensystem," *Deutschland-Archiv* 30, no. 6 (1997): 865.

2. Manfred Gerner, *Partei ohne Zukunft? Von der SED zur PDS* (Munich: Tilsner, 1994) (in the very title of the book); Patrick Moreau and Jürgen Peter Lang, *Was will die PDS?* (Berlin: Ullstein, 1994), p. 458.

3. Jürgen Raschke, "SPD und PDS: Selbstblockade oder Opposition?" *Blätter für deutsche und internationale Politik* 39, no. 12 (December 1994): 1453–1464; Manfred Gerner, "Antagonismen der PDS: Zum Pluralismus der SED-Nachfolgepartei," *Deutschland-Archiv* 29, no. 2 (March–April 1996): 239.

4. Viola Neu, "Das Korsett der alten Ideologie," *Die politische Meinung*, no. 369 (August 2000): 59; Wilfried Schulz, "PDS-Programmdiskussion—eine Frage der Glaubwürdigkeit," *Deutschland-Archiv* 33, no. 2 (March–April 2000): 179.

5. Manfred Gerner, "Widerspruch und Stagnation in der PDS," *Zeitschrift für Politik* 45, no. 2 (1998): 181; André Brie and Thomas Flierl, " 'Wir verteidigen eine Partei, die es noch nicht gibt': Berlin und die Zukunft der PDS," *Blätter für deutsche und internationale Politik* 46, no. 8 (August 2001): 952.

6. Norberto Bobbio, *Which Socialism?* (London: Polity Press, 1987); Uwe-Jens Heuer, "Zur Demokratiefrage und heutigen Aufgaben der PDS, zugleich zum Verhältnis von Demokratie und Diktatur," in *Gegenmacht Demokratie. Demokratisierung gegen Macht* (Berlin: PDS Grundsatzkommission, 1994), p. 7.

7. Michael Benjamin, "Dissens und Konsens in der Strategiedebatte," *Pankower Vorträge* (Berlin: Helle Panke e.V.), vol. 5 (1997), p. 35; Sahra Wagenknecht, *Antisozialistische Strategien im Zeitalter der Systemauseinandersetzung. Zwei Taktiken im Kampf gegen die sozialistische Welt* (Bonn: Pahl-Rugenstein Nachfolger, 1995).

8. Gero Neugebauer, "Die PDS zwischen Kontinuität und Aufbruch," *Aus Politik und Zeitgeschichte*, B5 (2000): 40.

9. André Brie et al., eds., *Zur Programmatik der Partei des Demokratischen Sozialismus. Ein Kommentar* (Berlin: Dietz Verlag, 1997); Dieter Klein et al., *Reform-Alternativen: Sozial—ökologisch—zivil* (Berlin: Dietz, 2000).

10. Ingo Wagner, "Moderner Sozialismus als sozialistische Moderne," *Marxistisches Forum*. nos. 17–18 (February 1998): 32; Eva Sturm and Eberhard Schmidt, "Ein Kommentar zur Programmatik der PDS oder das Problem der Diskursunfähigkeit," *UTOPIE kreativ*. no. 84 (October 1997): 83.

11. PDS Programmkommission, "Thesen zur programmatischen Debatte," *Pressedienst PDS*, no. 47 (26 November 1999): 4.

12. Michael Benjamin, Uwe-Jens Heuer, and Winfried Wolf, "Votum zu den Thesen der Programmkommission der PDS," *Pressedienst PDS*. no. 47 (26 November 1999): 34–36.

13. PDS Programmkommission, "Thesen," pp. 25–29; Benjamin, Heuer and Wolf, "Votum," pp. 47–48.

14. Horst Kahrs, "Was kommt nach den 'Reformern' in der PDS?" *UTOPIE kreativ*, nos. 115–116 (May–June 2000): 438.

15. PDS Programmkommission, "Zum Stand der programmatischen Debatte und der eigenen Tätigkeit," PDS Online, p. 3, available at http://www.pds-online.de/programm/programmkommission/dokumente.

16. Helmut Holter, "Die PDS als Zukunftspartei," November 1999, available at http://www.pdsmv/de/diskussion.

17. Frank Berg, "Politikwechsel und Reformpolitik: Der Fall Mecklenburg-Vorpommern," *UTOPIE kreativ*. nos. 115–116 (May–June 2000): 442.

18. Ibid., p. 443.

19. Ibid., p. 445.

20. "Wahlen 2000," *Blätter für deutsche und internationale Politik* 46, no. 1 (January 2001): 128.

21. Michael Schumann, "Es geht um die Verteidigung der UN-Charta! Nicht um Plädoyer für Kampfeinsätze!" *DISPUT*. no. 4 (April 2000): 24–26.

22. "Nein zu UN-Militäreinsätzen—Internationale Krisen und Konflikte friedlich lösen. Beschluß der 3. Tagung des 6. Parteitages," *DISPUT*. no. 4 (April 2000): 32–33.

23. Neu, "Das Korsett der alten Ideologie," pp. 57–63; Kahrs, "Was kommt," pp. 437–441; Andreas Fraude, "Ende einer Ära: Die 3. Tagung des 6. Bundesparteitages der PDS," *Deutschland-Archiv* 33, no. 3 (2000): 363–365.

24. Wilfried Schulz, " 'Für Gabi tun wir alles.' Vom Cottbuser Bundesparteitag und dem Doppelcharakter der PDS," *Deutschland-Archiv* 33, no. 6 (2000): 883.

25. Rüdiger Dambroth. "Parlamentarische Bündnisbestrebungen von SPD und PDS im Wahljahr 1998," *Politische Studien* 49, no. 360 (July–August 1998): 28.

26. PDS, "Tätigkeitsbericht des Parteivorstandes," *DISPUT*. no. 10 (2000): 60.

27. André Brie, *Ich tauche nicht ab. Selbstzeugnisse und Reflexionen* (Berlin: Edition Ost, 1996), p. 258.

28. Alexander Gauland, "Konservativ sein heißt," *Blätter für deutsche und internationale Politik* 44, no. 1 (January 1999): 10–11.

29. Gerner, *Partei ohne Zukunft?*

30. Manfred Wilke, "Die Diktaturkader André Brie, Gregor Gysi, Lothar Bisky und das MfS," *Politische Studien* 49, no. 360 (July–August 1998): 66.

31. Koch-Baumgarten, "Postkommunismus im Spagat," p. 872.

32. Neugebauer, "Die PDS zwischen Kontinuität und Aufbruch," p. 43.

33. Oskar Lafontaine, *The Heart Beats on the Left*, trans. Ronald Taylor (Cambridge: Polity Press, 2000), p. 48.

34. Brie and Flierl, " 'Wir verteidigen eine Partei, die es noch nicht gibt,' " p. 942.

35. Ibid.

36. "365 839 mal Danke an die Berlinerinnen und Berliner (23. 10. 2001)," available at http://www.pds-online.de/wahlen/aktuell/wahlen_berlin; "Wahlen 1999 (II)," *Blätter für deutsche und internationale Politik* 45, no. 2 (February 2000): 256.

37. "Nur, weil der Kanzler beleidigt ist," *Süddeutsche Zeitung* (31 October 2001); PDS, "Es geht auch anders: Nur Gerechtigkeit sichert Zukunft! 2. Tagung des 7. Partei-tages (6. und 7. Oktober 2001, Dresden)," http://www.pds-online.de/partei/strukturen/parteitag/0702/beschluss.htm

38. PDS, "Koalitionsvereinbarung zwischen SPD und PDS. Präambel" (8 January 2002), http://www.pds-online.de/politik/themen/senatsbildung_berlin; PDS, "Aus dem Abgeordnetenhaus: PDS im Senat von Berlin" (17 January 2002), http://www.pds-berlin.de/politik/dok/020117vitae.html.

39. David Patton, "The Rise of Germany's Party of Democratic Socialism: 'Region-alised Pluralism' in the Federal Republic?" *West European Politics* 23, no. 1 (January 2000): 144–160.

40. Tony Blair and Gerhard Schröder, "The Way Forward for European Social Dem-ocrats" (June 1999), http://www.xs4all.nl/~adampost/arc000006.html

41. Stephen Padgett, "The Boundaries of Stability: The Party System before and after the 1998 *Bundestagswahl*," *German Politics* 8, no. 2 (August 1999): 104.

42. Richard Stöss and Oskar Niedermayer, "Zwischen Anpassung und Profilierung. Die SPD an der Schwelle zum neuen Jahrhundert," *Aus Politik und Zeitgeschichte*, B5 (2000): 3.

PDS Chronology, 1989–2001

1989
8–9/16–17 December: Last party congress of SED becomes foundation congress of PDS, adopting transitional name SED-PDS; Gregor Gysi elected chairman.

1990
20 January: Calls for dissolution of party congress rejected by party executive (Partei-vorstand).

4 February: Name change from SED-PDS to PDS adopted by party executive.

24–25 February: PDS congress adopts party program, constitution, and platform for Volkskammer elections.

18 March: Volkskammer elections: PDS wins 16.4 percent and is relegated to opposition role. End of Prime Minister Modrow's government.

31 May: "Independent Commission for the Investigation of the Property of Parties and Mass Organizations of the GDR" established by the Volkskammer.

4 August: Foundation of the electoral alliance Linke Liste/PDS gives PDS first foothold in West Germany.

2 December: First elections in united Germany. PDS wins 11.1 percent of the East German vote and achieves representation in the Bundestag as the 5 percent rule is applied separately to East and West Germany. Its overall support of 2.4 percent includes 0.3 percent in West Germany.

1991
9 June: Electoral appeal of PDS has sunk to 6.5 percent in the East and 0.5 percent in the West, according to opinion polls.

21–23 June: PDS congress represents 242,000 party members. Delegates approve new party constitution to be adopted by plebiscite of members; three drafts for new party program presented.

27 September: New party constitution approved in a plebiscite by 126,355 of 130,848 participating party members (96.5 percent).

14–15 December: Party congress expresses intention to build PDS organization in West Germany.

23 December: PDS membership has declined to 172,579.

1992

27 February: A committee of the Brandenburg Landtag, chaired by Lothar Bisky (PDS), investigates allegations that Premier Manfred Stolpe (SPD) had illicit contacts to the Stasi in his role as church official in the GDR. A final report exonerating Stolpe is presented on 16 June 1994.

24 May: Success in local government elections in Berlin (11.3 percent and 170,799 votes) signals an end to the downward trend of the PDS's electoral fortunes.

12 July: Foundation of the Committees for Justice initiated by Peter-Michael Diestl (CDU) and Gregor Gysi (PDS) as attempt to form a social movement beyond the narrow clientele of the PDS.

25–26 October: André Brie steps down as chairman of the Berlin party organization, as he had concealed past activities as IM (informal contributor) of the Stasi. He subsequently loses his position as deputy chairman of the entire PDS.

19–20 December: The program commission adopts a draft of a new party program. An alternative draft by Michael Benjamin and Sahra Wagenknecht (Communist Platform) is withdrawn.

31 December: PDS membership has declined to 146,742.

1993

29–31 January: The new party program is approved by a 90.5 percent majority of congress delegates. Lothar Bisky is elected to succeed Gregor Gysi as PDS chairman.

26–27 June: Platform for 1994 Bundestag elections adopted.

19 September: Elections in the West German city–state of Hamburg: PDS gains no more than 0.5 percent.

2 October: "Ostdeutsches Kuratorium der Verbände" founded as umbrella organization for diverse interest groups expressing East German grievances.

5 December: Local government elections in Brandenburg show a recovery of the PDS to 21.2 percent; Wolfgang Thierse (SPD) and Konrad Weiss (Alliance 90/Greens) reject all forms of cooperation with PDS.

1994

16 February: The Ingolstadt Manifesto presented by PDS chairman Gregor Gysi calls for a New Deal and a New Social Contract.

12 June: In elections to the European Parliament the PDS achieves a share of the vote of 4.7 percent.

26 June: Before the Landtag elections in Saxony-Anhalt the PDS offered "toleration" of a minority government of SPD and Alliance 90/Greens excluding the CDU. The acceptance of this offer by SPD and Alliance 90/Greens ("Magdeburg model") triggers debates inside the PDS about its future role as opposition.

11 August: Rudolf Scharping, SPD chairman, confirms in the Dresden Declaration the rejection of any cooperation between his party and the PDS. On 5 December, the SPD party executive restates there would be no joint initiatives or coalitions with the PDS, neither at the federal nor the state level.

11 September: Support for the PDS increases in Landtag elections in Brandenburg (to 18.7 percent) and Saxony (to 16.5 percent).

16 October: In elections to federal parliament, the PDS gains 4.4 percent. In spite of its failure to reach 5 percent, the party qualifies for representation in the Bundestag by winning four direct mandates. After regional elections in Thuringia the PDS remains excluded from negotiations between CDU and SPD. In Mecklenburg–West Pommerania, SPD leader Harald Ringstorff makes talks with the PDS conditional on clarifying political statements that do not eventuate.

1995

27–29 January: Party congress adopts "Five Points" distancing the PDS from Stalinist positions; PDS decides to commit resources to the growth of its very small West German branches.

19 February: The strategy debate of the next two years is initiated with a paper by Lothar Bisky and André Brie: "Germany Needs a Neo-Socialist Alternative"; on 25–26 February a conference of the Communist Platform attacks the paper as "accommodation to the system in order to join government coalitions."

18 May: An appeal of 38 signatories ("In Great Sorrow") is published in *Neues Deutschland*; it expresses concerns about any weakening of the party's opposition concept.

6 June: The foundation of the Marxist Forum is announced by Uwe-Jens Heuer and other signatories of the appeal "In Great Sorrow."

16 June/18 July: The dispute over party property ends after five years with a compromise between the Independent Commission and the PDS that is confirmed by the Berlin Higher Administrative Court.

22 October: Elections to the Berlin Chamber of Deputies: The PDS achieves a total of 14.6 percent (2.1 percent in West Berlin; 36.3 percent in East Berlin).

28 November: New SPD chairman Oskar Lafontaine meets PDS chairman Gregor Gysi; 14 December: SPD leader Harald Ringstorff (Mecklenburg–West Pommerania) meets Gysi; 28 December: SPD leader Manfred Stolpe (Brandenburg) meets Bisky and Gysi.

11 December: In anticipation of controversies around the fiftieth anniversary of the foundation of the SED in 1946, as a merger of KPD and SPD in East Germany, the Historical Commission of the PDS presents its theses.

1996

20 January: Marxist Forum criticizes PDS plans to participate in government: There are people in the PDS who no longer assume the necessity of a different society.

27–28 January: The party congress adopts a strategic objective for the elections of 1998: to overcome the conservative government majority in cooperation with SPD and Greens.

20–22 April: The fiftieth anniversary of the foundation of the Socialist Unity Party of Germany renews controversies about 1946 merger of KPD and SPD, regarded by many Social Democrats as a *Zwangsvereinigung* (coercive merger).

7 May: "Brief aus Sachsen" (Letter from Saxony) by Christine Ostrowski and Ronald Weckesser demands end of attempts to build PDS branches in the West and the development of the PDS as an East German regionalist party. In response, party strategist André Brie demands patience and persistence in building the party in West Germany.

21 November: Discussion among Alliance 90/Greens about the options of ending CDU government in Berlin with help of PDS. On the other hand, prominent former East German dissidents Vera Lengsfeld, Günter Nooke and Angelika Barbe leave Alliance 90/ Greens and SPD to join the CDU in protest against improving relations between their parties and the PDS.

19 December: A strategy paper by SPD Deputy Chairman Wolfgang Thierse (supported by four of five Eastern regional SPD chairmen) argues that cooperation with the PDS was inevitable in the East though not desirable nationally.

1997

9 January: PDS Chairman Lothar Bisky launches the volume *Zur Programmatik der Partei des Demokratischen Sozialismus: Ein Kommentar*. Without claiming to prepare the replacement of the 1993 party program the *Kommentar* consolidates the dominance of "modern socialist" concepts in the PDS. The Erfurt Declaration of unionists, social democrats, and clerics describes the PDS as an acceptable part of an intended "Alliance for Social Democracy."

17–19 January: The party congress, held in Schwerin, adopts objectives for the elections of 1998–1999 and declares the PDS ready for direct and indirect government participation.

2–3 September: Strategy Conference of PDS adopts statement "For fundamental change of policies with the PDS."

1998

4–5 April: The party congress, held in Rostock, adopts the Rostock Manifesto calling for a Pilot Project East in order to maximize its appeal to East German voters in national elections and especially to the electorate of Mecklenburg-Vorpommern regarding the regional elections, both to take place in September 1998.

27 September: Elections to Germany's parliament: For the first time the PDS overcomes the 5 percent threshold and qualifies as a full parliamentary party (*Fraktion*). The national total of 5.1 percent includes 1.2 percent in the West and 21.6 percent in the East.

27 September: After the regional elections to the Landtag of Mecklenburg–West Pommerania, SPD and PDS negotiate the formation of government to be approved by party

congresses in late October and starting to work on 3 November. In the "Schwerin model," the PDS is for the first time included in a Land government, whereas the "Magdeburg model" of 1994 only involved toleration of a minority government of SPD and Alliance 90/Greens by the PDS.

1999

15–16 January: The party congress resolves to appoint a program commission and to initiate a program debate.

6 June: The PDS fails in its attempt to gain representation in a West German regional parliament. With 2.9 percent (1995: 2.4 percent) it cannot reach the required 5 percent in the city–state of Bremen.

13 June: With 5.8 percent of the German vote in the European elections, the PDS is, for the first time, represented in the European Parliament. Its six MEPs join the United European Left/Nordic Green Left.

1 July: In the second half of 1999, the Rosa Luxemburg Foundation receives, for the first time, financial support from the German parliament for its programs of political education and research. The foundation connected to the PDS has achieved a status similar to foundations connected to other parties with stable representation in the Bundestag.

September: Regional elections in Brandenburg (5 September: 23.3 percent), Thuringia (12 September: 21.3 percent), and Saxony (19 September: 22.2 percent) result in increased support for the PDS without, however, leading to the party's inclusion in more Land governments.

19 November: The majority of the program commission presents its "Theses," whereas a dissenting minority publishes its "Vote to the Theses."

2000

27 February: With only 1.4 percent of the vote, the PDS fails to reach the 5 percent required to win representation in the Landtag of the West German state of Schleswig-Holstein.

7–9 April: PDS party congress is held in West Germany (Münster) for the first time. Two-thirds of the delegates reject a motion by the party executive to accept, on a case-by-case basis, German participation in military intervention, provided they are mandated by the UN Security Council.

14 May: With only 1.1 percent of the vote, the PDS fails to reach the 5 percent required to gain representation in the Landtag of North Rhine–Westphalia, West Germany's most populous state.

14–15 October: PDS congress in Cottbus elects the chairwoman of the Thuringia branch, Gabi Zimmer, to the position of PDS chairwoman. Outgoing chairman Lothar Bisky and parliamentary leader Gregor Gysi step down from national roles to concentrate on regional politics in Brandenburg and Berlin, respectively.

2001

27 April: PDS president Gabi Zimmer presents draft party program. The adoption of a new program is deferred until 2003, after the Bundestag election of 2002.

26 May: Party strategist André Brie demands, in an interview with the *Berliner Zeitung*, that the PDS prepare itself for government participation at the federal level by 2006.

6–7 October: PDS congress in Dresden condemns the terrorist attacks on New York and Washington of 11 September. At the same time the congress resolution warns against the danger of a "spiral of violence" resulting from military responses by the United States.

23 October: The PDS achieves 22.6 percent (1999: 17.7 percent) in elections to the Chamber of Deputies of Berlin; it remains the strongest party in East Berlin with 47.6 percent (1999: 39.5 percent) and increases support in West Berlin to 6.9 percent (1999: 4.2 percent).

30 October: The PDS remains excluded from the formation of the state government of Berlin by the decision of the SPD to negotiate with Alliance 90/Greens and FDP about the formation of a coalition. The Berlin branch of the SPD followed advice from Chancellor Gerhard Schröder, head of Germany's federal government, to exclude the PDS because of its criticism of U.S. military action in Afghanistan.

2002

8 January: Negotiations between SPD and PDS, initiated by SPD leader Klaus Wowereit after the failure of talks with Alliance 90/Greens and Free Democrats, lead to an agreement for the formation of a government coalition for the city state of Berlin. Social Democrats and Democratic Socialists agree on a strategy of balancing budgets and lowering expenditure for public services.

17 January: The Berlin Chamber of Deputies elects a state government formed by SPD and PDS. Former PDS chairman Gregor Gysi holds one of three PDS ministerial positions as Bürgermeister and Senator for the Economy, Labor and Women's Issues.

Bibliography

Adolphi, Wolfram. "Bestandene Reifeprüfung—und nun erst recht ruft das Leben. Acht Notizen zum Schweriner Parteitag der PDS." *UTOPIE kreativ*, no. 77 (March 1997): 5–10.

Adolphi, Wolfram. "Kommunikationsstörung. PDS am Jahreswechsel." *UTOPIE kreativ*, no. 101 (March 1999): 61–69.

Averesch, Sigrid. "Gysi beantragt Verfahren gegen sich selbst." *Berliner Zeitung* (18 August 1998): 6.

Backes, Uwe. "Überblick: Linksextremistische Parteien in Deutschland: Sehnsucht nach 'Sinnstiftung.' " *Das Parlament* 44, no. 1 (15 April 1994): 2.

Backes, Uwe and Eckhard Jesse, eds. *Jahrbuch Extremismus und Demokratie*, vol. 9. Baden-Baden: Nomos, 1997.

Barker, Peter, ed. *The Party of Democratic Socialism in Germany: Modern Post-Communism or Nostalgic Populism?* Amsterdam: Rodopi, 1998.

Bastian, Jens. "The *Enfant Terrible* of German Politics: The PDS between GDR Nostalgia and Democratic Socialism." *German Politics* 4, no. 2 (August 1995): 95–110.

Behrend, Manfred, and Helmut Meier, eds. *Der schwere Weg der Erneuerung. Von der SED zur PDS. Eine Dokumentation*. Berlin: Dietz, 1991.

Beinert, Heinz, ed. *Die PDS—Phönix oder Asche? Eine Partei auf dem Prüfstand*. Berlin: Aufbau-Verlag, 1995.

Benjamin, Michael. "Dissens und Konsens in der Strategiedebatte." *Pankower Vorträge*, no. 5. Berlin: Helle Panke e.V., 1997, pp. 24–46.

Benjamin, Michael. "Konsens und Dissens in der Strategiedebatte." *Pankower Vorträge* (Helle Panke e. V., Berlin), no. 5 (1997): 24–46.

Benjamin, Michael. "Über Kommunismus und 'Antistalinismus'—Antwort an Kurt Gossweiler." *Kommunisten in der PDS. Sonderheft der Mitteilungen der Kommunistischen Plattform der PDS* (June 1995): 10–12.

Benjamin, Michael, Uwe-Jens Heuer, and Winfried Wolf. "Votum zu den Thesen der Programmkommission der PDS." *Pressedienst PDS*, no. 47 (26 November 1999): 33–48.

Benser, Günter. "Zusammenschluß von KPD und SPD 1946: Erklärungsversuche jenseits von Jubel und Verdammnis." *Hefte zur DDR-Geschichte*, no. 27. Berlin: Forscher- und Diskussionskreis DDR-Geschichte, 1995.

Berg, Frank. "Politikwechsel und Reformpolitik: Der Fall Mecklenburg-Vorpommern." *UTOPIE kreativ*, no. 115–116 (May–June 2000): 442–453.

Bergner, Christoph. "Das Magdeburger Experiment." *Die politische Meinung* 41, no. 315 (February 1996): 13–19.

Betz, Hans-Georg, and Helga A. Welsh. "The PDS in the New German Party System." *German Politics* 4, no. 3 (1995): 92–111.

Bisky, Lothar. "Die PDS trägt Dissens und Konsens seit ihrer Gründung in sich—und sie lebt davon!" *Pankower Vorträge* (Helle Panke e.V., Berlin), no. 5 (1997): 5–23.

Bisky, Lothar. "Für eine gerechte Verteilung von Arbeit und Reichtum." *DISPUT*, no. 4 (1998): 6–14.

Bisky, Lothar. "Kommunen stärken—Gesellschaft von unten verändern: Zur politischen Situation und zur Strategie der PDS bis 1998." *DISPUT*, no. 2 (1996): 5–12.

Bisky, Lothar. *Wut im Bauch. Kampf um die PDS: 29. November bis 7. Dezember 1994.* Berlin: Dietz, 1995.

Bisky, Lothar, et al., eds. *Rücksichten. Politische und juristische Aspekte der DDR-Geschichte.* Hamburg: VSA, 1993.

Bisky, Lothar, et al., eds. *Unrechtsstaat? Politische Justiz und die Aufarbeitung der DDR-Vergangenheit.* Hamburg: VSA, 1994.

Bisky, Lothar, Gregor Gysi, and Hans Modrow. "Sozialismus ist Weg, Methode, Wertorientierung und Ziel." *DISPUT*, nos. 3–4 (1995); reprinted in Beinert, Heinz, ed. *Die PDS—Phönix oder Asche?* Berlin: Aufbau-Verlag, 1995.

Bisky, Lothar, et al., eds. *Die PDS—Herkunft und Selbstverständnis. Eine politisch-historische Debatte.* Berlin: Dietz, 1996.

Blair, Tony and Gerhard Schröder. "The Way Forward for European Social Democrats" (June 1999). (Available at http://www.xs4all.nl/~adampost/arc000006.html).

Bobbio, Norberto. *Which Socialism?* London: Polity Press, 1987.

Bohl, Friedrich, and Rudolf Kraus, eds. *SPD und SED. Die politischen Verstrickungen der SPD in die SED-Diktatur.* Bonn: CDU/CSU-Fraktion im Deutschen Bundestag, 1990.

Bortfeldt, Heinrich. "Pyrrhussieg der Reformer." *Deutschland-Archiv*, no. 3 (1995): 228–230.

Bortfeldt, Heinrich. *Von der SED zur PDS—Aufbruch zu neuen Ufern? Sommer/Herbst 1989—18 März 1990.* Berlin: Kommission Politische Bildung des Parteivorstandes der PDS, 1990.

Bortfeldt, Heinrich. *Von der SED zur PDS: Wandlung zur Demokratie?* Bonn: Bouvier, 1991.

Braumann, Marcel. "PDS weit weg. Sachsens Sozialisten streiten über Tariflöhne." *Neues Deutschland* (4 February 1997):8.

Brie, André. "Ankommen in der Bundesrepublik." *Blätter für deutsche und internationale Politik* 41, no. 10 (October 1996): 1161–1165.

Brie, André. "Der zweigeteilte Parteitag. Versuch eines Beitrags gegen neue Legenden." In *Die PDS—Herkunft und Selbstverständnis. Eine politisch-historische Debatte*, edited by Lothar Bisky et al., pp. 52–65. Berlin: Dietz: 1996.

Brie, André. *Ich tauche nicht ab. Selbstzeugnisse und Reflexionen*. Berlin: Edition Ost, 1996.

Brie, André, and Thomas Flierl. " 'Wir verteidigen eine Partei, die es noch nicht gibt': Berlin und die Zukunft der PDS." *Blätter für deutsche und internationale Politik* 46, no. 8 (August 2001): 942–954.

Brie, André, et al., eds. *Zur Programmatik der Partei des Demokratischen Sozialismus. Ein Kommentar*. Berlin: Dietz Verlag, 1997.

Brie, Michael. "Die PDS—Strategiebildung im Spannungsfeld von gesellschaftlichen Konfliktlinien und politischer Identität." In *Die PDS im Parteiensystem*, edited by Michael Brie and Rudolf Woderich, pp. 14–51. Berlin: Karl Dietz Verlag, 2000.

Brie, Michael, Martin Herzig, and Thomas Koch, eds. *Die PDS: Postkommunistische Kaderorganisation, ostdeutscher Traditionsverein oder linke Volkspartei? Empirische Befunde und kontroverse Analysen*. Cologne: PapyRossa, 1995.

Brückom, Axel. "Jenseits des 'Magdeburger Modells.' " In *Jahrbuch Extremismus und Demokratie*, edited by Uwe Backes and Eckhard Jesse, 9: 174–187. Baden-Baden: Nomos, 1997.

Butterwegge, Christoph. *Jungsozialisten und SPD*. Hamburg: W. Runge, 1975.

Chrapa, Michael. "Interne Konfliktpotentiale und Modernisierungschancen der PDS: Situation, Anforderungen, Optionen." *UTOPIE kreativ*, no. 113 (March 2000): 276–283.

Claus, Roland. "Die PDS und die anderen. Parlamentarische Arbeit zwischen Ausgrenzung, Wettbewerb und Kooperation." *UTOPIE kreativ*, no. 112 (February 2000): 144–148.

Crome, Erhard. "Linke Positionen, linke Politik. Zur Programmdebatte der PDS." *UTOPIE kreativ*, no. 120 (October 2000): 972–980.

Dambroth, Rüdiger. "Parlamentarische Bündnisbestrebungen von SPD und PDS im Wahljahr 1998." *Politische Studien* 49, no. 360 (July–August 1998): 28.

Ditfurth, Christian von. *Ostalgie oder linke Alternative: Meine Reise durch die PDS*. Cologne: Kiepenheuer & Witsch, 1998.

Elm, Ludwig, Dietmar Keller and Reinhard Mocek, eds. *Ansichten zur Geschichte der DDR*, vol XI. Bonn and Berlin: Bundestagsgruppe der PDS, 1998.

"Erfurter Erklärung." *Blätter für deutsche und internationale Politik* 42, no. 2 (February 1997): 251–254.

Falkner, Thomas. "Von der SED zur PDS." *Deutschland-Archiv* 24, no. 1 (1991): 30–51.

Falkner, Thomas, and Dietmar Huber. *Aufschwung PDS: Rote Socken—zurück zur Macht?* Munich: Droemer Knaur, 1994.

Fraude, Andreas. "Ende einer Ära: Die 3. Tagung des 6. Bundesparteitages der PDS." *Deutschland-Archiv* 33, no. 3 (2000): 363–365.

Fraude, Andreas. *"Reformsozialismus" statt "Realsozialismus"? Von der SED zur PDS*. Münster and Hamburg: LIT Verlag, 1993.

Funke, Manfred. "Patchwork-Sozialismus im Robin-Hood-Look." *Die politische Meinung*, no. 346 (September 1998): 19–21.

Gansel, Norbert. "Die Strategie in der Diskussion der Jungsozialisten." In *Überwindet den Kapitalismus oder Was wollen die Jungsozialisten?*, edited by Norbert Gansel, pp. 79–100. Reinbek: Rowohlt, 1971.

Gauland, Alexander. "Konservativ sein heißt." *Blätter für deutsche und internationale Politik* 44, no. 1 (January 1999): 10–11.

Gehrcke, Wolfgang, ed. *Stalinismus. Analyse und Kritik*. Bonn: Pahl-Rugenstein, 1994.

Gerner, Manfred. "Antagonismen der PDS: Zum Pluralismus der SED-Nachfolgepartei." *Deutschland-Archiv* 29, no. 2 (March–April 1996): 227–239.

Gerner, Manfred. "Entscheidung vertagt. Die 2. Tagung des 4. Bundesparteitags der PDS." *Deutschland-Archiv* 29, no. 2 (March–April 1996): 172–178.

Gerner, Manfred. *Partei ohne Zukunft? Von der SED zur PDS*. Munich: Tilsner, 1994.

Gerner, Manfred. "Widerspruch und Stagnation in der PDS." *Zeitschrift für Politik* 45, no. 2 (1998): 159–181.

Gesellschaftsanalyse und Politische Bildung e.V. *ReformAlternativen: Sozial-ökologisch-zivil*. Berlin: Karl Dietz, 2000.

Gesellschaftsanalyse und Politische Bildung e.V. *Zur Programmatik der Partei des Demokratischen Sozialismus*. Berlin: Dietz, 1997.

Gibowski, Wolfgang G. "Election Trends in Germany: An Analysis of the Second General Election in Reunited Germany." *German Politics* 4, no. 2 (August 1995): 26–53.

Gibowski, Wolfgang G. "Social Change and the Electorate: An Analysis of the 1998 Bundestagswahl." *German Politics* 8, no. 2 (August 1999): 10–32.

Glotz, Peter. "Wir Sozialdemokraten wären am liebsten die einzige linke Partei." In *Die PDS—Phönix oder Asche? Eine Partei auf dem Prüfstand*, edited by Heinz Beinert, pp. 98–105. Berlin: Aufbau-Verlag, 1995.

Grebing, Helga. "Probleme einer Neubestimmung demokratisch-sozialistischer Politik nach 1945." In *Zwangsvereinigung?* edited by J. Klotz, pp. 27–29. Heilbronn: Distel Verlag, 1996.

Grönebaum, S. "Wird der Osten Rot?" *Zeitschrift für Parlamentsfragen*, no. 3 (1997): 407–425.

Gysi, Gregor. *Das war's. Noch lange nicht!* Düsseldorf: Econ Verlag, 1997.

Gysi, Gregor. "Die Oppositionspolitik der PDS im Deutschen Bundestag." *DISPUT*, no. 2 (1996): 13–17.

Gysi, Gregor. "Die PDS—die Herausforderung von links." *DISPUT*, no. 4 (1998): 43–55.

Gysi, Gregor. *Ingolstädter Manifest. Wir—mitten in Europa. Plädoyer für einen neuen Gesellschaftsvertrag*. Berlin: PDS, 1994.

Gysi, Gregor. *Zwölf Thesen für eine Politik des modernen Sozialismus. Gerechtigkeit ist modern*. Berlin: PDS, 1999.

Gysi, Gregor, and Thomas Falkner. *Sturm aufs Große Haus: Der Untergang der SED*. Berlin: Edition Fischerinsel, 1990.

Gysi, Gregor, et al. *Wir brauchen einen dritten Weg. Selbstverständnis und Programm der PDS*. Hamburg: Konkret Literatur Verlag, 1990.

Gysi, Gregor, et al., eds. *Zweigeteilt. Über den Umgang mit der SED-Vergangenheit*. Hamburg: VSA, 1992.

Herzog, Roman. "Rede von Bundespräsident Roman Herzog auf dem Bürgerrechtler-Kongress der Konrad-Adenauer-Stiftung am 23. Juni 1998 in Leipzig." *Presse-*

mitteilungen des Bundespräsidialamtes. Berlin: Bundespräsidialamt, 23 June 1998.

Heuer, Uwe-Jens. "Eine Glosse zum Avantgardismus." *UTOPIE kreativ*, no. 89 (March 1998): 86–87.

Heuer, Uwe-Jens. "Macht, Recht und Unrecht in Geschichte und Gegenwart." In *Rücksichten. Politische und juristische Aspekte der DDR-Geschichte*, edited by Lothar Bisky, Uwe-Jens Heuer, and Michael Schumann, pp. 40–62. Hamburg: VSA-Verlag, 1993.

Heuer, Uwe-Jens. *Marxismus und Demokratie.* Baden-Baden: Nomos, 1990.

Heuer, Uwe-Jens. "Programmdiskussionen gestern und heute oder: Wandel durch Annäherung. Teil 2." In *Nachdenken über Sozialismus*, edited by Klaus Höpcke et al., pp. 251–267. Schkeuditz: GNN, 2000.

Heuer, Uwe-Jens. "Rechtsstaat und Unrechtsstaat. Zur PDS-Debatte." In *Die PDS—Herkunft und Selbstverständnis*, edited by Lothar Bisky et al., pp. 374–378. Berlin: Dietz, 1996.

Heuer, Uwe-Jens. "Zur Demokratiefrage und heutigen Aufgaben der PDS." In Uwe-Jens Heuer and Harald Werner. *Gegenmacht Demokratie—Demokratisierung gegen Macht*, pp. 5–21. Berlin: Grundsatzkommission der PDS, 1994.

Heuer, Uwe-Jens, Eckehard Lieberam, and Gregor Schirmer. "Zur Regierungsbeteiligung der PDS." *DISPUT*, no. 8 (1996): 7–8.

Hildebrandt, Axel. "Eine Debatte zu drei Fragen." *DISPUT*, no. 2 (1996): 20–21.

Hilsberg, Stephan. "Strategien gegen die PDS." *Neue Gesellschaft/Frankfurter Hefte* 43, no. 1 (January 1996): 921–925.

Historische Kommission beim Parteivorstand der PDS, eds. *Der Stalinismus in der KPD und SED—Wurzeln, Wirkungen, Folgen. Materialien der Konferenz der Historischen Kommission beim Parteivorstand der PDS am 17/18. November 1990.* Berlin: PDS, 1991.

Historische Kommission beim Parteivorstand der PDS. "Zur Geschichtsdiskussion in der PDS (1993)." In *Die PDS—Herkunft und Selbstverständnis. Eine politisch-historische Debatte*, edited by Lothar Bisky et al., pp. 374–378. Berlin: Dietz, 1996.

Holter, Helmut. "Die PDS als Zukunftspartei." November 1999 (available at http://www.pdsmv/de/diskussion).

Holter, Helmut. "Innerparteilich ist einiges zu klären." (Interview mit Helmut Holter). *Frankfurter Rundschau* (14 October 2000): 5.

Höpcke, Klaus. *Geordnete Verhältnisse.* Schkeuditz: GNN, 1996.

Höpcke, Klaus, et al., eds. *Nachdenken über Sozialismus.* Schkeuditz: GNN, 2000.

Hora, Friedrich. "Diskriminierung eines ganzen Berufsstandes—Berufsverbot für DDR-Pädagogen." In *Weissbuch 3: Bildungswesen und Pädagogik im Beitrittsgebiet*, edited by Gerd Buddin, Hans Dahlke, and Alfred Kossakowski, pp. 11–24. Berlin: KOLOG, 1994.

Hüning, Hasko. "PDS-Systemopposition oder Reformpolitik?" *Deutschland-Archiv* 23, no. 11 (November 1990): 1670–1678.

Institut für Marxismus-Leninismus beim Zentralkomitee der SED. *Geschichte der deutschen Arbeiterbewegung in 15 Kapiteln. Kapitel XII. Periode von Mai 1945 bis 1949.* Berlin: Dietz, 1968.

Jesse, Eckhard. "SPD and PDS Relationships." *German Politics* 6, no. 3 (December 1997): 89–102.

Kahrs, Horst. "Was kommt nach den 'Reformern' in der PDS?" *UTOPIE kreativ*, nos. 115–116 (May–June 2000): 437–441.

Karau, Gisela. *Die Affäre Heinrich Fink*. Berlin: Spotless, 1992.

Klein, Dieter. "Die PDS zwischen Ideologie und politischer Realität." In *The Party of Democratic Socialism in Germany: Modern Post-Communism or Nostalgic Populism?* edited by Peter Barker, pp. 109–127. Amsterdam: Rodopi, 1998.

Klein, Dieter. "Fertige Lösungern—das wäre wieder der Anfang von alten Strukturen." In PDS. *Materialien: Außerordentlicher Parteitag der SED-PDS. Berlin, Dezember 1989*, pp. 41–56. Berlin: Dietz, 1990.

Klein, Dieter, et al. *ReformAlternativen: Sozial—ökologisch—zivil*. Berlin: Dietz, 2000,

Klein, Markus, and Claudio Caballero. "Rückwärtsgewandt in die Zukunft. Die Wähler der PDS bei der Bundestagswahl 1994." *Politische Vierteljahresschrift* 37, no. 2 (June 1996): 229–247.

Kleßmann, Christoph und Martin Sabrow. "Zeitgeschichte in Deutschland nach 1989." *Aus Politik und Zeitgeschichte*, B39 (1996): 3–14.

Koch-Baumgarten, Sigrid. "Postkommunismus im Spagat. Zur Funktion der PDS im Parteiensystem." *Deutschland-Archiv* 30, no. 6 (1997): 864–878.

Lafontaine, Oskar. *The Heart Beats on the Left*. Translated by Ronald Taylor. Cambridge: Polity Press, 2000.

Land, Reiner, and Ralf Possekel. "PDS und moderner Sozialismus." In *Die PDS. Postkommunistische Kaderorganisation, ostdeutscher Traditionsverein oder linke Volkspartei? Empirich Befunde und kontroverse Analysen*, edited by Michael Brie et al., pp. 112–30. Cologne: PapyRossa, 1995.

Lang, Jürgen P. "PDS: Linke Protestpartei oder Verfassungsfeind? Mehr auf Ostdeutschland ausgerichtet." *Das Parlament*, no. 15 (15 April 1994): 13.

Lengsfeld, Vera. "Kein Pardon für die PDS." *Die politische Meinung*, no. 365 (April 2000): 70–72.

Lieberam, Ekkehard. "Regierungsbeteiligung und linke Gesellschaftsstrategie." *Mitteilungen der Kommunistischen Plattform der PDS* 11, no. 8 (August 2000): 1–6.

Lösche, Peter. "Die verborgenen Veränderungen unseres Parteiensystems." *Universitas—Zeitschrift für interdisziplinäre Wissenschaft* 53, no. 627 (September 1998): 813–821.

Luft, Christa. *Abbruch oder Aufbruch? Warum der Osten unsere Chance ist*. Berlin: Aufbau Taschenbuch Verlag, 1998.

Luft, Christa. "Endlich den Osten als Chance begreifen." *DISPUT*, no. 4 (1998): 26–28.

Luft, Christa, et al. "Rostocker Manifest: Für einen zukunftsfähigen Osten in einer gerechten Republik." *DISPUT*, no. 4 (1998): 31–37.

Malycha, Andreas. *Auf dem Weg zur SED. Die Sozialdemokratie und die Bildung der Einheitspartei in den Ländern der SBZ. Eine Quellenedition*. Bonn: J.H.W. Dietz Nachfolger, 1995.

Marxistisches Forum. "Erklärung des Marxistischen Forums: Unsere Sorgen sind nicht geringer geworden." *Marxistisches Forum*, no. 10 (1996): 1–3.

Marxistisches Forum. "Unsere Sorgen sind nicht geringer geworden." (Statement by the Marxist Forum of 14 October 1996). *Marxistisches Forum*, no. 10 (November 1996): 1–3.

Minnerup, Günter. "The PDS and the Strategic Dilemmas of the German Left." In *The Party of Democratic Socialism in Germany: Modern Post-Communism or Nostalgic Populism?* Edited by Peter Barker, pp. 209–220. Amsterdam: Rodopi, 1998.

Modrow, Hans. *Aufbruch und Ende*. Hamburg: Konkret Literatur Verlag, 1991.

Modrow, Hans. "PDS am Beginn einer komplizierten Wegstrecke." *DISPUT*, no. 2 (1996): 3–4.

Moreau, Patrick. "Das Wahljahr 1994 und die Strategie der PDS." *Aus Politik und Zeitgeschichte*, B1 (7 January 1994): 21–26.

Moreau, Patrick. *PDS—Anatomie einer postkommunistischen Partei*. Bonn and Berlin: Bouvier, 1992.

Moreau, Patrick. "Transnationale Vergleiche." In *The Party of Democratic Socialism in Germany: Modern Post-Communism or Nostalgic Populism?*, edited by Peter Barker, pp. 128–155. Amsterdam: Rodopi, 1998.

Moreau, Patrick, and Jürgen Peter Lang. *Linksextremismus: Eine unterschätzte Gefahr*. Bonn: Bouvier Verlag, 1996.

Moreau, Patrick, and Jürgen Peter Lang. *Was will die PDS?* Berlin: Ullstein, 1994.

Moreau, Patrick, and Viola Neu. *Die PDS zwischen Linksextremismus und Linkspopulismus*. Sankt Augustin: Konrad-Adenauer-Stiftung, 1994.

Müller, Werner. "SED-Gründung unter Zwang—Ein Streit ohne Ende? Plädoyer für den Begriff 'Zwangsvereinigung.' " *Deutschland-Archiv* 24, no. 1 (January 1991): 52–58.

Nelken, Michail. "Schwierigkeiten einer Emanzipation. Zur Stalinismusdebatte in der PDS." In *Die PDS—Herkunft und Selbstverständnis. Eine politisch-historische Debatte*, edited by Lothar Bisky et al., pp. 66–86. Berlin: Dietz, 1996.

Neu, Viola. "Das Korsett der alten Ideologie." *Die politische Meinung*, no. 369 (August 2000): 57–63.

Neu, Viola. "Zurück zur SED." *Die politische Meinung*, no. 343 (June 1998): 51–56.

Neugebauer, Gero. "Die PDS zwischen Kontinuität und Aufbruch." *Aus Politik und Zeitgeschichte*, B5 (2000): 39–46.

Neugebauer, Gero. "Hat die PDS bundesweit im Parteiensystem eine Chance?" In *Die PDS: Empirische Befunde & kontroverse Analysen*, edited by Michael Brie, Martin Herzig, and Thomas Koch, pp. 39–57. Cologne: PapyRossa, 1995.

Neugebauer, Gero. "Zur Akzeptanz der PDS in der politischen Konkurrenz." In *Die PDS im Parteiensystem*, edited by Michael Brie and Rudolf Woderich, pp. 140–148. Berlin: Karl Dietz Verlag, 2000.

Neugebauer, Gero, and Richard Stöss. *Die PDS. Geschichte. Organisation. Wähler. Konkurrenten*. Opladen: Leske + Budrich, 1996.

Nick, Harry. "Die Marxsche Lehre im Lichte des sozialistischen Disasters." *Marxistisches Forum*, nos. 15–16 (December 1997): 1–58.

Nick, Harry. "Sozialistisches Ziel und praktische Politik." *Marxistisches Forum*, no. 10 (November 1996): 4–8.

Niedermayer, Oskar. "Das intermediäre System." In *Politisches System. Berichte zum sozialen und politischen Wandel in Ostdeutschland*, edited by Max Kaase et al., 3: 155–230. Opladen: Leske + Budrich, 1996.

Niedermayer, Oskar. "Die Stellung der PDS im ostdeutschen Parteiensystem." In *The Party of Democratic Socialism in Germany: Modern Post-Communism or Nostalgic Populism?* edited by Peter Barker, pp. 18–37. Amsterdam: Rodopi, 1998.

Niedermayer, Oskar. "Party System Change in East Germany." *German Politics* 4, no. 3 (December 1995): 75–91.

"Nur, weil der Kanzler beleidigt ist." *Süddeutsche Zeitung* (31 October 2001).

Ostdeutsches Kuratorium der Verbände, *Mitteilungen Nr. 1*, Berlin: GBM, 1993.

Ostdeutsches Kuratorium der Verbände. *Mitteilungen Nr. 2.* Berlin: GBM, 1994.

Ostrowski, Christine. *Im Streit.* Querfurt: Dingsda-Verlag, 1993.

Ostrowski, Christine, and Ronald Weckesser. "Brief aus Sachsen. Für einen eigenen Weg statt 'links von der SPD.' " *Neues Deutschland* (8 May 1995).

Oswald, Franz. "The Party of Democratic Socialism: Ex-Communists Entrenched as East German Regional Protest Party." *Journal of Communist Studies and Transition Politics* 12, no. 2 (1996): 173–195.

Padgett, Stephen. "The Boundaries of Stability: The Party System before and after the 1998 *Bundestagswahl.*" *German Politics* 8, no. 2 (August 1999): 88–107.

Padgett, Stephen, and Thomas Saalfeld. "Introduction." *German Politics.* Special Issue on "*Bundestagswahl* '98: The End of an Era?" 8, no. 2 (August 1999): 1–9.

Patton, David. "The Rise of Germany's Party of Democratic Socialism: 'Regionalised Pluralism' in the Federal Republic?" *West European Politics* 23, no. 1 (January 2000): 144–160.

PDS. "Aus dem Abgeordnetenhaus: PDS in Senat von Berlin" (17 January 2002), (Available at http://www.pds-berlin.de/politik/dok/020117vitae.html).

PDS. "Das PRESSEDIENST—Antragsheft zum Schweriner Parteitag." *Pressedienst PDS*, nos. 50–51 (13 December 1996): 1–64.

PDS. "Es geht auch anders: Nur Gerechtigkeit sichert die Zukunft! 2. Tagung des 7. Parteitages (6. und 7. Oktober 2001, Dresden)." http://www.pds-online.de/partei /strukturen/parteitag/0702/beschluss.htm

PDS. *Europawahlprogramm der Partei des Demokratischen Sozialismus.* Berlin: PDS, 1999.

PDS. "Koalitionsvereinbarung zwischen SPD und PDS. Präambel" (8 January 2002). (Available at http://www.pds-online.de/politik/themen/senatsbildung_berlin).

PDS. *Materialien: Außerordentlicher Parteitag der SED-PDS, Berlin, Dezember 1989.* Berlin: Dietz, 1990.

PDS. "Nein zu UN-Militäreinsätzen—Internationale Krisen friedlich lösen. Beschluß der 3. Tangung des 6. Parteitages." *DISPUT*, no. 4 (April 2000): 32–33.

PDS. *Opposition gegen Sozialabbau und Rechtsruck. Wahlprogramm der PDS 1994 (Entwurf).* Berlin: PDS, December 1993.

PDS. *Partei des demokratischen Sozialismus. Programm und Statut.* Berlin: PDS, 1998.

PDS. *Programm der Partei des Demokratischen Sozialismus.* Berlin: PDS, 1993.

PDS. *Programm der Partei des Demokratischen Sozialismus. Entwurf.* Berlin: PDS, 27 April 2001.

PDS Programmkommission. "Zum Stand der programmatischen Debatte und der eigenen Tätigkeit," pp. 1–6 (Available at http://www.pds-online.de/programm/ programmkommission/dokumente)

PDS. *Rostocker Manifest: Für einen zukunftsfähigen Osten in einer gerechten Republik,* Berlin: PDS, 1998.

PDS. *Wahlprogramm der Partei des Demokratischen Sozialismus zur Bundestagswahl 1998.* Berlin: PDS, 1998.

PDS Programmkommission. "Thesen zur programmatischen Debatte." *Pressedienst PDS*, no. 47 (26 November 1999): 2–32.

Prinz, Sebastian. "Kein Bad Godesberg, kein Westfälischer Frieden. Die PDS nach ihrem Münsteraner Parteitag." *Politische Studien* 51, no. 372 (July–August 2000): 96–110.

Raschke, Jürgen. "SPD und PDS: Selbstblockade oder Opposition?" *Blätter für deutsche und internationale Politik* 39, no. 12 (December 1994): 1453–1464.

Scharping, Rudolf, et al. "Dresdner Erklärung der SPD vom 11. August 1994." Documented in *Blätter für deutsche und internationale Politik* 40, no. 1 (January 1995): 119–120.

Scherer, Klaus-Jürgen. "Die SPD und die PDS." In *The Party of Democratic Socialism in Germany: Modern Post-Communism or Nostalgic Populism?* edited by Peter Barker, pp. 182–193. Amsterdam: Rodopi, 1998.

Schmidt, Ute. "Sieben Jahre nach der Einheit. Die ostdeutsche Parteienlandschaft im Vorfeld der Bundestagswahl 1998." *Aus Politik und Zeitgeschichte*, B1–B2 (1998): 37–53.

Schröder, Richard. "SED, PDS und die Republik." *Neue Gesellschaft/Frankfurter Hefte* 43, no. 1 (January 1996): 912–921.

Schulz, Wilfried. " 'Für Gabi tun wir alles.' Vom Cottbuser Bundesparteitag und dem Doppelcharakter der PDS." *Deutschland-Archiv* 33, no. 6 (2000): 882–886.

Schulz, Wilfried. "Nachdenken über Sozialismus." *Deutschland-Archiv* 33, no. 4 (2000): 602–608.

Schulz, Wilfried. "PDS-Programmdiskussion—eine Frage der Glaubwürdigkeit." *Deutschland-Archiv* 33, no. 2 (March–April 2000): 177–179.

Schulz, Wilfried. "Zur Stalinismusdebatte in der PDS." *Deutschland-Archiv* 29, no. 2 (March–April 1996): 257–261.

Schulze, Jörg. "Ganz in Rot: SPD-Parteitag in Güstrow." *Freitag* (6 November 1998): 6.

Schumann, Michael. "Es geht um die Verteidigung der UN-Charta? Nicht um Plädoyer für Kampfeinsätze!" *DISPUT*, no. 4 (April 2000): 24–26.

Schumann, Michael. "Wir brechen unwiderruflich mit dem Stalinismus als System!" In *Materialien: Außerordentlicher Parteitag der SED-PDS, Berlin Dezember 1989*, by PDS, pp. 41–56. Berlin: Dietz, 1990.

Schumann, Michael. "Zur Auseinandersetzung der PDS mit dem Stalinistischen Erbe." *UTOPIE kreativ*, nos. 81–82 (July–August 1997): 164–168.

Schütt, Hans-Dieter. *Zwischen Baum und Basis. Gespräche mit Gabriele Zimmer*. Berlin: Karl Dietz Verlag, 2000.

SED/PDS. *Materialien: Außerordentlicher Parteitag der SED/PDS. 8./9/. und 16./17. Dezember 1989*. Berlin: Dietz Verlag, 1990.

Seite, Berndt. "Die PDS im Bonner Machtkalkül." *Die politische Meinung* 41, no. 323 (October 1996): 5–7.

SPD. "Beschluß des Parteivorstandes der SPD zum Umgang mit der PDS vom 5. Dezember 1994." Documented in *Blätter für deutsche und internationale Politik* 40, no. 1 (January 1995): 123.

Stöss, Richard and Oskar Niedermeyer. "Zwischen Anpassung und Profilierung. Die SPD an der Schwelle zum neuen Jahrhundert." *Aus Politik und Zeitgeschichte*, B5 (2000): 3–11.

Sturm, Eva, and Eberhard Schmidt. "Ein Kommentar zur Programmatik der PDS oder das Problem der Diskursunfähigkeit." *UTOPIE kreativ*, no. 84 (October 1997): 81–88.

Thierse, Wolfgang. "Strategiepapier 'Gesichtspunkte für eine Verständigung der ostdeutschen Sozialdemokraten zum Thema Umgang mit der PDS.' " *Frankfurter Rundschau* (19 December 1996).

Uschner, Manfred. *Die roten Socken*. Berlin: Dietz Verlag, 1995.

Valtin, Kathrin. "Das erste Mal: PDS-Parteitag in Parchim." *Freitag* (6 November 1998): 6.

Wagenknecht, Sahra. *Antisozialistische Strategien im Zeitalter der Systemauseinandersetzung. Zwei Taktiken im Kampf gegen die sozialistische Welt*. Bonn: Pahl-Rugenstein Nachfolger, 1995.

Wagenknecht, Sahra. "Wir müssen aus der Defensivstellung herauskommen." *Kommunisten in der PDS. Sonderheft der Mitteilungen der Kommunistischen Plattform der PDS* (June 1995): 31–35.

Wagner, Ingo. "Moderner Sozialismus als sozialistische Moderne." *Marxistisches Forum*, nos. 17–18 (February 1998): 1–32.

"Wahlen 1990 (III)" *Blätter für deutsche und internationale Politik*, 36, no. 4 (April 1991): 508–511.

"Wahlen 1994 (I)." *Blätter für deutsche und internationale Politik*, 40, no. 1 (January 1995): 124–128.

"Wahlen 1998 (I)." *Blätter für deutsche und internationale Politik*, 44, no. 1 (January 1999): 126–128.

"Wahlen 1998 (II)." *Blätter für deutsche und internationale Politik*, 44, no. 2 (February 1999): 253–256.

"Wahlen 1999 (I)."*Blätter für deutsche und internationale Politik*, 45, no. 1 (January 2000): 127–128.

"Wahlen 1999 (II)." *Blätter für deutsche und internationale Politik*, 45, no. 2 (February 2000): 253–256.

"Wahlen 2000." *Blätter für deutsche und internationale Politik*, 46, no. 1 (January 2001): 127–128.

Weber, Hermann. *Die Sozialistische Einheitspartei Deutschlands 1946–1971*. Hanover: Verlag für Literatur und Zeitgeschehen, 1971.

Weiss, Konrad. "Die Tradierung totalitärer Strukturen in der PDS." *MUT*, no. 372 (August 1998): 26–35.

Weizsäcker, Richard von. *Vier Zeiten. Erinnerungen*. Berlin: Siedler, 1997.

Welzel, C. *Von der SED zur PDS. Eine doktringebundene Staatspartei auf dem Weg zu einer politischen Partei im Konkurrenzsystem? (Mai 1989 bis April 1990)*. Frankfurt: Peter Lang, 1992.

Wiesenthal, Helmut. "East Germany as a Unique Case of Societal Transformation: Main Characteristics and Emergent Misconceptions." *German Politics* 4, no. 3 (December 1995): 49–74.

Wilke, Manfred. "Die Diktaturkader André Brie, Gregor Gysi, Lothar Bisky und das MfS." *Politische Studien* 49, no. 360 (July–August 1998): 39–69.

Wittich, Dietmar. "Mitglieder und Wähler der PDS." In *Die PDS: Postkommunistische Kaderorganisation, ostdeutscher Traditionsverein oder Volkspartei? Empirische Befunde und kontroverse Analysen*, edited by Michael Brie, Martin Herzig and Thomas Koch, pp. 58–80. Cologne: PapyRossa, 1995.

Woderich, Rudolf. "Ost-Identität—Residuum der Vereinigung oder Phänomen der 'langen Dauer?' " *UTOPIE kreativ*, no. 105 (July 1999): 51–60.

"Wörlitzer Erklärung." *Blätter für deutsche und internationale Politik* 42, no. 2 (February 1997): 254.

Zessin, Helmut, Edwin Schwertner, and Frank Schumann. *Chronik der PDS 1989 bis 1997*. Berlin: Dietz, 1998.

Ziblatt, Daniel F. "The Adaptation of Ex-Communist Parties to Post-Communist East Central Europe: A Comparative Study of the East German and Hungarian Ex-Communist Parties." *Communist and Post-Communist Studies* 31, no. 2 (1998): 119–137.

Ziblatt, Daniel F. "Putting Humpty-Dumpty Back Together Again." *German Politics and Society* 16, no. 1 (Spring 1998): 1–29.

Index

About the Author

FRANZ OSWALD is Senior Lecturer, School of Social Sciences, Curtin University of Technology, Perth, Australia. His publications include *The Political Psychology of the White Collar Worker in Martin Walser's Novels*.